BROKEN PIECES OF BEAUTY

By
Thelma Quinn

Artwork By Christy McSwiggan

Manufactured in the United States by:
VISION PUBLISHING GROUP
Griffin, Georgia

Edited by Mona Cook
Cover design and original artwork by Christy McSwiggan

ISBN 1-892861-01-1

DEDICATION

This book is dedicated to the Lord Jesus Christ, who has been all things wonderful and beautiful to me. I pray that Christ will receive all the glory and honor due Him from my life. I seek no glory for myself and pray my Lord will accept my offering and will carry this writing wherever He will.

Jesus stands at the door and knocks. Won't you open the door and invite Him in? He will be your dearest Friend and never forsake you nor leave you comfortless.

God bless you.

Destiny Quinn
Newton, Texas, 1998

ACKNOWLEDGEMENTS

I want to thank all of the many people who have been a part of my life. Especially my children, who grew up the hard way without the many securities most children enjoy these days.

Most of all, I want to thank Mona Cook for the many sacrifices she made toward this cause. She has been a soul sister to me and her faithfulness has been an inspiration to my life. I would also like to thank her son, Kevin, who played a significant part as well.

Words can't express how my heart has been blessed by all of these dedicated people. They mean so much to me and to the Lord.

CONTENTS

INTRODUCTION

I never gave much thought about prisons until someone I loved was incarcerated in the Wall Unit at Huntsville, Texas for the crime of murder. When I drove by them on the highway, I would shudder thinking how lonely and hopeless these outcasts of society must feel. Prison seems so final after judgements have been handed down. The offender then becomes a number instead of a name. Before God sent me to Ted, I tried very hard to shut him out of my mind because of the hopelessness of the situation. My dream of sharing our lives together died when he was given a life sentence. The idea that God would send me to him after all that I had suffered at the hands of his brother was unbelievable and hard for me to accept. All I wanted was to be free to worship Christ without ever being afraid anymore. After I surrendered to the call of God, I became confused when I would see the news reports on TV and in the newspapers. Many times I had to fall on my knees and pray, questioning the Lord's wisdom of sending me to Ted. I was so torn apart knowing that Ted nor I could relive the past and that God was the only one Who could draw the curtain down on our sins of yesterday. Only then could we continue on for Jesus' sake.

We send missionaries to foreign lands and yet the mission field is here all around us. But most of us don't want to get involved. Our Father also walks the halls of these places - these prisons - seeking to save the lost. God uses people like me to go for Him. I was reluctant and didn't want to expose my heart to the hopelessness of heartache; sometimes very near to the despair that I knew I would have to suffer for Jesus' sake. I couldn't believe there could be any beauty found behind the walls of a prison. But God always knows best.

Two of God's children were praying many miles apart. An inmate was praying that God would send him someone to love as he looked from a window in his cell above the prison yard where visitors met for a contact visit. Many miles away, a woman knelt in prayer asking God to fill her life with purpose and meaning in order to bring glory to His Name. God heard their prayers and brought them together in a miraculous way to begin a beautiful love story, which had started many years ago. He hid them beneath His mighty wings in the years ahead as He began the process of healing their wounds.

As God promised in Malachi 4:2 of the King James Version of the Bible, "But unto you that fear My Name shall the Son of Righteousness arise with healing in His wings." Psalms 63:7 also states, "Because Thou hast been my help, therefore in the shadow of Thy wings will I rejoice." Ted and I claimed the promise of God in Isaiah 40:31 which gave us hope in our hearts, "But they that wait upon the Lord shall renew their strength; they shall mount up with wings as eagles; they shall run, and not be weary; they shall walk and not be faint."

This is our love story and it deals with two types of prisons. It is a unique love story that describes the sufferings along with the heartaches, which are filled with incredible drama and mystery. It also tells of the many adversities that were faced all because of my love for the Lord. It is filled with the Holy Spirit as He moves in miraculous ways that may seem unbelievable to an ordinary person.

Our love story begins on my fifty-seventh birthday.

CHAPTER 1

COVENANT OF GRACE

The bright sunlight streamed through the windows of my bedroom awakening me from my rest on July 30, 1989. Although it irritated me with its brightness, I immediately became aware of the special importance of that day. "Get up, sleepy head, it's the Lord's day again. Not only that, but it's also your fifty-seventh birthday. The children will be calling soon and besides that, you have a busy day ahead," my angel seemed to say. I felt like a child again as I thought about presents and I jumped to my feet joyfully.

As I made my way to the kitchen and started the coffee making, I walked into the living room. I smiled as I looked around the living area marveling at how wonderfully God had blessed my life since Jacob passed away. Some years back the Lord had promised, "Destiny, you will live here someday." My heart sang with joy again as it had on that day and I saw how perfectly everything had fallen into place. I experienced so much joy as I was fixing up the house, hanging new curtains and arranging the furniture. Two weeks had gone by since Isabella and Steve had moved to Jasper, leaving me their new home to live in and to call my own. It is such a happy thing to see my dream come true and especially one I had only dreamed about for many years. "Thank you, Father," I cried happily. "Praise Your name for all the beautiful gifts that You have given to me." As I sipped my coffee, I thought about the last few months of my life. A lot of things had happened in the short time since Jacob had died in February of this year. Steve and Isabella had invited me to live in their home since the company that he worked for insisted that they move into the company house near the farm. I had sold the little house Jacob and I owned and came to live with them in March.

A continual burst of activity took place when I moved into their home as they helped me to establish a small fried pie business.

I looked across the peaceful countryside and thought how lovely and serene it was with my neighbor's cows grazing lazily in the green grassy fields, little birds chirped away as they flew near the porch and a peaceful feeling filled my heart. `How could I ask for anything more than this,' I thought? `Dreams do come true, don't they, Father, and I am a prime example of that.'

Happy memories of Sunday mornings before the children moved away went through my mind and I missed Steve and Randall singing in the bedroom as Steve prepared the music for the church choir. Music had filled the house as we dressed for church. As I remembered, suddenly I felt empty in my heart and worthless now that my life was in order. I suddenly realized that my life had no real purpose. Just to fry pies for a living seemed so cold and unfeeling. What kind of sacrifice could be found for Christ in frying a few pies? Isn't there something more to life than living for yourself? Then I reminded myself that I should be grateful that I had such an easy life.

The empty feeling persisted as I dressed for Sunday school. It was as if I was only going through the motions. I tried to tell myself that I should be excited instead of allowing myself to get into such a foul mood. After all, it was my birthday and I should be celebrating.

"Snap out of it, Destiny, this mood will pass when you get to church," I told myself. As I drove down the country road toward Newton, I reminded myself of the freedoms I enjoyed now. I am free to worship God without fear anymore. I don't have to be afraid to go home following the worship service any longer. Not so long ago I wasn't able to do that. Before Jacob found Christ, he made me tremble in fear. Our life together had been a battleground because Jacob didn't want me to live a dedicated life for the Lord. A part time church member was quite enough he thought, not an active member who was faithful. The Lord had used my talents over the years even though Jacob moved his family from pillar to post. No matter how far he took us, the Lord had a place where He could use me and the children in the church. The place I usually filled was at the piano. When the needs of the church began demanding too much of our time, Jacob would move us to another town in the hope that we would turn our attention on him. Of course it didn't work out the way he wanted because the Lord would always use us wherever we moved.

I won't complain now that those days are over. Because of them, I have learned how very precious the freedom to worship God really is. I will never forget the past even though it has left many open wounds, which will take time to heal. In the meantime, I must take each day as it comes and allow the Lord to use my testimony for others who may be suffering the same way that I had.

As I drove up to the front of the church and walked inside, my friends shook my hand and greeted me. I sat in the pew where I usually sat every Sunday which was near the front close to the piano. Still in this strange state, I played the piano and I am not even sure of what I played nor even if it was suitable. I couldn't seem to pull myself together and even when I took my seat later, I moved without emotion. Our pastor took his place in the pulpit and I followed along with the scriptures he read. Still unable to find the spark so needed right at this moment that would excite my thoughts, I turned my head toward the Church Covenant that hung on the wall.

As I read the Covenant, I thought wistfully, `Father, I do these things, but I feel the emptiness in my heart as if I didn't have anything to live for anymore. My life doesn't seem to have a purpose anymore even though everything seems to be in order, but there is no challenge anymore.' Suddenly without warning the Lord spoke to me and said, "Go to Ted, he needs you." My heart began racing madly at the sound of His voice. Then I thought about my pride and began making excuses as to why I shouldn't go. Then I looked around at the congregation who hadn't noticed my behavior. I wanted to tell them what I heard, but I couldn't disrupt the service and I couldn't ignore His command even though I wanted to. First, I felt hurt that God would send me to Ted. "Father, why are You sending me to Jacob's brother who is in prison," I cried? "I have always cared for Ted, but he is in prison for shooting and killing his wife. He received a sentence of ninety-nine years and You know, Father, that he may never get out. How could You do this to me since I have just been set free to serve You, Father," I pleaded. "What possible good can I be?" So many questions ran through my mind as I tried to find the perfect excuse to offer Christ, but I was only considering myself and the sacrifices that I would have to make if I surrendered to the Lord and I had plenty of excuses to offer Him. Each one of them were reasonable excuses that I had heard others offer.

Then I thought, `Lord, what about my family and friends? The children will think I have lost my mind completely. Will their faith withstand the reproach they are sure to bear when tongues start wagging and spreading gossip about their mother? Will they turn against me because I have brought shame on them and the grand-children? Lord, Mark and Sam are ministers of the Gospel.

They pastor churches and if I surrender to Your call, won't it affect their ministry? What else can I say to convince you that I am unable to hold up under such a mission?'

Jesus replied in a soft and gentle voice and I heard authority in His voice as He said, "My grace is sufficient to meet your every need." I became weak as my heart softened and I knew then without a doubt that He would keep His promise. "Lord, we have come so far together and You have proved Your love to me time and time again. How can I refuse You now that You have sent me on a mission for Your sake? I am not even sure that Ted will want me anyway, but Joyce, my oldest daughter, tells me that he continually inquires about my welfare. She called Ted as soon as she got home from Jacob's funeral. She said that You placed it on her heart to contact Ted at the prison and tell him that his brother had died. Now they enjoy a sweet relationship through letters, but I didn't think that I should get involved with Ted, at least not right now, because Jacob hasn't been dead very long. Besides that, Lord, when I prayed asking you to fill my life with purpose I was thinking about helping some young mother, perhaps someone like myself, who is facing some of the same things that I have when Jacob fought against my serving You in spite of his threats to hurt me. To serve You in that manner wouldn't take much time or effort. I could go on enjoying my freedom. Don't You see if I do what You ask I will suffer. If I get involved with Ted I will be hurt again because our relationship is bound to stir up the old feelings that we once had for each other," I cried out to God.

"Oh, God," I sobbed in heartbreak, "I don't want to suffer anymore. The Quinn family put me through the fire and I thought that pain was over. I don't know if I can bear the sleepless nights and the despair that lies ahead of me. I certainly didn't realize when I prayed that You would fill my life with a purpose that would demand twenty-four hours a day, Lord." I prayed. "Nevertheless, my God, I will surrender to Your call and I will be faithful to Your cause. But please help me bear this cross no matter the cost and I will place my loved ones in Your capable hands to help them understand that You called me to serve You today in this manner."

The power of God's grace gave me strength immediately and when the church service was over, I went home with a new commitment. I thought, `Father, I don't even have Ted's address so I can write to him. I won't worry about it right now though since I have plenty of time and Ted really isn't going anywhere. Besides, Father, maybe You will change Your mind and release me from Your call once You consider how hopeless the situation really is and the trouble that it can cause.' As I went about my usual activities, I tried not to think much about Ted.

CHAPTER 2

TESTING OF GRACE

Monday morning began as usual and as soon as I cleared the table, I started preparing more fried pies and storing them in the freezer. Sometime that morning Isabella came by unexpectedly. I heard her drive up and she burst through the door excitedly and she looked surprised. Then she exclaimed, "Mamma, guess what, you got a letter from Uncle Ted in the mail today."

My mouth felt dry and I could hardly stand up because my legs felt like jelly. I thought I was going to faint so I sat down at the table. My hands trembled as I opened Ted's letter and thought, `Lord, you sure didn't waste any time. Evidently this letter was already on the way when You spoke to me yesterday. Your grace is amazing, Father. You confirmed Your will, but I am nervous because I don't know how to tell Isabella what happened yesterday in a way she would understand.'

Isabella waited patiently for me to read Ted's letter aloud. We were both so excited, but I was afraid I would blurt out my story before I read the letter. `He has a beautiful handwriting,' I thought. Then I started reading it to Isabella out loud. It seemed like I could hear his voice speaking in his familiar tone, as I read: "Dear Destiny, Hello, it's me, Ted. It's been so long since I've seen your pretty face and I know you're surprised to get this letter." Isabella giggled thinking her Uncle Ted was romantic, but it was hard to disguise my true feelings from her as I continued reading the letter.

He wrote about Joyce and the great blessing she had been to him. He wrote about the call she made when Jacob died. "As I told Joyce, I wish I could have put my arms around my brother one more time and tell him that I loved him. Joyce is the only friend I have now, Destiny. A woman stood by me during the trial and visited me at the prison until a few months ago. One day she said, "Ted, this is my last visit today. The Lord is sending someone else to you." I couldn't imagine whom God would send to take her place because she had stood by me for five years. I decided that she couldn't see any future in visiting a man who was serving ninety-nine years and that it was just an excuse to be free of me without hurting my feelings. Oh, how mistaken I was though because God sent Joyce right away. Of course, my own daughters deserted me for the crime I had done, but I can't blame them."

Ted went on to say, "Destiny, any old saying comes to mind that I heard years ago, `If you dance, sooner or later you will have to pay the fiddler.' I am paying the price now because I danced and committed a terrible crime. I hope that you will write sometimes and pray for me. The Lord has saved my soul, Destiny, and I love Him with all my heart." Then he signed it, "With love, Ted." Ted didn't know how right his friend had been when she told him that God would send someone into his life, but why did she feel it was necessary for her to bow out of his life, I wondered?

Even though I was reluctant to tell Isabella my testimony, I knew that I couldn't avoid it. Such an amazing miracle had happened yesterday and I couldn't keep it to myself any longer now that God had confirmed His will through Ted's letter. This was undoubtedly my first test as well as testing the power of God's marvelous grace. Even though I was troubled about the whole situation with my lack of understanding, I felt a surge of power suddenly sweeping over my body as I began my testimony to my daughter.

Broken Pieces of Beauty

"Isabella, I have something to tell that will be very difficult for you to understand. I have experienced many miracles in my lifetime, especially years ago when the Holy Spirit spoke to me at the New Salem Baptist Church when He said that I was bound for hell because I was lost. I thought that I was safe since I had been baptized as a small child and I was so good that I could look down on those who weren't saved. The Holy Spirit showed me the fires of hell as I sat on that pew. I saw hell so plain, Isabella, that I knew I was going there if I didn't repent of my sins and give my heart to Christ. I gave my all to Jesus that day and He saved my soul. Many miracles happened after that, but until yesterday I hadn't heard Him speak to me like He did the day when I received Christ as my Savior," I testified. Isabella was very attentive as I continued my testimony, all the while the Holy Spirit gave me a calm, steady voice and encouraged me to go on. "As you know, yesterday was my birthday and I should have been happy, but a strange thing happened before I went to church. I suddenly felt empty and my life seemed worthless. Isabella, I realized that I didn't have anything to live for anymore. Suddenly I realized I was an empty shell, only going through the motions and pretending to be happy."

Isabella watched me carefully as I continued, "I played the piano in a daze, not really sure how, because I seemed to be in some sort of a trance. After the song service, I took my seat apart from the other members. I felt so alone with no real purpose in my life. I couldn't seem to become interested in the sermon either, so I started reading the Church Covenant on the wall, thinking that somehow it would have the answer that I needed to bring me out of the terrible mood I was in.

As my attention turned toward the Covenant that gave instructions on how a Christian should live, suddenly the same Holy Spirit spoke to me as He had when He convicted me of my sins so long ago. He said, "Go to Ted, he needs you." Oh, Isabella, it stunned me so because I wasn't expecting that."

Tears welled up in Isabella's eyes as they did in mine and the Holy Spirit bore witness that my testimony was true. "I immediately looked around the church to see if someone had said those words to me or if the church had heard the Lord speak as I had. I knew they hadn't even before I looked around, but I needed to be completely sure in my own mind. Once I realized that it was, in fact, my Lord that spoke, my first reaction was to jump to my feet and tell the church what had happened. I didn't, however, because I knew they wouldn't understand or believe my testimony. They would think that I had imagined the whole thing. I almost burst into tears because I was so afraid, not only of the voice that spoke the command even though His voice was gentle and kind, but the Lord was sending me into a strange world that I had never been in," I cried.

"Oh, Mamma," Isabella cried, "I can't believe God would do this to you. You have been through so much with Daddy and the whole Quinn family. Everyone knew that you and Ted had special feelings for each other all those years. I was just a baby when we lived at Fort Worth, but I remember Daddy's anger when Ted showed you affection when you were so sick. We moved back to Cleveland, but Daddy accused you of such terrible things. Mamma, you suffered so much because of Ted until Daddy died and now the Lord wants you to go to him! I can't believe it. Are you going? Joyce writes to him and that should be enough."

I prayed in my heart that the Holy Spirit would comfort my daughter. Oh, how much I needed comforting and the wisdom to understand what was going on myself, yet I knew that God was so much wiser than I and He knew what was best. Even though I don't understand right now, I did know that I must keep my faith in God. So I said, "Baby, don't you see, Ted's letter only confirms God's call. I know it is troubling to you, but don't you realize how bewildering it is for me as well. Just to think of going to a prison terrifies me. Why, I have never been inside a jail before either. The thought scares me, but I realize that I must take one step at a time and place all my faith and trust in God. Isabella, we have to be strong and trust in God. He didn't leave me without His promise to supply all my needs with His glorious grace. After I became so disturbed by His call to go to Ted, I began offering every excuse that I could think of with the hope that they were good enough. He listened, then He said, "My grace is sufficient to supply all of your needs." At that point, I surrendered to His call. Oh, Isabella, God has been with me all these years and He has never left me to suffer alone. He has stood between Jacob and I when he threatened my life. He has given me the sweet assurance that He is with me now. His grace is powerful and until you have tried the Lord like I have, you can't walk blindly by faith as I am doing right now. I pray that you will accept my testimony and support me. I am going to need all the love and support of my family to carry out this mission the Lord has sent me to do."

Isabella said sobbing, "Mama, I just want you to be happy, but I wanted you to find someone that would take care of you. Ted can't help you, Mamma. You know he is going to be in prison for a long time. It is just not fair, Mamma. You deserve better, but if this is what it takes to make you happy, I won't fight against it." Isabella left shortly still disturbed by everything I had told her. We held each other and cried. She said, "I love you, Mamma, and I will stand by you even though I don't understand what is in the mind of the Lord."

Isabella drove away and I was alone again and I fell on my knees and started praying. "Father, the first test of fire is over, but I know there are many more to come. Oh, God, grant me the grace to stand faithful for the cause of Christ, my Lord. Take my life and use it for Your glory. Take my hand and lead me every step of the way and I will praise Your Holy Name forever, in Jesus' Name," I prayed.

My faith faltered at the thought of answering Ted's letter. Eventually I must tell Ted that God had sent me to him, but I told myself there would be plenty of time for that later. Actually, I avoided that issue. I was reluctant to let Ted know what the Lord wanted me to do since I still couldn't believe the Lord would actually require so much of me.

I decided that it would please the Lord if I wrote about Jacob instead of myself, although I did tell him about my accomplishments in the pie business, as well as some of the other ways that God had blessed my life. I told him about Jacob and our last days together and my living with him on the truck for four years, but I didn't mention anything that would give him any notion that I had any intention of changing my lifestyle. The idea of giving my all to Jesus through a commitment to Ted meant giving up my newfound freedom. I felt my freedom was being threatened and I felt sorry for myself. I had sacrificed all those years to serve the Lord and He was really putting me to the test, if only to see if I would follow Him in spite of where He sent me. "I will tell him in my next letter, Jesus," I reasoned with God. "If I tell him now it would be too much of a shock and he would think that I was crazy or decide that I was taking advantage of him."

I couldn't understand the way I felt about Ted, though. For some strange reason I was feeling love for him. It is true that Ted and I had been attracted to each other over the years, but I didn't trust him even then. He knew that it was wrong to care for his brother's wife and to have the feelings that he did. Even after he married, we were attracted to each other and even though we tried not to let it show, others sensed it. Jacob was jealous of Ted all those years and he would taunt me about it, even though Ted nor I ever did anything behind Jacob's back nor Ted's wife. I had been too afraid of the way we felt about each other and was afraid the wall of defense we put up would eventually break down, so we kept our feelings inside, even though Ted took advantage at times to let me know that he cared.

Neither Ted nor I would dare to be alone and his folks saw to it that we weren't. When Jacob and I would visit his folks and Ted was there, we were watched very carefully to make certain that Ted and I had no opportunity to be alone together.

"Have you really brought us together now, Father," I would ask? "You know it doesn't seem right. We are free to love each other now, but, Lord, we aren't free completely. We can't enjoy a normal relationship, Father, and we are going to suffer so much. How can we bear the pain we are bound to face in a sweet relationship built on faith alone? I am not even sure Ted will be strong enough to bear such a cross himself because he hasn't been saved very long and even though I have been for many years, my faith falters when I think of what lies ahead. Oh, Father, it will take a boundless supply of grace on both our parts to get us through the sleepless nights that will be often filled with tears and heartache as we trust in Your wisdom for the choice You have made in both our lives."

I was sure that Ted only wanted a friend when he wrote to me and he never suspected that God had begun a well-devised plan. When I sent my first letter off, I tried to forget it, but the Holy Spirit dealt with me continually.

`Surely the way I feel isn't one sided and surely the Lord has placed the same love in Ted for me that He has in me for him,' I thought.

Ted answered my letter right away. I could hear his voice clearly in my mind as I read the lines. I could see him smiling as he spoke to my heart, "Say, Destiny, did you know that you wrote to me on my birthday?" Ted continued, "It was a beautiful birthday present and I can't think of anything more precious than this gift you have given me. I will always cherish it, Destiny. Not only because you cared enough to write, but you told me so many things that you and Jacob did since I saw you last. You must have some beautiful memories of you and Jacob traveling across country in a truck. Do you ever wish that you could go back again when you meet one on the highway? Those trips took you to a lot of places that very few people have ever been. I will bet that you have a lot of stories that you could tell to the grandchildren about the places you've seen as well as the adventures that you experienced as you traveled to Newfoundland on a huge ferry and to parts of Canada."

Ted went on to tell me how he had ruined his life by allowing Satan to get control of him. Instead of turning to God when his troubles started, he was rebellious and his heart was filled with hate. "I tried to find you and Jacob when things got so bad, but I couldn't. I felt like Jacob could help me because he was much wiser than I ever was," Ted wrote.

My heart went out to Ted as he continued and I felt sorrow in my soul that no one listened to his cries for help. "Destiny, Jesus saved my soul here in this prison. I thought I was doomed to spend eternity in hell. Tears of repentance streamed down my cheeks while I pleaded for mercy time and time again. One night while I prayed, Jesus saved me and freed me from the terrible sins that I had committed. He took away all the hate in my heart and filled it with peace and love for everyone. I am not the same old Ted that you once knew, Destiny. I just want to live for Jesus now. I won't fear what man can do to me because I have been saved by the blood of the Lamb. I can't undo what I have done and I'll have to spend the rest of my life in prison, I suppose, but I deserve the sentence I received. It is so wonderful that God has blessed me through you and Joyce. I can't believe the happiness that I have found. Praise His Holy Name forever!"

Ted's testimony touched my heart so that I wept. A member of my family was suffering and I cried out to God to grant him peace. As I prayed, I asked God to help me express correctly in words the beautiful miracle at church on my birthday. It was still fresh in my mind, but would Ted understand? I was afraid he would think I was forcing my attention on him. How will he receive my testimony that God told me to go to him and God had filled me with love for him at the same time? My hands trembled as I began my letter, but the Holy Spirit brought many precious memories about the past to my mind. "We have always had a special bond, Ted," I wrote, "and I have always loved you through the years. I have never understood why because I loved Jacob, too. It is very strange that we were drawn to each other over the years and yet I resisted any advances that you made toward me. Jacob was jealous of your attention and he was suspicious every time you came around. Everyone watched us so closely that we couldn't have done anything wrong had we have wanted to. You know, Ted, we were never alone at any time, but even in a crowd everyone knew there was something between us. My mother and sister told me one day that you loved me. They could feel it and others did too. Now we are free to express our true feelings to each other, but I feel so strange telling you now."

I was leading up to God's call and fear crept into my heart. "Lord, what if Ted rejects me and he doesn't feel the same as I do? Yet, I know I must place all my faith and trust in You, Jesus. Besides, if he doesn't want me I will be free from my commitment to You. I will tell Ted about my experience and just leave Ted in Your hands," I decided. Then I repeated how God sent me to him on my birthday. "I am so afraid of the idea of prison, Ted. I made every excuse that I could think of to get out of this commitment. The Lord listened to all those feeble excuses, which I thought He would accept. I just wanted to serve Jesus, but in my own way, a way that wouldn't require too much time. I didn't want to hurt anymore, crying out in hopeless despair during all the sleepless nights. If I surrendered my all to Christ, I would suffer twenty-four hours a day. I am committed to my promise to the Lord, Ted," I told him. "I will always love you as a sister and as a woman. God promised to supply all our needs with the right supply of His marvelous grace. I have learned through the years that I can depend on Christ, Ted, so whether you reject my love or accept the things I have told you, I will continue living for Jesus. I don't understand why God brought you into my life again, but I do know and trust that God knows what He is doing and He knows best. I am sure the things I have written will be a shock to you, but what has happened lately has stunned me as well. God bless you. Write and let me know how you feel soon. I will be anxiously waiting to hear from you." Then I signed it simply, "Love, Destiny."

Ted answered my letter right away. You could hear the excitement in every word he wrote. He wrote about our love for each other over the years, a tender and sweet love that we couldn't express. A tenderness that God held in reserve to be expressed in the fullness of time. "Although a strong attraction for each other grew and in spite of everything, you resisted me and stayed true to Jacob, Destiny. In my young mind I loved you in spite of you being my brother's wife. I have wanted you since I was a teenager even then knowing my feelings were wrong. You sent me home time after time saying, 'Go home, Ted.' I still feel the same way about you now, Destiny. You will always be the most beautiful woman on earth in my heart. I will never reject you, Dear. I will love you all my life and not as a sister-in-law either, but I love you and I am very happy that you love me too. I am the happiest man in the world because my beloved Destiny is finally mine at last!" Hidden secrets weren't hidden anymore and I felt free as I rejoiced. I didn't allow myself to think about Ted in the past and the thought that our lives might be united like this was inconceivable. Only God in Heaven knew the way that we felt. He knew that I had been faithful to Jacob as well. I couldn't live with myself if Ted or I had cheated on our mates. I loved my Lord Jesus with all my heart. My life had been spent in winning Jacob to Christ and all of my attention was in that direction as well as bringing up our children to know the Lord. As the years went by, I didn't see Ted after Mom and Dad passed away. Now it seemed like a dream instead of a reality that Ted and I would be together. It didn't matter that he was in prison either. Just to be loved by him was sufficient.

Ted added, "Destiny, when I read your letter, I was stunned. I do believe that God sent you to me in answer to my prayer for so long now. It is incredible that God would send someone to love me and even more incredible that He would send you, the only woman I have adored for many years and the only woman on earth I could trust. Oh, Destiny, I would place my life in your hands. I will be good to you and I will never hurt you. I just want to make you as happy as possible. I am the richest man in the world that I know, and I don't even have a penny in my pocket. God bless you, my sweet Destiny. I love you with all my heart." Ted drew two tiny hearts together, an emblem that he has continued in each letter to me.

The Lord brought sunshine into our lives by the wonderful miracle that He performed on my birthday in 1989. Suddenly, both our lives started changing into a world of beauty that had gone unnoticed before. I rejoiced that God had chosen me to serve Him this way. We never know the joy that can be ours until we go willingly for Jesus' sake. "Father, we don't know why You brought us together, but we will gladly accept our love for each other as a gift from You. When the storms of life close in, we will hide beneath the shadow of Your Mighty Wings and there we will find comfort and peace. Show us the way gently, my Lord, and lead us with Your Hand of mercy. We love you, Father, and we praise Your Name for all the beautiful blessings that You have extended us by Your glorious grace," I prayed.

CHAPTER 3

WALKING IN GRACE

Truly Ted and I had entered a story book world. We had found true happiness at last. I realized that we weren't young any longer, yet we were as happy as if we had never experienced love before and were just discovering how beautiful it is. We wrote all of the lovely things young lovers are too shy to write about such as the beauty of God's creation through new eyes of understanding. The roses were more beautiful than I had ever seen. Their sweet aroma made me smile with a greater appreciation for the Lord. Loving Ted gave me the ability to describe many scenes of beauty. The fields were splashed with brilliant colors that only the great Master Artist could paint. Golden reeds stood tall among the green grass of the fading summer. They swayed yielding to the gentle breezes. The tiny stars twinkled brightly on a clear night as I looked toward heaven into the Face of God. I praised Him for the sheer wonder of it all.

My life was filled with laughter and singing as I walked with Christ daily. I learned how lovely life could be as if I had only just discovered how gentle Christ was. Free at last to walk in freedom and to love Ted to a greater depth was a glorious feeling. Beautiful rainbows appeared without warning as my Father renewed His Covenant of grace now and then. I needed these lovely things in my life and in my heart as I entered into the strange and often times frightening world of the prison. The contrast is overwhelming to a woman all alone, but God was faithful to His promise that He would supply His grace, which would strengthen me when I called on His Name.

Ted put my name on his visitors' list so I started making plans to visit him. We could have one contact visit a month during those days. It had to be a member of his family on these special visits. Ted could hold me in his arms and kiss me for one minute, then we had to sit at a table opposite each other and be together for two hours as we visited. He gave me all the instructions I would need, what to carry and this was my driver's license for identification and a small billfold to carry some change in. I would have to know his Texas Department of Corrections number also. The thought of guards everywhere really frightened me.

Ted wrote stating, "I can hardly wait to see you again." I couldn't wait either, but the closer the day approached for our visit, the more I became excited. The last time we had seen each other was when Dad passed away and I only saw him briefly then. The thought of seeing him after all these years was more like a dream than a reality. It was as though we were living out a love story with every event in order just like the Lord had planned.

I sent Ted a picture of myself taken just recently so he would know what I looked like and he was pleased. The only picture I had of him was a small snapshot that I had taken many years before of him and his brother, Jacob. I had a couple of his school pictures, which Mom had given me when he was a boy. One was when he was a teenager with the sweet smile of innocence on his handsome face. Joyce had a newspaper clipping of Ted that a photographer had taken of him in the prison yard. It was a hazy photo, but I could tell that it was Ted walking across the yard. I didn't really care what he looked like, though. My only concern at that time was that I was going to see the man I really loved again.

I worried about my appearance like any woman who loved a younger man when she was already fifty-seven years old. Ted was seven years younger and I knew there wasn't any way to hide the wrinkles in my face. I had lived a hard life with Jacob and looked years older than I really was, but every night I prayed that God would make me beautiful in Ted's eyes. My self-esteem at that point was very low, but the sweet Holy Spirit would comfort me saying in a soft gentle voice, "Ted will think you are beautiful. He always has you know." "Yes, Father, I know Ted has always seen me through blind eyes. Only You could have make him love me in the way he has for so many years. It is truly marvelous how true love is able to endure through the years and not lose the beauty that You placed in our hearts. Oh, Jesus, help me to be all things sweet and lovely to Ted now that I am free to love him completely," I prayed. Isabella said, "Mamma, let me go with you to see Ted this time. You are so nervous that I am afraid you will have a wreck and besides, your old Pontiac isn't dependable. It will be my joy and pleasure to be with you on your first date." Her suggestion eased my mind because I was beside myself with happiness and told her that it was a wonderful idea if Steve didn't mind. Steve grinned and said, "I don't mind. She wouldn't listen if I told her she couldn't go."

I was like a young girl on her very first date when I started getting dressed to go and see Ted. I was so nervous I don't know what I would have done if Isabella hadn't been there to calm me down. Isabella was pretty excited too. Laughing happily, she said, "Mamma, I never dreamed the time would come when I would help you get ready for a date. Just sit down and I'll fix your hair before you fall apart." She helped me choose the dress that I would wear while I fussed and fretted almost in tears. She held me by the shoulders and said, "Mamma, calm down or you will be sick." I told her, "I'll try, but it's hard to be calm when in just a few hours I'll be with Ted again. I still can't believe it's actually happening and I can hold him close the way I always wanted to."

We finally got off to Huntsville, but my nerves were in a state of shock by the time we arrived. We parked the car and got out and I looked up at the guard post and shuddered. Once inside, my mind went blank and I couldn't remember Ted's TDC number, but the guard wrote his number down on a piece of paper and said, "You will need it when you get inside." Isabella took my arm and led me inside through barred doors that were opened electronically by a guard on a crosswalk suspended over us. Then we entered another door and waited in line to show our ID to another guard.

Once the guard checked us in, I requested a contact visit. The guard said, "You can have one, but your daughter can't go in with you. She can visit if you take a regular visit, though." My heart was sick because I wanted to be with Ted after not seeing him in such a long time and then being unable to touch him. Isabella smiled and said, "Mamma, take a contact visit, I don't mind. I'll wait for you at the park tables I saw under the trees. It's nice out there and I can rest from our trip while I wait for you."

The guard wouldn't let Isabella wait for me. They sent her outside and I waited in the waiting room with the other visitors who were just as anxious as I was. It seemed like an eternity before they called out Ted's name. Then they gave me a piece of paper to present to another guard. They told me where the visiting area was and I walked outside into the bright sunlight and saw Isabella sitting on a park bench smiling reassuringly as I started down the sidewalk to where Ted waited for me.

A brisk autumn wind caught the slip of paper and sent it sailing down the sidewalk to add to my fears. Finally, I retrieved it before I reached the corner where another guard tower was located and fear wrenched my heart as I walked under it. As I continued around the building and down the sidewalk, it seemed as though my legs felt like rubber and wouldn't hold me up. I was afraid that I would stumble since I was so nervous and excited at the thought of seeing Ted again. I thought as I looked down at my feet, 'Destiny, I know that you are in a hurry, but walk carefully or you might trip and fall.'

When I reached the small building in front of the entrance to the yard where the visitors met, a guard checked my ID again, then another guard led me to the table they had assigned for us and told me that Ted would be here shortly. I waited anxiously and prayed as I looked around, "I'm so nervous, Father, and so afraid. There are so many guards everywhere I look with guard towers on every corner and entrance. There are rolls of barbed wire on top of the hurricane fence around the yard where the picnic tables are. The canopies are nice, though, and protects me from the sun. This is such a strange place that I unfamiliar with and I can't believe my loved one really lives here, but I know he does. Ted and I have waited so long for this moment and now that it has come we will need Your glorious grace in a special way. Help us be strong now and not fall apart when we see each other for the first time after so many years."

My heart raced with joy when Ted suddenly appeared just outside the gate. A guard searched him before he would let him enter the yard where I was. As Ted entered the yard through the gate, I stood on my feet and held my breath, unable to speak. I wanted to run into his arms, but fear of the guards caused me to hesitate after making a few steps toward him. Ted walked fast, almost running while he held his eyes on me. Then he held me in his arms and kissed me. Then we looked at each other and our tears trickled down our cheeks freely because God had finally brought us together after so many years.

Ted smiled happily and said, "You just fit inside my arms and it seems like you were always meant to be there." I don't understand the ways of God and the love He places in our hearts for certain people, but both of us found the sweetest peace we had ever known before. Ted hadn't changed that much, maybe a little thinner than when I had last seen him. His hair was thinning too, but I didn't care. He didn't seem to mind the wrinkles in my face either or my gray hair that I had been so concerned about. We were so excited to finally be together and the way we had aged didn't seem to matter at all.

"They won't let me hold you in my arms but one minute, Darling, but I wish I could hold you like this forever and never have to let you go. Only these prison walls will every separate us again, Destiny. No one can keep us from expressing our love for each other anymore," Ted whispered in my ear with his cheek pressing against mine which were both moist with our tears.

"I love you so much, Darling," Ted said tenderly as he looked into my face. "I love you Ted and always will," I promised. Time seemed to stand still while we held each other, but the short time we were allowed passed very quickly. We were trembling and teary-eyed as Ted took my arm and seated me across the table from him and reaching across the table wiped away the tears on my face with loving tenderness. We just gazed into each other's eyes for a while and many previous memories rushed through my mind. Days of long ago became very real again as if all the terrible things that had happened were only a bad dream.

Our ties were very strong and go back to Mom and Dad and Jacob and I getting married when we were just kids and Ted only nine years old. I stood before Mom's mirror on my wedding day while Ted stood watching with curiosity. Then at the chapel when Jacob and I were taking our vows, I turned my head toward the small group that sat behind us and Ted was watching attentively. "Oh, Ted, we have loved each other so many years," I cried through my tears. "I can't believe so much has happened over the years and then God's marvelous grace would bring us together again like this," I sobbed. Ted took my hand in his and said, "It's so wonderful to be with you like this. I feel like a new man since Christ came into my life, Precious, and I've been born again with the past being forgiven and a new life just beginning. We can't erase what has been done, but we can learn from our mistakes and not repeat them."

Ted turned in his seat and pointed toward a barred window above. He said, "That is where I have often stood and looked out over the yard where we are. I ached in my heart and prayed that one day God would send someone to love me again. I could picture in my mind visiting at one of these tables just like we are now." He smiled and thanked God for hearing and answering his prayer. Tears welled up in my eyes as his testimony touched my heart. God sent his sister-in-law and neither of us suspected He would.

"Isn't it strange how marvelous God is, Ted? When you were praying that God would send someone to love you, I was praying that God would fill my life with purpose. We were many miles apart, Ted, and I'm so glad that distance didn't matter to the Lord. I was very sincere when I prayed, Precious, and I did want God to give my life purpose, but I thought more about just serving Him a few hours each day, not a full surrender to heartache that would keep me on my knees constantly. Only God knows how much pain I will suffer and He must supply the grace He promised or I'll go down in utter defeat," I said, still uncertain and unable to comprehend the great power of my Lord and Master.

"I am still walking in a dream world too, Honey," Ted said smiling. "I remember how Jacob treated you in the past and the way you stood by him. I have complete faith and trust in you because you were a good wife to my brother. There were many times I would bite my lip when he was cruel to you. It made me furious when Mother would run you down and try to make you look bad in my eyes. Pauline just couldn't understand why I defended you all those years and she was jealous because I cared for you so much. She would accuse me of having feelings for my sister-in-law that I shouldn't have. She was right, I guess, but I wasn't even ready to admit to myself how much I did care for you. I loved Pauline and Jacob, but I loved them in a different way," Ted said thoughtfully.

Ted smiled and said, "Destiny, I did have special feelings for you when I was just a teenager. I thought you were the most beautiful woman in the world. Do you remember when we lived near Port Lavaca and I brought my friends by your house so they could get a look at you? Then, over the years I worried about you and even after Pauline and I married, I would lie awake many times wondering if you were cold or hungry. I drove by your house many times when Jacob was gone at night just to see if you were all right. When I tried to be near you when I knew Jacob was gone, you always said emphatically, 'Go home to your wife and family, Ted.' I asked God to send me someone to love me, Darling, and Jesus sent the very best, the one I had loved all the time. Oh, I'm so glad He sent you to me. God performed a beautiful miracle in my life, Destiny!"

Ted said, "Honey, when you start to the car stop by the telephone booth near the entrance and look up at the building and watch for my hand waving through a broken screen. Tell Isabella I want to wave to her and tell her that I love her." "I will," I said excitedly.

Broken Pieces of Beauty

Everything about our new life was filled with beauty almost as though we were living out a fairy tale and a beautiful love story. There is so much mystery surrounding our lives that it is unbelievable. However, the Lord doesn't do things halfway and He does all things well. He has many beautiful surprises for those who place their trust in Him by faith.

I looked at my watch and discovered our two hours were almost over. Then Ted took my hands in his and said, "Darling Destiny, let's pray." Tears fell when he prayed thanking God for His rich blessings and His grace that had brought us so far and that we needed so much when we had to part. He prayed for our family and the forgiveness of our sins and that somehow his children would forgive him for the terrible thing he had done. Ted and I began learning how great God's grace truly is during that first meeting. The first true test came when a guard walked over to our table and said it was time to part.

When I stood up with Ted at the end of the table, I trembled and my legs didn't want to hold me up as we said our good-byes. Our eyes filled with tears and with trembling lips we kissed and held each other tightly. I was stammering as I said, "I'll be back soon, Darling." Then he smiled and said, "I love you," one more time. Ted walked hastily toward the gate where he would be searched again before going back inside the Wall Unit. I walked out the gate, which clanged shut behind me and startled me for a moment. Then I realized that sharp clanging noises were being heard from all over the prison. As I drew near the area where Isabella waited, I saw her sitting at the table smiling at me. I told her what Ted had told me about waiting near the telephone booth and we watched for him and his hand to wave through the window up above. I thought excitedly, 'This is just like a love story with knights in shining armor.'

I looked up after a short time and saw Ted's hand appear. Isabella and I laughed happily as we blew kisses and waved goodbye and then we went on to the parking lot. We went across the street to eat before we started the trip back to Newton. I could see the area clearly where Ted said his cell was located from the window where we sat. I was happy, but my heart ached terribly. I looked toward the building where my Darling was confined and wondered if his heart was aching like mine.

I thought about the power of God's grace and prayed in my heart, `Father, my heart hurts so much that it feels as if it will burst. It's a sweet hurt though, because Ted and I are so in so in love with each other and it's wonderful. I do believe You are taking us down a path of beauty we have never experienced before.'

CHAPTER 4

COMFORT FROM THE HOLY SPIRIT

A sweet Spirit filled the church the following Sunday after my first visit with Ted. I wanted to shout to the world about the joy Christ had brought into my life, but I knew that very few would share my happiness since Ted was in prison. I also realized that it would require a lot of faith on their part to believe that God had truly sent me to Ted during the church service on my birthday. Surely they could see how happy I had been lately, but I was reluctant to tell them my story. It was very hard to keep it to myself as I was very proud that Ted and I had finally found each other. I didn't want folks to think that I was ashamed of Ted, but for now I would be silent. They would find it out eventually.

Thoughts of Ted ran through my mind during the worship service. I prayed that God would keep Ted safe from harm and let him know that I loved him. I also prayed that God would give us the strength to endure the trials ahead, especially when our story began spreading throughout the small community where I lived and the church. Sweet memories of God's call still lingered in my mind like a lovely song that you can't dismiss from your mind. I stood alone as usual apart from the others when we stood for the dismissal prayer. My eyes were wet with tears as I prayed silently. Then suddenly to my surprise, Jesus spoke softly in my ear, "You are loved." His sweet tender voice melted my heart and tears of joy streamed down my face as I knew then without a doubt that God was pleased with me.

God sent His glorious grace in such a beautiful way, but I knew if I told the church they would accuse me of hearing things. It is very hard for most folks to believe that

Jesus speaks to certain ones in an audible voice. The church members didn't hear Him speak. They had their heads bowed in prayer and no one noticed me. I couldn't see the glory of God in the church, but His Holy presence filled the church and I trembled amazed with wonder and joy. 'Heaven must be rejoicing right along with me,' I thought. His sweet voice had spoken softly and gently and I cried softly praying, "Oh, Father, Your very presence is so profound and the church doesn't realize that Christ is here. Let others doubt, Father, even if they refuse to believe in miracles. They say they do, but I don't believe they will think that the things You say to me are a miracle, but I do. You healed the blind and raised the dead by speaking to them long ago, so why can't Your children be content and happy to hear Your sweet voice as I did this Lord's day? I really don't have a thing to ask You for only to hear Your sweet voice say, 'You are loved.' Oh, my Lord, I love You with all my heart." I rejoiced all the way home as God blessed my heart with hope and the assurance that He was with Ted and I, no matter what trials lay ahead. My greatest trial would be when the children made plans to gather home on Thanksgiving. I dreaded telling them about God sending me to the prison where Ted was confined. Ted and I discussed that subject on our visit.

He said, "Destiny, even though I'm the kids' uncle they may not like the idea of your visiting me. Sam and Mark are preachers and they pastor churches. Their ministry could be affected because their members might not understand. How strong is your faith, Precious? Can it hold up if they turn their backs on you for the decision that you've made? If you should change your mind, Darling, I would understand. I replied, "I'm certain God sent me to you and I surrendered my life to Christ. I won't turn away from my Lord for anyone, Darling. He promised to send His grace when I needed Him, so God will deal with the children. God's marvelous grace has been there for me since Jesus saved my soul, even through the hard times with Jacob. Yes, I will follow Christ, even if it becomes a cross that I must bear." Ted smiled and I knew he was proud of me. Most of all I knew in my heart that I had won the respect of the man I loved. Ted took my hands in his and said, "Darling, let's stand by each other and follow the convictions of our hearts. Even if some of the children don't agree with our decision and they write a letter asking me to let you go, I won't as long as you feel the way you do. I won't listen to anyone but you, but if things get too overwhelming and you can't continue bearing this heavy burden, then tell me so and then, Darling, I will release you from any promise that you've made to me. I have witnessed others in this prison that have made commitments they couldn't keep. Many marriages have fallen apart because the pressures were too great. I can't blame the women for giving up in defeat. These men have brought confinement on themselves for the crimes they have committed."

Ted continued talking and I listened silently, "Precious, you deserve better than I can offer you. You came to me to share my life, but you aren't guilty of anything wrong. I need you more than I can say, but I love you so much and I am so ashamed that I ruined our chance to be together by the sin that I have done. I pray that God will grant you the power to bear up under the strain of the heartache and despair which can be overwhelming at times. Until you came into my life, I didn't have anything to live for. No one has ever loved me like you do and given as much as you have, my Beloved." "I love you, my Darling Ted, I always will. I am very glad that you are mine," I told Ted softly.

The children gathered home for Thanksgiving. Joyce and Isabella already knew about Ted, but the boys didn't yet. After dinner, I asked them to gather around because I had to talk to them. They stood around the bar and stood quietly while I began my testimony. They were very quiet and the silence was deafening. Mark's eyes were damp with tears and he was the first to speak. "Mamma, I can't judge what God has done. All I can do is place you in God's hands. I know the Lord calls us to serve Him and Ted does need help, but why does it have to be you, Mamma? You have been through so much. I didn't want you to tie yourself down to anyone or marry again. I wanted you to live out your days in peace without problems and the thought of what lies ahead stuns me, but only God knows what He wants for you."

Sam stood silently listening and I felt that he was struggling for the right thing to say. Finally he said, "Mamma, I agree with Mark. I will place you in God's hands and pray for you. They began talking about the power of God to save the lost no matter what a person has done. Through Ted, they learned things about the purity of Jesus' blood and its' power to save regardless of what sin a person had done in the flesh. Mark said, "God said that He would forgive any sin except one and that was blaspheming the Holy Spirit which God wouldn't forgive." Wayne, my oldest, laughed happily and remarked, "Just look how happy Mamma is. She is happier than I've ever seen her. Whether it is Ted or Christ that placed this glow of happiness on her face, I glad for Mamma. She deserves happiness no matter who put it there." My heart rejoiced and the boys seemed content.

We went to visit Jacob's grave later that day. Joyce brought a monument from Louisiana to place at his head. We took food and drinks to have a picnic later. The little kids played games and the grownups joined them. They played while I enjoyed their being together. I thought as I stood near Jacob's grave, "Jacob, aren't you proud of your family?" I just knew that he smiled down from Heaven as he watched them play. If he were here, he would be running and playing too and I could almost hear him laughing heartily.

Joyce kept to herself because she was upset. She saw the marker for Ted's grave next to mine. "Don't worry, Joyce," I told her, "I'll pay for Ted's funeral." She had helped pay for Jacob's funeral, but only the marker for his grave. She couldn't argue the point because she knew it was true.

Joyce pouted the remainder of the evening while the rest played games and enjoyed being together. Most of the children went their separate ways later that night. Joyce and Gentry didn't because they planned to leave in the morning. When things settled down later that night, Gentry and Joyce sat at the table and Joyce started crying. "You don't love Daddy, Mamma, and I wonder if you ever did. You talk about Daddy like he was bad, but he wasn't, he was good. I don't know why you are so excited about Uncle Ted when he doesn't have anything to offer or help you because he's probably going to spend his life behind bars for what he did. He won't even come up for parole until 2004 and you may die before then and you'll have wasted your life away for nothing." Gentry agreed with Joyce and said, "I wish I hadn't agreed to let her write to Ted in the first place. I even let Darlene write also which was a mistake. I shouldn't have let my daughter get involved with a criminal even though he is a member of the family."

I stood on my feet and held the back of my chair to help steady me instantly realizing my faith in God was being severely put to the test. "You children don't realize that I didn't run to Ted on my own. You haven't been listening to my testimony that God sent me to him. This wasn't my idea, far from it, I can assure you, because my little world of contentment has turned into something I'm not familiar with. I was very afraid when God sent me to a prison. My God, Gentry, I'd never seen the inside of a jail before and the idea of going to a strange place like the Wall Unit in Huntsville was very frightening. I couldn't believe that God would lay such a burden on my shoulders so soon after Jacob passed away, especially since I was having trouble just adjusting to his death.

"God me a promise and a Covenant with me as I cried out to Him that I wasn't able to endure the trials I knew I would have to face if I accepted His call. He told me that His grace would supply my every need then. Don't you understand that God never sends His servant on a mission without equipping that person with whatever is needed. I couldn't refuse Jesus, Gentry, because He has never forsaken me through the hard times when I went against Jacob to serve Him and bring our children up to know Christ as their Savior. The Lord intervened many times and stood between Jacob and myself. Many times Jacob threatened to leave me and take the kids away from me, sometimes even threatening to take my life as well. I have been so terrified at times that I couldn't speak when Jacob was really angry. Gentry, don't you realize that I have experienced the great power of God's grace all through the years and without that great power and grace I would not be standing here tonight. I know the voice of Jesus, my Redeemer and the Great Shepherd who sent me to the prison with the promise to be with me."

Gentry's heart hardened and his voice became accusing as he stated, "I don't believe God spoke to you. It was the devil. You are going against everything you have taught all these years and you have listened to the devil. God wouldn't send you to such a place." His words stung and hurt severely, but I wouldn't relent. I knew positively that God had called me to serve Him in this manner. God's grace is powerful and I relied on His grace to make my speech steady without faltering or being weak. Boldly, I looked into the face of my daughter and son-in-law and said, "I will stand with my God no matter what you believe. If I lose all my children and they turn their backs on me, I will still trust and follow Jesus wherever He leads me. I love every one of you and I had hoped that you would stand with me because I am facing a cruel world that has the same views as you do. The time will come when you will realize that you have judged me wrongfully. I am not going to argue with you any longer. I am going to bed." Then I turned away and went to the bedroom leaving them sitting at the table, but I heard them discussing the terrible things Mamma was doing lately.

It had been a trying day, weary and exhausting, so I went to bed early. As I laid my head on the pillow I prayed, "Father, bless my family. Please help them understand and believe this glorious thing You have done for Ted and I. If only they will believe that You sent me into Ted's life and believe that it was You who did this beautiful miracle instead of viewing these things from the fleshly mind. I realize this thing You have done is hard for them to accept because they only see the bad side and the shame that I have brought upon them, my Father. In time, Father, open their eyes that they might clearly see. In the meantime, my Father, I will trust in You to send Your glorious grace to them that they too might believe."

Gentry came to my room several times during the night waking me up and trying to convince me that God didn't call me at all. It was Satan instead, but I held firm knowing in my heart what was true. When I got up the next morning, Joyce and Gentry were loading up their car. Joyce didn't speak or say goodbye, but Gentry came back inside three times trying to change my mind. Tears stung my eyes as they drove away. I pleaded with Jesus to help them understand this stand that I had taken for my Lord and Savior who had called me to serve Him in this way.

Another giant mountain had been crossed, I thought, but it has left my hurt and bruised. I was certain that God in His own time would bring them to the understanding and knowledge that God had really called me to serve Him in this manner.

The victory would come when God was ready. It wasn't long before I received a letter from Joyce. She was still angry and accused me of not loving her Daddy. I understood that she grieved for the loss of her father, but to accuse me of never loving him simply wasn't true and she knew it, but would not accept. I answered her letter and said, "Yes, Joyce, I did wrong when I compared Ted to Jacob when you were at home. I had hoped my children would understand because they witnessed first hand his abuse with cruel words as well as his threats until he was finally saved. I am still angry because he left me with some many debts to pay, which could have been avoided, if he had not chosen to ignore them. Now they are my burden. Jacob thought problems would disappear if he refused to face them. He didn't want the responsibility placed on his shoulders and when any sort of problem came up, he escaped on his truck leaving me to deal with it. I always made up excuses for Jacob because I loved him, but since he died I have had to face up to so many things that I didn't allow myself to deal with in the past. We all grieve in different ways, Joyce. There are times when I hate Jacob for leaving me without anything. I have experienced so many mixed emotions of love, bitterness and regret. There are so many broken pieces of my life, which can never be mended.

Through Ted I found a ray of hope that I have never known. God gave me someone who loves me and has for all these many years. I am sure Jacob loved us in his own way, but he wasn't perfect and I refuse to place him on a pedestal now that he is gone. God did send me into Ted's life and I will not turn back now. I hope that you will understand in time because I love you so much. Of all my children, I thought you would be happy for me. After all, it was you that pleaded with me to write to Ted. I did love your father and I gave him the best years of my life. Now I just want to be happy in the few years remaining that I have left on this earth."

My heart was broken because Joyce wouldn't or couldn't understand. I loved her and had always depended on her through the years. She had helped me with the babies when she was just a baby herself. She didn't seem interested in boys until she met Gentry. She had reached out to Ted first which made me proud and happy because she had always been so kind and understanding.

I realized then that only the Holy Spirit could help her believe my testimony by opening her heart and mind to bring her to the knowledge and understanding that God had sent me to Ted. Joyce would be the first of many as my faith was put on test. `Would I really be able hold out through these storms and trials for Christ's sake,' I asked myself?

The Holy Spirit began dealing with Joyce through dreams. I was surprised, but I realized that God's grace is a powerful force and always knows what is needed in every situation. When our problems overwhelm us and we can't find a solution, all we need to do is place them at the feet of Jesus and He will work them out for us. I felt caught in the middle of everything going on in my life right then while I was desperately trying to hold fast to my call from the Lord and at the same time loving my children with all my heart, but it hurt terribly when they questioned that God had called me. The children couldn't comprehend our situation any more than I did. I acted entirely upon faith alone, but the children didn't seem to have grown enough in faith to accept this fact nor even try to understand what was really happening. Through this first test that I was facing, however, they would learn much more about the Holy Spirit's power.

Joyce called one day not too long after and told me about her dreams. She said the Lord sent her these dreams to show her how wrong she had been.

Her first dream was about her Grandmother Quinn who had died in 1979. She was my mother-in-law and I called her Mom. Joyce said, "Mamma, I saw Grandmother in a very strange place. She wandered aimlessly alone as if she were lost. She seemed to be searching for someone, but could not find them. She had such a sad look on her face that it broke my heart. I thought about her children and the things that have happened since she died. If she knew about Ted, it would break her heart. As she drew near, I called out to her, 'Grandmother, is it really you?' Oh, Mamma, she didn't hear me. She just turned away and continued her search in the mist." Joyce cried, "Mamma, do you think Grandmother was searching for her children?" I told her, "I don't know, Honey. Many times she asked me to pray for them, especially Ted." Joyce said, "Mamma, I hope Grandmother finds rest and her soul is at peace." I said, "I do too, Joyce, and I believe if she can see from heaven that I have gone to Ted she would be happy." Then Joyce said, "Mamma, I dreamed about Daddy, too. In this dream, I was at a prison, which I assumed to be where Ted is confined. I walked through white sliding doors into a waiting area. A guard checked me in and directed me to another waiting room that was solid white also. I sat alone on a white bench and cried. I didn't understand why I was there, but I knew that Ted must be there. Suddenly Daddy appeared, but I was mad at him, so I turned my back on him. He was so handsome in his navy blue suit. He was young again, Mamma, and he glistened as if shimmering lights gleamed from his clothing and his handsome face. He flew like an angel and showed me what he could do. He fluttered near my face as he tried to draw my attention. He said happily, 'Look, Joyce, I can fly. Don't be sad for me because I am very happy. I fly anywhere that I want to and I see places that I have never seen. There are so many wonders in the universe to discover, Joyce. Please don't cry for me because I am finally free to explore God's creation and I am excited. Your mother deserves some happiness too, Joyce. She has been through so much. Don't fight against her now.' Then Daddy disappeared and I woke up knowing that Daddy had found what he had searched for all of his life. Mamma, I won't fight against you anymore. I know now that it is God's will that you be with Ted." "Glory to God," I cried thanking God for His love. A love strong enough to bring peace between the two of us when only God could have resolved the situation. Now my daughter and I received healing beneath the Wings of God. There is no sweeter place to find comfort than in the mighty arms of the Lord. The Holy Spirit knows the mind of our Father and He knows what to do. It pays to wait on an answer from heaven and not act rashly on your own.

CHAPTER 5

GRACE THROUGH FIRE

"Please, Father, be kind and patient with me as I meet those who oppose Your will for me. The children know about it, but the church doesn't know yet except for Mikie and J. T. Father, I was not afraid to tell them, but some will ridicule and reproach me for my commitment to Ted. I am unsure of my ability to stand bravely so that You won't be ashamed of me. You promised that the Holy Spirit would give us the words to speak when we are in the midst of people who will not understand. Lord, help me to speak with grace and confidence that will leave no doubt that You sent me to someone in prison," I prayed realizing the greatness of the witness that I wouldn't be able to resist or ignore.

I also realized that God's grace was powerful, but so far my witnessing had only just begun. It was ever my desire to be a faithful witness like the many that had gone before me. It was a real challenge just to give my testimony to my family, but to tell my friends and acquaintances what God had done was going to be an even greater challenge and would have to be approached differently. What glory would the Lord receive from the witness He gave to me if I kept His call a secret?

So I decided to tell my former pastor about God sending me to Ted first. He had retired from the ministry since his health had worsened over the last few years. He had been my friend for many years and I believed that he would understand the Lord's call to me. He had always regarded me favorably as being faithful to the church and to the Lord. So one Sunday morning as I sat on the pew in front of him, I leaned over and whispered to him, "Bro. William, I want to tell you how the Lord spoke to me a few weeks ago right here at the church and He sent me to Ted, Jacob's brother, who is in prison at Huntsville." Bro. William leaned over and whispered in my ear saying, "I won't tell a soul and I promise to keep your secret." It was very hard to control my emotions and hold back the tears that were so close to the surface. I didn't have the opportunity to explain my feelings because the service started. I walked to the piano hurt and confused, but I realized that it was be very hard for these folks to believe that God would send me on such a mission since they didn't hear God when he spoke to me. They would think like so many others would when I told my story that God couldn't possibly send a woman to a prison and only the devil would do such a thing.

"How can I convince them, Father," I pleaded in tears. "Must I go through the fires of hell to prove my love for You? I need their support and prayers," I beseeched Him earnestly. "Oh, God, stand by me and give me the courage to give my testimony bravely," I cried. I realized my mission had only just begun and I was already suffering. Folks that I thought would be strong failed me unexpectedly. Yet God had sent the Holy Spirit to give Joyce comfort. Now I must place my trust in God and let Him reveal His will for me to others.

The news spread quickly throughout the community that Isabella's mother was visiting a man in prison, but the church didn't mention it much at first. As time went by, Bro. William would tease me when I settled in my pew. He would ask, "Well, Mrs. Quinn, did you go to the pen yesterday?" His questioning stung my heart as I pictured Ted in a hog pen. It would bring tears to my eyes and I would feel like an outcast, but I bit my lip and didn't say anything.

Bro. William wasn't the only one who objected to my mission for Christ. My sister, Heather, rejected my testimony also thinking that I made up the story, I'm sure. She tried to convince me that Ted was a murderer and didn't deserve my care or the help that I gave him. She pitied her sister who beamed with happiness. She thought her sister had stars in her eyes and couldn't see clearly. Heather wanted me to be happy, but she couldn't believe that I could be happy with Ted. "How could you possibly find any happiness with Ted when you know he will spend his life behind the walls of a prison," she asked, concerned about me. "I know you love him, Destiny, but what possible good can he ever be to you. He can't help you or take care of you. You are wasting your life for nothing and that is a shame. You have so much to offer a good man, but you are throwing your life away. I am really concerned about you and I wish that you would listen to me," Heather pleaded. "Oh, Heather, you are not listening to me. God sent me to Ted," I cried trying to get through to her. She truly wasn't listening. It was as if she had closed her mind and heart to my testimony. She had helped me in the past by sending me money, but eventually she stopped and like so many, she fell by the wayside.

Times got hard for the both of us when the summer months set in. The pie business fell off and it didn't pick up again until fall.

Ted and shared our first Christmas together in 1989. We looked forward to the holiday with hope in our hearts. We were together as a family and we shut the world out and even though other family members were excited as they visited their loved ones at tables near us in the prison. Our relationship grew in beauty as time went by and this

Christmas had a special meaning to both of us, even though we had to be cautious about the way we presented ourselves since we were supposed to be sister and brother until the Lord saw fit to change it.

Ted was beside himself with joy because he received a beautiful Bible for his Christmas gift from Isabella and myself. “Destiny,” Ted exclaimed happily, “this Bible has everything in it to guide my understanding. I am very protective of it and I place it carefully back in the box when I have finished studying it. I want to thank you and Isabella for this beautiful gift. I will treasure it always. I have been so richly blessed since you came into my life.” Then tears began to well up in Ted’s eyes. His lips trembled as he stated, “You will always be my precious gift from Heaven, Darling. Whether it is Christmas or any other special day except for the gift of salvation, you are the most treasured gift that I ever received. When I think of God’s great love and the love He bestowed on me through you, I can’t help but cry in joy unspeakable.”

Tears of joy wet my cheeks as well and then holding Ted’s hands in mine, we prayed thanking God for all the wonders He had done for us. We parted with a smile on our faces, but our hearts longed for the freedom to one day be together always.

As I walked down the sidewalk and waited on the hill to wave goodbye once more, I thought how lovely our life was now, even though we both suffered pain, I was beginning to learn what the meaning of beauty was as our love story began to unfold. Although our love began many years ago, through the Lord we had discovered the deep feelings that we had experienced then was truly love. A love that had been kept in reserve until God saw fit for it to be expressed in His own time and for His own reasons, I was sure. “Go with God, my own true love,” I whispered as I waved goodbye. "I love you," I shouted as Ted walked up to the guards who led him back inside the old Wall Unit.

Because of the beauty of our lives together, I often fought back tears as I made my way toward the car. The old red brick wall always looked so lonely as I walked down the sidewalk time and time again. `This is not an easy life,' I thought, `but through God's grace, we will bear the hurt and pain for the beauty of our love.' My heart was heavy as I approached Livingston and then my sorrow changed to ecstatic joy as a beautiful rainbow appeared far away. Suddenly, I realized that God was confirming His Covenant with me once again and with the realization, I began to praise His Holy Name. "Truly You are my Master, my Lord and King forever," I cried. My tears fell all the same, but this time they were tears of joy instead of pain and heartache.

The rainbow was such an unusual one and quite different from any I had ever seen before. It rose above the tree line and it looked like a giant steeple on a church. The colors were deep and vibrant and reached toward Heaven. They were blue, gold, green and purple and made a picture of mysterious beauty and wonder. The Holy Spirit touched me greatly and my heart pounded loudly. I knew that it would evaporate soon, so I wanted to drink in all of its' beauty so I wouldn't forget the wonder I saw. I praised God for the lovely miracle that He sent in His mercy knowing how much I needed to be lifted up. As the rainbow faded, I knew God was pleased with me, but I would still need His assurance every step of the way.

When I got home, I gathered some things and walked across the yard to Granny Smith's house. Granny and I would spend this Christmas together, and she stated laughing as I went inside saying, "Come on in, Destiny. It looks like us two old widow women will spend Christmas together this year." I laughed too, but that thought hadn't occurred to me. "Granny, I can't think of a nicer way to spend Christmas than with you," I told her. It's nice to have someone to share Christmas with. Now, neither of us will be alone."

I spent the night with Granny on the weekends a lot when her sitter was off. Neither Granny nor I cared much for television, so Granny told me many stories about her life, mostly about her childhood. She would rock gently in her wheelchair while memories of the past flooded her mind. A gleam of pride shone in her eyes as she pointed toward the location of the old homestead. She said that her parents moved to Newton from Mississippi in a covered wagon.

They had built a house, but one day her mother gathered their laundry and she and the kids carried it to the creek nearby to do their washing. They saw smoke rising above the treetops. Granny sighed, "We ran home as fast as we could, but we couldn't save our home. It burned to the ground in a very short time. The neighbors all pitched in and helped us build another house. I am glad we had a few things left that we had taken to wash in the creek," Granny said thoughtfully.

Granny chuckled softly, then wiping a wisp of hair from her face, she held out her hands and turned them over as if she were looking for a scar of some sort, she began a story about a flock of geese her mother raised. "It was one of my chores to pick goose feathers now and then. Oh, I hated that job because the geese pecked my hands and arms so severely that they bled. At the time I wasn't thankful for my soft feather bed and pillows, but when our house burned, we had to sleep on bedding made with pine straw. So, the next time Mama told me to pick the geese, I didn't mind," Granny stated wistfully.

Thelma Quinn

It was twilight and as the sun set beneath the tree line, I said, "Granny, are you getting tired?" She glanced out through the glass storm door as she rocked back and forth, then replied, "No, I want to stay up until it is dark. Some of the kids might stop by on their way home." So I relaxed in the big over stuffed chair and listened as Granny continued with her many precious memories of the past.

Granny turned her wheelchair slightly toward the kitchen table as if in memory she could picture her husband, Durham, sitting there. I knew Steve and his folks had built Granny this new house and they had built it on the same spot where the old homestead had stood. For a moment she smiled and her eyes twinkled, then she chuckled and said, "You know, I don't know how I ever managed to marry Durham. Lord, I was so shy when I was a girl. When a boy came to visit, I would hide from him. I acted so silly, but times were different then," she said blushing at the thought.

Granny waved her hand in the direction of the fields where J. T. and Mikie, Steve's mother and dad, graze their cows, then she said, "Durham had farmed this land and their roots were in this valley. They had brought up seven children, three girls and four boys. Some of them lived nearby and two boys had moved away." Granny pointed toward the dining table and said sadly, "Durham died right there at the supper table." She added tearfully, "We were about to start eating. Durham had turned thanks when he suddenly leaned forward with his head lying on the table. I pulled the chair backward and gently laid it back and then placed his head on a pillow, then ran to Mikie's seeking help. My husband was dead and it was a great loss." I sympathized with Granny because I had experienced the same kind of sudden loss when Jacob died.

"Granny, you have been a marvel and so blessed by the Lord. You have set such a great example for others to follow. Now, my Darling, it is bedtime and I am exhausted. Let's turn in now because tomorrow is Christmas and it will be a big day for all of us," I said light heartedly. She agreed as she glanced toward the road once more. Then she turned to me and said, "Be sure to lock the wooden door."

I helped Granny dress for bed and kissed her good night. Then I retired in the guestroom with my writing material. As I lay propped up on the pillows, I wrote to Ted telling him the stories that Granny had told me earlier and then went to sleep myself. Christmas morning came quickly and it was a lovely day. Granny's children came by at different times throughout the day. Some brought food, all brought gifts and Granny was thrilled. "It is a wonderful Christmas," she remarked often during the day. Later in the day Mikie went out in her back yard to burn some trash in a barrel. The wind blew in strong from the north and the fire got out of control. The dry winter grass spread the fire quickly and while Steve's Aunt stayed with Granny, I helped fight the fire. Mikie was so upset because she hadn't acted wisely and our efforts didn't help much. We eventually just let it burn itself out. "Don't get upset, the grass will grow again," J. T. told her. It did, of course, but we had all learned how quickly a trash fire can get away from you.

With a new year just around the corner, I felt a change in the air. I needed to be around people since I was so lonely. As my friends fell by the wayside, I decided to close my little pie business since it hadn't expanded all during the fall and I decided to find a job as a nurse's aid and just fry a few pies to supplement my salary. I knew it would be hard work, but at least I would have a steady salary. So I applied at the nursing home in our area on the first of January. I received a call immediately and was hired on January 2, 1990 and went to work right away. The work was very hard and it was all I could handle. I didn't try to fry pies any more, instead I turned all my interests to patient care.

It didn't take very long for the word to get around that I went to Huntsville to visit an inmate. The Administrator called me to her office one day and began telling me her thoughts on the matter. She told me how afraid she was for me that Ted might get out and kill me too, like he did his wife. I thought this lady was a Christian so I tried to explain to her how the Lord had sent me to Ted while I was in church on my birthday a few months ago. "Don't you see," I said, "I didn't just decide to choose any man who was in prison. Ted is my brother-in-law and I have known him since he was nine years old. Ted and I were always close until he married. I don't know all the circumstances that caused him to shoot his wife. God didn't send me to him to judge him. He sent me to care for him." It was as though she hadn't heard a word that I said. She tried to smooth things over by saying, "Destiny, I am just concerned about you." "Don't worry about me," I said confidently. "I have never been afraid of Ted and I never will be. Anyway, I don't know why everyone is so worried that Ted will come home. It will be many years before he comes up for parole and I might be dead by then, so I wish folks would quit interfering in my life. We need your prayers just to endure the years ahead, not be persecuted and mistreated because we are doing our very best. I need my job, but if my way of life presents a problem, I can always leave here." She said quickly, "I don't want you to quit because you are a good nurse. Go back to work now." So I returned to work on the floor.

After orientating on all three shifts for several days, I finally settled on the night shift. Since I couldn't get off on weekends, the night shift worked out better for my needs. It was hard for me to make the trip to Huntsville on Saturday and then go to work that night and it was doubly hard to leave my job on Sunday morning and then dress for the morning service at church. I didn't know how long I could keep up such a pace, but the Lord gave me the strength to carry on.

Ted worried when we met on our visits and begged me to get more rest. I was exhausted by the time I walked up the sidewalk to the main entrance at the old Wall Unit, but Ted understood that our visits were very important to the Lord and I had promised God that I would be faithful to my commitment. "I'm sure it is a test or some sort of trial that I am going through right now, Ted," I explained on one of our visits. "The Lord has a purpose for everything He does. I believe we're all tried to see if we will be faithful even though times get rough. In time, the Lord will open up a door so my life can level out. Right now, I have to stand or I will bring shame on Christ and I couldn't bear that."

There was a lot of gossip going on at work and I wasn't surprised when one of the nurses met me in the hall and drew me aside. She started to cry, then she said, "Destiny, everyone is gossiping about you. It is none of their affair that you are in love with a man in prison. They don't have the right to interfere in your life. As for me, I think you are a very courageous woman." I couldn't believe that anyone cared that much for me. Carol clung to me while she cried helplessly. I comforted my friend and said, "Please don't cry, Carol. Everything will be all right. The Lord sent me to Ted and He will stand by me through these trials and tests. Any time God sends you on a mission, there will always be stumbling blocks and this path that He has chosen to send me on is sure to cause some people to react badly. They don't understand what they are doing. All they see is on the surface. It is sad to know there are those who judge you just as some are doing to me, but I still have some precious friends here who love me just like you. They wouldn't want to walk in my shoes or live all alone without someone you love so much and would love to live a normal life with, but true friends accept you the way you are."

Most folks wouldn't agree with my way of life nor would they believe that God had sent me into Ted's life. However, I did think folks should their own business. I had known there would be some that would whisper behind my back, but I didn't expect them to meddle in my life as though they had the right to. Not even my own children stepped that far out of line, so it astonished me to learn what was happening behind my back at work. I went about my work and avoided those who sneered and stuck up their noses at me. Actually, there was just a few that treated me badly and spoke hatefully every opportunity they could find.

While I worked in the nursing home, I had received my nurse's aid certificate. When the State sent their representative to give us our tests, another class started in the recreation room for those who wanted to study for their G.E.D. I worked the night before the State representative came, so I didn't go home after work because I wanted to study for my G.E.D. They called me out of class to take my tests and I passed them by a miracle even though I was completely worn out.

I was excited at the prospect of obtaining my G.E.D. I was fifty-seven years old with a hunger to learn. It seemed funny, I guess, to see a woman my age sitting in a classroom. The teachers were excited too, especially when they read an essay I had written. They told me I should write every day, but they didn't know I did. Ted was very proud of me and encouraged me to go on. He would say, "Darling, you can do anything you set out to do. Spread your wings, Sugar, follow your dreams and I will pray for you."

"Ted," I cried happily, "It is just like a dream. It has been fifty years since I have been to school, but I never dreamed this opportunity would come to me. You know when I was growing up that education wasn't that important. If you could read and write, our parents thought that was sufficient. I tried to stay in school, but Mamma took me out for two years in succession at mid term. All my friends passed me by and I finally gave up and stayed at home to help Mamma with the kids. Now the thing that I thought was gone forever is suddenly available to me. The Lord has opened so many doors of opportunity for me to explore that it leaves me breathless and amazed. Out of all I learned in class, the most impressive was a deep desire to write. Through my love for you the Lord taught me how to express my thoughts on paper."

Even though my life was filled with so many things to do, I was very happy. I didn't think there was going to be a big change in my immediate future, but storm clouds were forming. I felt uneasy when Isabella told me that Mikie and J.T. were going to need a place to live soon and how would I feel about the idea of them moving in with me. Isabella was trying to keep peace in her family I knew, but she didn't know how threatened I felt right at that moment. I didn't want to share my home with anyone, especially with Mikie and J. T. since I knew how easy gossip could get started. Isabella said, "Steve tried to get them to make this their home instead of building a new one. He told them that he didn't intend to move back, but they rejected the idea. Mikie wanted a new home built on the same spot where her old house is."

I fought to keep my composure even though bitter tears choked up inside me. 'Oh, my God, I feel so forsaken and everyone has lied to me,' I cried bitterly in my heart. 'Lord, I gave up my home even thought it wasn't much to look at upon a promise when I moved to Newton. It wasn't on their promise alone that I made that decision. I claimed Your promise that I would live here someday. Was I mistaken? Actually, You didn't say how long that I would live here, so I must depend on your wisdom in this matter and trust that You know what is best for all concerned.' "No, Isabella, I'll have to move out. I wouldn't feel comfortable living with J. T. and Mikie," I replied firmly. She was disappointed, but I couldn't help it, so Isabella left quite disturbed about the situation.

I struggled to get by with my small income, so when the summer months started and I had to use the air conditioner I didn't know how I would manage to pay the electricity bill. I could hold it down when I was alone, but when the children came home, they turned it up. One day while Isabella and Steve were home, I broke down in tears. I couldn't handle the pressure any more. Isabella went outside and told Steve I was crying. He ran in the house and held me while I cried. When I explained my situation, Steve said, "Come and live with us so you can get on your feet." It seemed to be the perfect solution for all concerned. Even though I felt defeated, the relief on Steve's face made me feel better. They move me to Jasper right away.

After I moved, Mikie and J. T. moved into Isabella and Steve's house. Then they began the process of tearing their house down. I stayed away from Newton except for driving back and forth to work at the nursing home. I attended the church at Newton as long as I worked there, but that would change as I made up my mind to make the best of my situation.

Even though Steve and Isabella were pleased that I didn't make a fuss about moving in with them so his parents could have a place to live; my sleeping in the daytime presented problems for them. They were very considerate and tiptoed around the house while I was resting, but it still caused a tense situation. I was tense and nervous myself, but somehow we would get through it.

My visits with Ted were so precious during those days. He was the only one who loved me unconditionally besides Jesus. "God is with you, Darling. Don't worry. He has His hand on us. Even though things look bad at this moment, He will take care of you," Ted said trying to reassure me.

During those trying times, Ted and I had dreams which we discussed, as we were sure they had some meaning. We weren't sure what they meant concerning our future. We didn't know why we were having them at a time when we were suffering so many disappointments. Through these dreams, we both realized that the Lord had brought us together for a reason far more important than having a secure future for myself. They gave us a vision that took preference over our frivolous desires and as we talked about them, we placed our own needs to the side.

Ted said, "Honey, I have had the same dream again that I had years ago before I was incarcerated in this place. I saw a huge field of cotton that was ready for harvest. The cotton bolls were large and they were white as snow. When I saw the inmates were dressed in white, I remembered my dream and decided that that was why I had the dream. I had the same dream again and it still troubles me. Do you understand why? Can you tell me what it means?"

As the Holy Spirit dealt with me, I trembled. His dream indeed held great meaning and to my way of thinking, the revelation was simple and easily defined. "Look around you, my Darling," I cried with emotion. "Can't you see the field of cotton all around you. You were placed in this field to reap the harvest of lost men who need Christ, Precious. Jesus reached down in His mercy and saved you, Ted. He has something He wants you to do for Him. This is truly a field ready for harvest. Now, the question is, what will you do about it, Darling?"

Ted didn't say much in answer to my question, only to say that he had to be careful. "I'm confined in this place, but I am not free to do very much. What do you think I can do? I don't want to be like some of those Bible toting inmates that walk around with a Bible tucked under their arms. You are looking at the scum of the earth, Destiny. Some of them are child molesters and I don't want to mess with them," Ted said defiantly.

"Well, Darling, why are you in this prison, then," I asked. "Is there any crime worse that the one that you did Ted? Besides that, I am not so sure that many child molesters have been caught or that the older generation just closed their eyes to such things in the past when a member of their family committed such an offense. So many things are being brought out now that our parents ignored. When a child complained that uncle so and so had been touching the private parts of their body, they were simply brushed off and told to be quiet, telling the child they had a big imagination. There are all kinds of excuses that we can offer God for not getting busy in the fields of cotton, but none of them are acceptable to Him. God didn't send us on a mission to judge anyone, Ted. He wants us to win the lost to Jesus Christ."

When Ted finally accepted that the things I told him were true, then the Holy Spirit would convict him and he would smile and take my hands in his and just hold them tight. Then he would jokingly remark, "Amen, Sister Quinn!" I couldn't get upset with him when he did that. He just didn't want to make a commitment to the Lord until he was sure. "When God makes His call sure, I'll surrender to Him, Destiny," Ted promised.

Ted said on one of our visits, "Darling, I dreamed about you last night. It Ws a beautiful dream with you all dressed up in a long white chiffon dress. You looked like an angel, Honey. You held your hands out and beckoned saying, "Ted, come with me." I was so amazed that I was speechless and then you disappeared," Ted exclaimed excitedly. "Honey, do you think the Lord sent you in a dream to give me hope and that through you, the Lord might let me go free," Ted asked?

"Oh, I wish it were true that you would go free, but I have a strange feeling that this dream has a different meaning. There is nothing that would make me any happier than to have you come home, Darling. All our hopes and dreams center around the day when you will be free and we can enjoy a wonderful life together. I can't keep back the tears when I think of all those years when we loved each other, but weren't able to express our love for each other until now. Still, we are bound to a certain extent, but at least we are free to hold each other for a little while without the weight of guilt bothering us. I believe God brought us together for a purpose. One that we don't know yet, but I am certain that in time the Holy Spirit will reveal it to us. There is no doubt in my mind, Precious, that the Lord is revealing these things to us through our dreams and through them He is confirming that we have a mission to do for Jesus' sake. We must wait upon Him and He will reveal His will in His own time," I told Ted confidently.

"Sweetheart, I have experienced strange dreams, too," I said excitedly. "I've actually had two dreams which trouble me. They were both so strange. In fact, I believe they were visions, not just ordinary dreams. I have problems when I try to understand them, so I'll tell you about them and maybe you can help me with the aid of the Holy Spirit and I can ease my mind."

"My first dream wasn't as puzzling as the second. In this dram I was walking up the sidewalk toward the entrance of the Wall Unit excited at the thought of seeing you again. As I walked up the hill and drew near the huge oak tree where roots protrude about the ground, I saw two men walking toward me. I knew somehow these men had something to tell me before I reached the old tree. I became quite nervous and afraid, very sure they were going to tell me that something about you. As I drew nearer, I decided that they were men of authority. One man especially because he was dressed in a neat gray suit. He was well groomed with his gray hair neatly combed. I slowed my pace as I drew closer because I had to force my feet to move," I continued. As I approached them, the one I thought was the warden and who held high authority stepped out to greet me. The other man stood behind him and I barely recall what he looked like. He seemed to be there for a witness or at least that is what came to mind. Anyway, he stood in the background and didn't speak. My full attention was upon the man in the gray suit, so I stopped and stood very still. He didn't introduce himself, but I realized somehow that this man didn't need to. The Holy Spirit bore witness that God had sent him and he began speaking. He said, 'Destiny, will you love and cherish Ted always, and stand by him through sickness and in health? Will you promise to be faithful to Ted and support him in Christ for the remainder of your life?" Without delay I answered, "Yes," while tears streamed down my face. Oh, Ted, I committed my life to the Lord again and dedicated my all to this ministry. Once the man said these things that he was sent to say, he and the other man walked away. I could hear them talking as they walked away from the prison and they simply vanished and I woke up and realized that I had had a dream," I told him quite mystified. As I continued telling Ted about my strange dreams, he sat breathless and quiet. "What a mystery, Darling. Honey, tell me about your other dream," Ted asked. I said, "Precious, this dream is even more puzzling and even though it must have been a dream, somehow I believe this one was a vision as well."

"This dream took place at the Wall Unit too, but this time I was in the parking lot. Isabella was with me and she drove the car. When she stopped the car, I opened my door and started to get out when I heard your voice behind me and I froze, unable to get out of the car. "What is Ted doing outside," I asked Isabella? I couldn't believe you were free. I turned my head in the direction that the voices were coming from and saw you walking toward the entrance, but you weren't alone. I called your name clearly, but it was as if I were apart from the actual scene and only watching these events and I sat in awe because these things were so mysterious." I watched Ted's reaction as I continued with my story. He was just as tense as I was and I had only begun.

"Ted, the mystery lies in the two people I saw. There is no doubt in my mind that both men were you. I saw you when you were just a boy and the other man was you, but you were very old and drawn. You were stooped and bent with age and I sobbed as I thought, 'Will Ted have to grow old and die in this place?' I called out your name again, but you didn't hear me. You walked hurriedly toward the Wall Unit while the young boy played around you instead of keeping step. You growled at him for misbehaving. You seemed to be in an awful hurry to get back in the Unit. Sugar, none of our dreams are silly, but they are unusual. They are disturbing, but I am certain that we will remember them as important before our lives are over," I assured Ted.

"My heart broke even after my dream was over and I sat up in the bed. Honey, you looked so broken and weary that I fell on my knees beside my bed and prayed for both of us and that God would keep us safely beneath His powerful Wings until He sees fit to end this strife. Fiery trials of life may confront us, Darling, but our love will be sustained and one day we will fly away on those same Wings that keeps us safe and heals our broken spirits now."

"Together forever, Precious Darling, No matter what our destiny is," Ted cried emotionally. "We have the Lord, our Savior, to hold us firmly by His glorious grace, Precious."

CHAPTER 6

THE BLESSINGS OF LOVE

When Ted and I were together, the whole world seemed at peace. Only Ted and I knew how much God had blessed our lives together and the many years we had kept apart for our families' sake. We couldn't avoid seeing each other at family gatherings and such, so we sat across the room from each other avoiding eye contact. At one time, the barrier broke down. It was all so long ago and Ted was my best friend. Lord, we were so young and I was so very ill. I needed a friend so much because Jacob didn't seemed to care. Because of Ted's care and him just being there for me, Jacob took me away. Ted finally married a girl less than a year later.

As the years went by, I didn't see Ted much, but when we met we knew that we had an affection for each other that no one could destroy. After Ted's marriage, I put all thoughts of him out of mind. Then after Jacob died, Joyce got in touch with him at the Wall Unit and at the very mention of his name, my heart ached. Would we ever be able to live like the people in love stories and finally find true happiness? We take our happiness now with gratefulness even if it is only to hold each other for a few moments once a week.

I believe that if the Lord didn't send us beautiful dreams and colorful rainbows now and then, we would have gone down in defeat. While the persecution continued at work and my friends began falling by the wayside, the sweet voice of Jesus would repeat again as He had done in church saying softly, "You are loved." When Ted would hold me in his arms and kiss away my tears, he would hold up my chin, smile and say, "Darling, let me see your pretty smile." I would always smile for him regardless of how much my heart ached. I have never loved anyone so much and I wanted to be his wife more than anything in the world. As long as I live, no other man could take Ted's place in my heart. Many times I would tell him how I felt about him and he would say, "Darling, let's not be too hasty, we have a long time before we can get married. You will always be my wife in my heart and the only woman I'll every love. I feel so helpless, Precious, since I can't be a proper husband to you as long as I'm doing time. I have so many years to serve yet, Baby, and I may not live that long. We'll know when it's time, Sweetheart. The Lord will let us know."

My greatest fear was that I would lose Ted again. This was the one thing I couldn't bear and I earnestly prayed about it. My suffering from the persecution and heartache was almost unbearable and Satan was using any opening to make me miserable with doubts and fears. At times, it seemed that Satan was winning the battle. Our marriage would somehow seal God's will and it wasn't long before the Holy Spirit made God's will known to both of us.

Ted and I had been seeing each other for almost a year when I went to visit him. As we sat across the table from each other, we both suddenly knew that the Lord wanted us to be married very soon. Ted took my hands and said questioningly, "Sugar, do you feel it, too? It's strange, Honey, but I'm so sure now that the Lord wants us to marry." "Yes, Darling, I feel it, too and God is receiving the glory. Everything seems to be happening according to God's plan even though I don't understand why our life together seems to be controlled by God's gentle hand. He seems to be smiling upon us," I replied smiling happily.

Ted said that he would get a legal document drawn up that would give Steve the authority to stand in his place and answer for him. He explained the procedures of a marriage by proxy and said, "Darling, very soon now you will be Mrs. Ted Quinn, just the way you always wanted to be," Ted said teasingly. We were so happy that it was hard not to show our emotions, but we had to because the guards would get suspicious. We were supposed to be brother and sister and if they found out we weren't, we wouldn't be allowed to enjoy our contact visits anymore.

Our way of life was so different from those on the outside of the prison walls where you are free to experience the beauty of a sweet relationship. With my loved one confined, we had to be cautious because the guards were always watching suspiciously. Ted and I wanted to shout it to the whole world that we were in love, that God had worked a miracle and brought us together. Instead, we had to behave as though nothing had happened with a large crowd of people all around us. We joined hands and prayed that God would bless our decision to be married, not only because we wanted to be husband and wife, but that He might receive glory from our marriage. The Lord blessed us with the sweetest peace that day and we both knew God was pleased.

We decided to wait until Ted could get the documents ready, which he would send me in the mail before we could set the date for our wedding, but paperwork didn't bother me at that time. I was the happiest woman in the world. I would finally be Ted's wife, even though our marriage would be an unusual one. I was walking on clouds when we met at the end of the table where Ted could hold me in his arms for one short minute. We were jubilant with joy and laughed when we kissed goodbye as we showered each other with kisses. "One day we'll be free to hold each other and never have to part anymore," Ted promised. Though we had to part again there was no crying this time. I floated down the sidewalk with a song in my heart and waited at the telephone booth as I had done so many times watching for his hand to wave at me through the broken window in the front of the Unit.

Very few people will experience such a beautiful relationship in their lifetime. God filled our lives with such beauty in the many small things, which made our lives rich and lovely. "It is like living in a land filled with magic and wonder, Father," I said happily to my Lord, as I blew kisses to my Darling who waved through the tiny opening in the broken window. Smiling, I thought, 'Only Ted would think of a small thing like that, like a knight in shining armor which he had been for so many years.' He made our love beautiful in spite of the fact that he was in prison and he never ceased in trying to keep that magic alive and beautiful in our lives together. Beauty will bring tears of joy to your eyes because of its very loveliness with no sadness in your heart, but this is really Christ lighting up your life. 'Don't feel sorry for me, world, I don't want your pity, because I'm the happiest woman on earth,' I was thinking as I walked to the parking lot.

It was terribly hot all the way back to Jasper. My little car didn't have an air conditioner. I had purchased it in January because my old car was worn out. I didn't know anything about cars so Sam met me at a small car lot his friend owned in Livingston one Saturday. Since the car was small and would be economical to run, I had purchased it never even considering the hot summer ahead. When Isabella decided to sell her little Spectrum, I asked Steve if I could buy it from them. I said, "Steve, if I can get back what I have paid on my car which is $500.00 and take up the notes on Isabella's car along with $500.00 down, will you sell her car to me?" He answered, "Yes," not dreaming that I could talk Sam's friend into such a deal.

That evening I called Sam's friend and told him what I had on my mind. I said, "My daughter has a 1988 Spectrum she wants to sell. It is a good dependable car and it has air conditioning. If I bring my little car back to you, would you give me back the $500.00 I paid on it?" To Steve's surprise, the kind man answered, "Yes, bring it back and I'll give you your money back." 'Thank you, Jesus,' I cried happily. The idea never crossed my mind that Sam's friend might refuse my offer. I was so naive about the ways of the world, just standing on my faith in God as I walked alone. Isabella followed me to Livingston on Monday and my friend handed me a check for $500.00. After I thanked him, he said, "I have a buyer for your car already. He's a school kid that needs an economical car." Then we drove back to Jasper in my new car. Oh, isn't it wonderful to enjoy the blessings of our Lord. When I visited Ted again, we decided to set our wedding date in July. I wanted it to take place on my birthday, July 30th, the date that God sent me to Ted, but for some reason we set the date on July 21st instead. It would take place on Saturday and I could leave as soon as it was over and go straight to Huntsville to my wonderful husband who would be anxiously waiting for me. Everything seemed to fall in order without any problem. We were like two children who placed their faith in God and never doubted that He was in full control of their lives and in every decision that we made.

Steve agreed to stand in Ted's place during the wedding ceremony and I asked Bro. Tom Brown, my pastor, at the church that I attended in Jasper to perform our ceremony. He said he would and it was wonderful feeling that everyone was happy for me around Jasper.

This wasn't the case at Newton, though, except for a few of my friends. A war raged bitterly as Satan fought God's will. The workers at the nursing home were split and some wished us well while others ranted and raved because I was marrying a man in prison. Because of that, my heart was heavy. Our marriage was unusual, but being apart from Ted was enough to tear my heart out without folks cruel tongues wagging, but the more it went on, the closer I drew to my Father and it made me love Ted even more. Since I didn't make much money, when I went shopping for my wedding dress, I didn't know how I would manage to buy something beautiful and still be able to pay for it. My heart ached at the sight of the price tags on the garments, but I finally found one that was just right for $23.00. It seemed as though Jesus told me that this was the one He wanted, just as if He had picked it out for me Himself. It was white which was not traditional as I had been married before, but it was as if Jesus seemed to say, "To Ted you are. You are that special lady he has dreamed of for so many years. Yes, you are like a virgin to Ted because you are a special bride sent by God." That thought made me happy and humble and I was grateful that Jesus came shopping with me when I bought my wedding dress.

On Friday morning, July 20, 1990, I asked my boss if I could take off on Saturday, my wedding day. Some of the nurses were at the nurses' station too, and my boss happened by at the right moment, I thought. She shouted loudly, "No, you can't be off," and one of the other nurses started screaming, "You are not actually going to marry that jailbird on death row, are you?" As I trembled with indignation, I said, "Ted isn't on death row and I don't know where you got that idea. It doesn't make any difference whether you let me off or not, I am going to marry Ted in the morning," and I walked out of the nursing home hurt and disturbed.

When I got to Isabella's, I slept for a while. It was my regular day off so there wasn't any pressure on me to get plenty of rest. There weren't many preparations to get together since I had planned a short simple ceremony without the usual fuss. That night Isabella and Daniel were sitting at the dining table. Isabella was make a white satin heart shaped pillow with lace trim. Daniel was very excited when I walked into the room. He excitedly told me, "Grandma, I'm going to be your ring bearer." The only ring Ted had given me was a small wedding band that one of the prisoners had made with a silver metal of some kind. I had been wearing it for sometime already because Ted and I pretended we were husband and wife. We were like children in so many ways and our love was so sweet and tender. When Isabella finished putting it together, I took my ring off and Daniel placed it on the little pillow and stood very still showing us how he would hold it. Tears choked up in me since I hadn't expected Isabella would do such an unexpected and lovely thing. 'My wedding would be beautiful,' I thought, in spite of the fact that Ted couldn't be there.

Later in the evening, Bro. Tom came by and talked to Steve about the wedding ceremony. Steve teased me by saying that he might back out, but I knew he wouldn't. He had gone through too much already to back out now. He had gone with me earlier to get our marriage license. The young lady who prepared the license hadn't ever heard of marrying by proxy. She laughed when she realized that Ted and I had the same last name. Then she asked if Ted and I were sister and brother. "Ted is my brother-in-law," I told her. She looked at me quite surprised, but she did the necessary paper work as she shook her head. Steve was sitting in a chair behind me since he had to be there to take Ted's place.

It was a first experience for that young lady, but it was also a first experience for us all. When God sent me into Ted's life, many such surprises took place in all our lives and in everything that surrounded us because our lives were so unusual. This would be the first time that Bro. Brown would perform a marriage ceremony by proxy too. He told Steve that he would call him Ted and that he must answer for Ted during the ceremony. I was so happy because it seemed as if I walked around with my head in the clouds. I would be Ted's wife tomorrow and that made me the happiest woman on earth.

Isabella brought out some net and some silk flowers. She was making a lovely wedding veil for her Mamma I discovered. I watched as she sewed the lace on the edge of the net with great love and care. All of these special things were unexpected and these special touches by my daughter filled my heart with joy and wonder. It was more like a dream than a reality. I hadn't expect anything beautiful to every happen to me. Before Jacob died, my life had been a battle just to survive. Now it seemed as if the Lord was blessing my life with all sorts of lovely things that I couldn't understand. God had already blessed me through my trying years with Jacob even though I hadn't known much true beauty, but He brought me through many trying experiences. Now with each beautiful experience that God brought into my life, I became afraid that they would suddenly be taken away. I was afraid to dream or truly believe that all these things were truly gifts from Heaven.

That night, I went to bed and fell asleep quickly. Isabella was up for quite a while though because I heard her in the kitchen as I drifted off to sleep. When I awoke on my wedding day, I went into the living room. When I saw the beautiful surprise my daughter had prepared in the dining room, I gasped in delight. She had covered the table with a lace tablecloth and then had placed Ted's and my family Bible on the table. There was also a small slender vase with a single rose. The table was set with silverware and plates with a beautiful wedding cake in the center of the table. It had blue roses and two hearts on the edge with "Best Wishes" written on one side and on the other side was written "Destiny and Ted." A bride and groom stood encased with roses and trim. Tears of joy and happiness streamed down my face. "Oh, Father, I don't deserve such a lovely blessing," I cried, "but I'm so happy that I just can't believe it." Isabella was beaming with happiness and God blessed her for the love she had expressed when she saw my happy face with tears of joy streaming down my face.

Isabella helped me dress and fussed over my hair. I was so nervous that I couldn't control my emotions. Another surprise was in store for me when my friends with whom I worked with came all dressed up for this special occasion. They told me that they wouldn't have missed it for the world even though our boss had threatened to fire anyone who took park in this marriage. They said she ranted and raved as she ran down the halls and refused to sign the check from our flower fund until the nurses put up such an uproar that she had to. Old Satan really put up a fight all the way, but God was the victor and His will won the final victory. I was even more surprised when J. T. and Mikie came too. I hadn't invited anyone, not even my children since they were all against my marrying Ted at least until he was free. I have never heard of a bride crying on her wedding day, but I did because it was such a beautiful experience. I needed Ted so much at this special time in my life, but I needed God's grace more then than at any other time. My heart ached for my loved one to stand before God and take his marriage vows with me like everyone else.

Steve programmed the sprinkling system to go off behind us at a certain time while the ceremony took place. We stood outside with our backs to the fields where small pine trees were growing. There weren't any bars or prison walls here as we stood in the open air between an oak tree and a magnolia tree.

Bro. Brown began with a prayer and then he asked if anyone present objected to this marriage. Daniel stood proudly with the little pillow in his hands wondering why his Grandmother was crying as she took her vows to Ted. Steve steadied me since my legs trembled beneath me and he answered for Ted with immaculate grace. Rainbows formed through the water of the sprinkling system reminding me of the Covenant God had made with me almost a year ago. Isabella played a song in the background softly which added to this beautiful moment as my tears streamed down my cheeks. All the years that Ted and I had known each other went through my mind as the words in the song spoke about enduring time. 'I will always love you, my sweet Ted,' I promised in my heart, `no matter how much suffering and disappointments we must endure. I will be your faithful companion until death and forever will I love you, Ted.'

When the ceremony ended, we went inside after Isabella took pictures. We cut the cake and Steve performed his duty just as if Ted was the one who stood with me. My friend Sue had brought a bottle of champagne which spewed all over the floor when it was opened. We laughed when Daniel remarked that it smelled like Uncle Bill. He always said whatever came into his mind and this time his remark made me feel happiness instead of so much heartache. Steve and I sipped from the wineglass as tradition taught with Isabella instructing us on what to do. As soon as the celebration drew near the end, I thanked my friends for coming and told them I needed to be on my way to Huntsville to see my husband. They understood my reason for leaving and hugged me wishing Ted and I great happiness. Even though my life was beautiful and exciting, they were glad that they weren't beginning a marriage like mine.

I wore my wedding dress and veil as I sat down in the seat of our little car. Finally, I removed my veil as I was attracting so much attention when I met the oncoming traffic. I was deliriously happy as I thought about Ted. I thought excitedly, 'Would he be watching for me and wave through the broken window as I walk up the sidewalk this time?' When I parked the car and started up the sidewalk my head was filled with happy thoughts. Suddenly Ted's hand appeared through the window waving vigorously. I waved and blew kisses to my husband and then entered the prison and signed in while the lady guard stared at me. She said, "You look just like a bride." I smiled happily, but I couldn't tell her that I was, at least not yet. Ted would have to give a copy of our marriage license to the warden's office before I could make the announcement that I was Ted's wife.

When the guard called out his name in the waiting room I walked hurriedly down the sidewalk to me my husband. "Hello, my Darling, you're mine at last," Ted exclaimed happily as he held me close. "I'm the happiest woman in the world and my dreams have come true, Precious. No matter what our future holds, we'll be together loving each other always," I promised. "You're a beautiful bride, Destiny, and I adore you so. I just wish I could have stood with you on our wedding day. I told a guard this morning that I was getting married today. She laughed and said, "Are you crazy, Ted? You're in prison." 'No,' I told her, 'while I'm talking to you, a wedding ceremony is taking place near Jasper and another man is filling in for me.' She couldn't believe my story, but I didn't care. I wanted the whole world to know my Destiny and I were being married today. While you said the vows and Steve repeated mine for me, I promised God and you all the things in our wedding ceremony, Darling," Ted exclaimed excitedly.

We shared a lovely visit; holding hands and praising our Lord for His beautiful gift of love with tender care, praying that God would bless our marriage even though we couldn't share a regular marriage such as others enjoy. Our life together began on faith in God alone and now we took hold of that faith and began a new kind of marriage without any pattern or example from anyone else. "Our life is a great adventure, Father," we both cried as excitement raced through us and we realized the dynamic power that God had on both our lives. "Keep us beneath Your Holy Wings, Jesus, and guide our paths. We don't understand all the whys yet, but we pray that one day we will. Right at this moment we are the happiest couple on earth, but we can't help but feel that You have placed us together for some purpose other than our need for each other," we agreed together in Christ Jesus.

When our visit ended, we parted with hope in our hearts, hopes of freedom coming soon as we dreamed of a bright future in spite of where we were. I walked on air with my head in the clouds as I made my way to the front of the Wall Unit, then sat on the park bench and waited for Ted's hand to appear again through the broken window before I went to the parking lot. Finally I saw his hand and I blew kisses to my Beloved, not knowing this would be the closing of a beautiful part of our love story. On my way home, a beautiful rainbow appeared once more and God renewed His Covenant with me that He was with us both. A beautiful chapter in our lives had ended, but I didn't know it then. As time went by, I learned that God had more in store for our future than this human heart could imagine.

I didn't get much rest before I had to return to the work at the nursing home. My boss wouldn't let me off on my wedding day, but by the grace of God I would survive through the night shift anyway. She did a cruel thing, but God is all in all even with her threatening all the nurses, they surprised me that night with a sweet reception. There were gifts on the table with a cake and refreshments. They laughed and said, "Well, we used one of the boss' sheets for a tablecloth." I was totally surprised as it was so unexpected. I was also concerned and quite worried that these friends were jeopardizing their jobs by showing me an act of kindness. Not once did it enter my mind that I would be the one to lose my job as I went naively on my way, but I realize now that God's grace blinded my eyes to the things that could have happened.

I worked my shift without any problem and then drove to Jasper. I worked for my employer the rest of July, but it wasn't easy. On August 2, 1990, I decided to place an application at the nursing home in Jasper. I placed one at one of the hospitals too. I didn't get a quick response so I called the other hospital located there and asked for the Director of Nurses. She had the sweetest, kindest voice and I needed that assurance so badly. It seemed like I had been beaten down so much lately and I was afraid of rejection again. I asked, "Do you hire nurse's aides at your hospital?" She quickly responded saying, "Yes, we do." "I'm looking for a job as a nurse's aid, but I have never worked in a hospital before, so I'm a little uneasy," I told her. "Why don't you come in and I'll talk to you," she said. "I will come right now if you have time to see me," I told her. She said, "Come on in, I'll put you down for an interview right away." It was like a dream come true for me because I had always dreamed of working in a hospital as a nurse all my life. I danced around rejoicing as if I had already been accepted, then reality set in and I became apprehensive. 'What if she won't hire me since I'm married to Ted,' I thought anxiously. 'Well, I'll know soon once I tell her about Ted,' I told myself.

I was nervous, but excited as I entered the hospital. My hand shook as I knocked on the door of the Director of Nurses' office, then a lovely lady beckoned to me saying, "Come in, Mrs. Quinn. My name is Beth and I'm happy to meet you," in a friendly voice. "My name is Destiny and I'm glad to meet you too. I need a job, Beth, but first I need to tell you that I'm married to a man in prison. If you have a problem with that, there's no reason to go on with this interview," I stated firmly. Beth looked at me puzzled and said quickly, "That would be discrimination and we don't allow discrimination to be practiced at this hospital. It's against the law as well, Destiny, and if anyone discriminates against you, I want to know about it. You are judged by your performance as a nurse and not who you are or the color of your skin." The mere idea shocked her that anyone would persecute another person because she is married to a man in prison. "Besides," she said, "It's nobody's business who you are married to."

I felt so relieved as if I had suddenly been set free. I had been so persecuted by some of the nurses at the nursing home that I had begun to believe I had committed some sort of terrible crime and needed to be punished for marrying Ted. It was hard not to cry when Beth hired me and asked me when I could start working. "I'll do what is right and turn in my resignation and give them two weeks to find someone to fill my place," I said. "In the meantime, on your days off, you can orientate here if want to," Beth stated. "I want you to orientate on all the shifts so we can decide which shift will be better suited for you," she added.

When I left the hospital, I was so happy that I was walking on a cloud and on top of the world. I hurried home to tell Isabella the wonderful news. Since I had been a small child, I had dreamed of being a nurse. I had admired them in their snow-white uniforms. My greatest dream was to be a nurse in some hospital, but my self-esteem was so low I didn't think I would ever be good enough to get a job in one. I praised the Lord all the way home that day. I just couldn't wait to tell Isabella and Steve about my good fortune. They were both very happy for me when I told them my good news. Now, I couldn't wait to tell Ted too. We'll have two things to celebrate this time, not only my new job, but also our birthdays.

When I turned in my resignation at the nursing home I took Daniel with me not intending to stay long. I wanted to pick up my paycheck at the same time. Daniel and I sat down and waited while my boss fumbled around delaying as long as she could. Then she began making excuses for the way she had treated me. She blurted out in front of Daniel that she was afraid that Ted would kill me when he got out of prison. Tears welled up in Daniel's eyes as I tried to explain again that Ted loved me and we had known each other since before I married his brother, Jacob. When we left, Daniel said, "Grandma, she doesn't know my Grandpa Ted. He wouldn't hurt anyone, especially you." I despised her for hurting Daniel. I said, "Son, that woman doesn't know what she is talking about." He cried a little and I did too. She was only one of the many others who made hurtful remarks like the one she had made on that day.

I walked on air as I made my way toward the entrance to the Wall Unit that coming Saturday. I had so many wonderful things to tell Ted that my heart raced wildly. Suddenly, I sensed something was terribly wrong. Then when I looked upward toward the window where Ted had always waved to me through the broken screen. My heart ached because I realized the window had evidently been repaired recently. 'Father,' I cried, 'It was just a little thing, not only was it just a romantic thing for Ted to wave to me through the small opening in the window, but I looked forward to it and it had become a beautiful part of our love story. Things change now and then, however, so we have to adjust, but it's sad, Father, and my heart aches.'

I didn't realize how great the changes would be for Ted and myself until he told me even more sad news when he held me close to him. I asked, "Honey, did you get in trouble because you waved to me through the window?" Ted replied, "No, Darling, everything is fine. They repaired the window last week, but that's not all that they did. Honey, they moved me to another cell in the back of the prison. It's more like a dungeon where I live now. All that I can see is one tiny star at night now, but I'm grateful for that. Things have completely changed from the way it was." "Oh, Ted, everything will be all right. We've had one beautiful year filled with little romantic things from God. He has blessed us so very much, but now our trials have really begun. We can overcome all things together, Precious. Our marriage is strong and our love has the strongest foundation of all," I cried.

Ted agreed with me that a chapter in our lives had come sharply to an end. He said, "Honey, I don't know why this vast change has taken place, but I'm sure the Lord knows why. There may be someone on that cellblock that He wants me to witness to. This is our first real trial and I feel sure there will be many more. Yes, Darling, our marriage will stand any test that comes along. Unless a marriage is tested in various ways through disappointments as well as the sunshiny days, how can we know its' strength, Darling? Hand in hand and heart to heart, we'll pray for strength to withstand the storms of life through the power of the Holy Spirit." "Darling, I have some wonderful news to tell you that will lift your spirits. By the way, Darling,

Happy Birthday! With all the sad troubling things which took place last week, Darling, we need to be celebrating some of the ways that God has blessed us too," I replied. "Well, Happy Birthday, Mrs. Quinn. You are a year older and you are still seven years older than I am," Ted said smiling. Then he chuckled as he stated with a grin, "You know how much I always liked older women, Destiny."

"Well, Smarty," I laughed, "I have wonderful news. I am a nurse at a hospital at Jasper now and I'm the happiest woman in the world." Ted chuckled lightly, then with a flirting grin, he stated firmly. "Well, my Smarty Pants, I'm very happy for you. I'm a proud man too because I have you. You are my angel of mercy as well as my Smarty Pants, Sugar." We laughed together like two teenagers and for a short time we enjoyed a mixture of life together in spite of our circumstances.

Our time was running out which seemed to fly by too quickly, so we held hands while Ted led in prayer before a guard walked over to our table to tell us we have five minutes. We relied on God's grace to give us the courage to kiss goodbye each time. Oh, how great His grace has been for both of us, but we didn't truly know how great it was until God brought us together to glorify His name.

His grace was marvelous while I stood on the small hill waiting for Ted to reappear as he walked from the building where we visited to where the guards would search him again before entering the Unit. We waved to each other one last time and blew kisses to each other, and then he would disappear inside while I walked in the opposite direction. My heart cried out in pain as I gazed at the blue sky, 'Oh, Father, hide us from the storms of life in the safety of Your powerful Wings. Heal our wounded spirit, Father, and make us fit vessels for Your glory. We aren't worthy, my Lord, but use us according to Your sweet will.'

CHAPTER 7

THE APPROACHING STORM

The hospital was a very exciting place to work. It could be very quiet at times and then suddenly, it would burst alive with activity in just an instant. At first, I felt lost until one of the aides took an interest in me. She showed me around where the supply areas were for one thing. I knew about patient care, such as bathing and grooming, but this wasn't the nursing home and things were much different. Either a patient was being discharged or one was being admitted. No matter how absorbed you were doing one thing, instantly you could be called to do something else. I loved the excitement, however, and it was a challenging work and it had its rewards too.

The Director of Nurses was ecstatic when I received my GED. She thought it was great and placed it in my file along with my Certification for my nurse's aid. My self-esteem grew because I had made so many accomplishments since Jacob died. I encouraged Isabella to get into nursing too. I believed that type of work would be perfect for her. She entered a nurse's aid class and the hospital hired her too. She loved working in the OB Department, especially in the care of newborns. She beamed happily with a tiny baby in her arms. I was the happiest Mamma on earth, I believed, and my life was beautiful.

The hospital wasn't like the big hospitals in those days. It had a family atmosphere. When you did well, you were praised and when you cried, someone cried with you. I never felt alone anymore because these folks made you feel needed and appreciated. It seems impossible that such a place could exist in those days and I learned very quickly the patients preferred the hospital too, because of the caring spirit. The Lord filled my life with so many great blessings that I didn't know how to handle them. My world was surrounded by caring folks now, which was quite a contrast from before. From Administration on down to other departments, I felt at ease. Everyone knew that I had a husband in prison, but I found out that I wasn't alone. I learned that most folks keep it a secret if they have a member of their family incarcerated in prison somewhere, and I felt so much better when some folks would tell me that they had a loved one in prison too. Even though my attitude about Ted was one of joy and pride and I didn't keep it a secret, I could relate to so many who were suffering shame instead of the happiness that Ted and I shared. I thought many times, 'Father, how will these inmates overcome their wrongs and straighten their lives out if their loved ones are so ashamed of them and hide them from the world? Castaways, indeed, but I refuse to treat Ted in this way even though he had committed a terrible crime.'

One morning Isabella said, "Mamma, how would you feel about living in a travel trailer? I found a nice affordable one and if you agree to buy it, Steve can park it by the shop." The idea excited me so we went to look at it. Steve moved it by the shop after I made the deal. Even though the payments put me in a strain to meet the notes, I was glad to have the privacy and not be an invader on my family anymore. Steve fixed it homey by raising the canopy. I set a table under it so I could write letters to Ted in the open air and I parked my car under it as well. Before long, however, the company Steve worked for complained and he moved it to Newton.

Steve set it up next to the fence on their property. Mikie and J. T. were building a new brick home on the old home place and living in Isabella and Steve's house. It was good to be home again, in spite of the fact that I didn't live in the house. Mikie and J. T. were my sweetest friends and we thoroughly enjoyed each other's company. We enjoyed making scrambled egg sandwiches when we got home from church on Sunday nights. It became sort of a tradition with Mikie and me.

I took out my fryer one day and made up some fried pies to sell. It had been quite a while since I had made any and the smell of them frying under the canopy filled the countryside with such a sweet aroma that it attracted our neighbors' attention. I made extra money by selling some at the hospital and I became so busy. I worked too many hours, but I sold every one I could package and distribute. Between writing to Ted every day and trying to keep up, I was under a lot of pressure.

On Saturday, I took my usual trip to Huntsville to visit Ted. Sunday would be Mother's Day and the church planned to have dinner at the church. They put in their request for some fried pies, so I made up a batch intending to get up Sunday morning early and fry them. Mikie's children came home, so her house was full.

When I got home from my visit with Ted that Saturday night, I was so exhausted that I crawled into bed. I dozed for a while, then around nine, Daniel knocked on the door. I opened the door sleepily, then Daniel said excitedly, "Grandma, did you forget, you know we pray for Grandpa Ted at nine o'clock when we can?" I replied fully awake then, "I'm sorry, Daniel. I didn't know if you'd remember since you're visiting Grandmother Stewart. Of course, we will pray for Grandpa Ted together." We went to the tiny bedroom and knelt beside the bed. We prayed that God would bless Ted and bring him home to us. When our prayer was finished, Daniel put his little arms around me and saying words of comfort that only a small child of great faith would say, he said, "Grandma, God will bring Grandpa Ted home to us someday!" Then he raced back to his Grandmother Stewart's house and I lay down again.

The air conditioner was running because it was a warm night. I drifted off to sleep with the television on as well. I don't know what time it was when I was suddenly startled by a loud commanding voice, so great that I sat straight up in my bed. The voice seemed to come through my bedroom window by my pillow, but it was the voice of a man that boomed throughout the trailer. "Get up, get busy," He commanded and immediately I thought, 'Someone must have called Mikie to tell me that I was needed at the hospital.' I didn't have a telephone, but no one was at the door. Mikie's house was dark, so I knew everyone there was sleeping. Then I thought to myself, 'That voice must have come from the television.' I got up and turned it off and lay back down, still exhausted and needing rest.

I fell asleep quickly and I'm not sure how long I slept until I was sharply awakened from my sleep with the same booming voice repeating the same message, "Get up, get busy." I sat up again in my bed quickly as before so startled by the commanding voice, which I knew of a certainty that it had authority. As I sat on the side of the bed, I thought, 'Someone is playing a trick on me and is trying to frighten me,' and I became very irritated. I looked out the window where the voice seemed to come from, but I couldn't see anyone and no one was visible anywhere. "Oh, Lord, I'm so weary, I need rest," I cried. 'I don't understand what is going on around here,' I thought, 'but I'm determined to get some sleep,' and I lay down again.

As before, I went back to sleep quickly and I don't know how long it was before I was again sharply awakened by the same command again. The voice was very loud and I couldn't ignore it or roll over and go back to sleep. It was as if I was having a bad dream or a nightmare. The voice seemed to fill the whole valley and I wondered why it didn't wake up Mikie and her family. As before, I sat up alarmed and startled, then aggravated. I hung my legs off the side of the bed. I sat there troubled, wondering how long this would go on when His voice spoke once more in the same manner and tone shouting, "Get up," a pause and then, "Get busy!" 'This isn't a dream,' I told myself, 'this is the Lord calling me.' I turned the porch light on and looked around just to be sure, but I knew in my heart it was a waste of time because He wasn't visible to my eyes. I picked up my Bible then and sat on the couch and began to read in hopes that somehow I could find an answer there.

My mother had told me long ago that if God called my name, ask Him what He wanted in the name of Jesus. I started my prayer with a plea for understanding, because I didn't see how I could do any more than I was already. The idea seemed preposterous that I must get busy and I reminded my Father of all the many things I was doing every day. Tears rolled down my cheeks because I was feeling sorry for myself and I thought, 'The Lord doesn't seem to care that I was already working my fingers to the bone. Not only was I standing on my feet and racing up and down the halls at the hospital doing patient care, coming home completely exhausted, most times working overtime when they were short handed. Besides that, I sold leather goods for the men in the prison. I even paid them for their work before I could collect the money from the customers. Not only that, Father, there's Ted whom I love and care for, frying pies on the side to help pay our bills and send him a little money to go into his trust fund. I'm running my legs off, Father, and I just can't see how I'll be able to get any busier than I already am, but if You will instruct me and guide me, I will do Your will. Somehow just let me know what it is You want me to do and I'll follow You so that I can be at peace again.' After that, I lay down again and slept without interruption, but when I woke up I felt awful and thought about the things that had taken place during the night.

When I walked out on the porch at Mikie's to fry some pies for the church dinner, Isabella asked, "Mamma, did you sleep well last night?" I immediately thought that she knew about last night. She had never asked me if I had slept well before so she must be in on a joke someone was playing on me. Since I was already quite irritated, I responded to her question quickly saying, "Well, if certain people would have let me sleep, I would have rested. Instead, I was awakened several times by a sharp commanding voice telling me to 'Get up, get busy.' Was it Bill or Randall, Isabella? Did someone call from the hospital and want me to come in?"

Isabella sat stunned and was very close to tears. Her lips trembled as she said, "Mamma, we were all sleeping. The hospital didn't call and no one went outside. I don't know who woke you up, but it wasn't any of us." I felt so ashamed because of my outburst, but I couldn't understand what was happening. Everyone in the house had heard me because I was so irritated and Mikie came out on the porch and took me by the arm and said, "Destiny, the Lord must have called you Himself. Maybe there's something He wants you to do." I really became frustrated after that as the tears stung my eyes, but I retorted hatefully, "What more can I do than what I'm already doing?"

Steve came out on the porch and said, "I'll look around the trailer. If someone has been fooling around, there are sure to be footprints." Mikie and I went with him, but there weren't any footprints anywhere, not even the paw prints of an animal. As we searched around the trailer, it became more and more puzzling and then I knew without any doubt that it was God who had visited me this Mother's Day morning. I couldn't imagine what God wanted me to do and as I went about my normal activities, I trusted that God would make His calling clear eventually.

In a short time I received a statement from the land tax office at Livingston, Texas. They notified me that the taxes hadn't been paid and that the interest was accumulating and it was already a sizable amount. I went to the couple who had bought Jacob's and my small frame house on a payment plan that I had financed for them and asked them why the taxes were delinquent. They only laughed and said, "We always pay our taxes late." I didn't think it was funny at all, because I couldn't pay such an outlandish figure on my pay as a nurse's aide. I went by Sam's and asked his advice right away. He said, "Mamma, they have broken their contract. They haven't kept the insurance up either, so I'll go by their house and talk to them about it." I knew it would place me in a bind just to catch up on the taxes and I didn't know which way to turn. Sam went to see the couple that had bought the house, and he brought back the key to our little house. I'd used the income from selling the house to pay the notes at the bank for Jacob's funeral expenses. I cried happily as I rejoiced. "Thank You, Father, all that remains is one more note at the bank. Help me make it through, Dear Jesus, and not just to meet my obligations, but also to increase my faith as I follow You," I prayed. Satan kept reminding me that God had promised that I would live in Isabella and Steve's house, but I refused to accept or believe it even though I was still living in the small travel trailer that seemed to smother me, making me feel all closed in like a prisoner. I would huddle in a corner of the couch and write long letters to Ted. This was the way that I escaped from reality. Memories of living in a truck still haunted me and the small, closed in trailer was a constant reminder of the way we had lived. "I must be free, oh, my God," I cried, "Take me back home, Father, where I can sit on the front porch feeling the gentle breezes and the freedom that I so long for. We can put this trailer up for sale and with Your help we can move back home. We can load up the little car when I finish my last shift for the week and eventually get everything back in place the way it used to be. We can start all over again, and I'll be closer to Ted as well. I can look for employment around Livingston at the hospital or the nursing homes. In the meantime, I can drive back and forth to the hospital at Jasper. I'll change my schedule at the hospital too. I can make doubles and complete my forty hours sooner and have the rest of the week to work around the house. Yes, we'll do that Father, because I truly believe You have opened this door for me. Surely, it's Your will and I'm excited about the idea of having my home again."

First of all I placed an add in the Peddler to sell the travel trailer, then I talked to the Director of Nurses about changing my schedule which she readily agreed to do so that I could begin my new schedule right away.

On Thursday, May 30, 1991, Mikie came over to my trailer and watched as I loaded up my car. She asked, puzzled, "Destiny, what are you doing?" I told her, "Mikie, I'm moving back home." She was very near tears as she said, "Destiny, why are you moving back to Goodrich? You can't move all by yourself." "I believe I can, Mikie, if I move a little at a time. I believe that I can do anything if I set my mind to it," I insisted. She helped me stuff everything I could get into the little hatchback, then shook her head as she waved goodbye and I drove out of the driveway. The nurses marveled when they saw how full my car was packed. They too wondered about a woman who would do what I was doing. I worked the evening shift, then climbed into my car and headed toward Livingston.

Thelma Quinn

Lord, I was just a determined woman I guess not dreaming what my little house looked like. In my mind, I expected it to look just like it had before I left. My mind was made up to move back regardless of the house's condition though. My, how happy and hopeful I was as I thought about going home. It was around 2:00 A.M. when I drove up in front of the house. Looking at the dark house with only the street light and a full moon to help me see, I thought, `I'm not afraid to go inside, Father. This is my home, regardless of the condition that it's in. The screen on the front storm door is torn and hanging in tags and some of the windows don't have any screens on them at all and, Father, it makes my heart ache to see the horrible condition the renters have left the house in. How can people live like pigs in a sty? The little wood frame house did furnish them shelter, but they didn't appreciate it, I guess.'

Tears streamed down my face as I made my way through the waist high tall weeds in the yard. The weeds were dense, and as I walked through them, it was kind of frightening as they seemed to try to pull me down. They were so thick that I had to stretch my hands in front of me so that I could clear a path up to the front porch. Although I stumbled a few times as the weeds wrapped around my ankles, sheer determination carried me to the front door steps, which were also sadly in need of repair. It was good to hear the boards on the porch creak again as I made my way to the front door. The neighbor's dog started barking threateningly as I unlocked the front door nervously. When I pushed it back and went inside I stood for a moment thinking, `Lord, it's so good to be home again.' It was a beautiful moonlit night so that I could see a little inside and the street lamp helped too. I looked around the place where Jacob and I had spent our last year together. The moonlight streamed through the windows and cast shadows throughout the house, but I could see enough to find my way around the tiny two-bedroom house. I took a quilt and a pillow and made a pallet on the floor in the bedroom where Jacob and I had slept before he died. I opened the screenless windows to get a little fresh air inside because the house was musty from being closed up. I was so tired and weary that the thought of mosquitoes didn't even bother me and I fell asleep quickly.

I woke up with the bright sunlight streaming in on my face. "Get up, get busy, you sleepy head," I heard my angel say cheerfully. `Yes, I have a lot of work to do,' I told myself. Excitedly, I jumped to my feet, not knowing where to start and I decided to go to the truck stop first and fill my thermos with coffee. Then I went to the hardware store and bought some supplies and hurried back home to start my project of getting the house livable.

My neighbor and friend that lived nearby brought a battery lamp for me to use until I could get the power turned on. She helped me while her husband cut down the high weeds with his tractor. We worked feverishly that day and my hopes were high and I believed my decision was pleasing to the Lord. That night, I sat on my pallet and started a letter to Ted. I always wrote to him every day no matter where I happened to be. I would tell him the things that I had done during the day and he said it was a blessing, because through my experiences he could picture us sharing our lives together. The lamp gave just enough light for me to see. As I headed the letter and started to write the date, I suddenly realized I had returned home on May 31st, which would have been mine and Jacob's forty-second wedding anniversary. Chill bumps covered my arms and I started crying. "Why, Father, why have I returned home on this special day without even realizing what date it was? Father, can it be possible that You sent Jacob to lead me home so I could feel contentment and be at peace?" As I prayed, I felt warm and safe as I sat on the floor gazing out the window toward the spot where Jacob died in the back yard. I thought of God and His power over our lives, of the many great mysteries that our human minds couldn't understand.

As in all my letters to Ted, I wrote from the heart, and I poured out my heart to Ted that night, just as the Holy Spirit led me to write. After the letter was finished, I felt peace as though the letter had been addressed to heaven. I prayed for understanding and the courage which I would need in the coming days. Then I turned out the light and slept peacefully. The sunlight awakened me again and thoughts of seeing Ted today were exciting. I jumped up quickly and began getting ready for our visit. It wouldn't take very long to reach Huntsville because it was only about a forty-five minute drive and I would also be able to work some more when I got back. I walked on air as I crossed the parking lot thinking Ted would be proud of me because of my decision to move back home. As I so often did, I talked to my Lord deep in thought as I strolled along, `Father, Ted hasn't seen the little house that we lived in since before his brother died. It's so sad that they lost all contact with each other years ago. Families split up over things that are not really important just like our family had done. Then one day you wake up and find that it's too late after a member of your family dies. I pray that somehow our family will be brought together in peace, even though so many broken pieces remain. There is nothing impossible for You, my Lord, because You spoke the universe into existence. Your mercy is long suffering even as You gently lead Ted and I, even though our past sins continually haunt us and we're unable to understand how You can love us at all. Surely, Father, there's some work that You would have us to do, for You to keep us alive as You have done.' As I walked up the sidewalk toward the visiting area, my heart raced when I saw

Ted sitting at the table smiling and waving to get my attention. When I checked in and walked outside into the yard, Ted was standing by the table and watching as I crossed the yard hurriedly and went straight into his waiting arms. He embraced me, and covered my face with kisses. Then smiling, he held my face and said proudly, "You are some kind of woman, Destiny, and there's no limit to your faith when you make up your mind to do something. I trust you are making the right decision to move back to Goodrich, but Darling, I can't help but worry about you doing it without any help from your boys." As we sat down opposite each other, Ted looked into my eyes adoringly, and it was as if he was just seeing me as a strong determined woman who wasn't dependant on anyone for her survival unless it was absolutely necessary to ask for help. Ted smiled and said, "Darling, it really takes a tremendous amount of courage to step out on faith the way you do. I pray for you every moment and it hurts that I can't be out there to help you. My constant prayer is that God will protect you from harm. I became so heartbroken and so helpless the other day when the Lord spoke to my heart, saying, `Ted, don't worry and fret about Destiny, she is mine and I will take care of her every need.' Suddenly the burden was lifted and I placed you in God's loving hands, Darling. I have peace now concerning you and the sweet assurance that God loves you, my Darling wife, even more than I ever could, even though I would give my life for you, Precious." It was a very emotional moment and tears filled my eyes. As I struggled to regain my composure, I said, "Darling, I love you so very much and it's a wonderful feeling to know that I can make you proud of me, but I also pray that I can please the Lord too. I don't understand why I felt such a sense of urgency to make a home for us when I realize you have years to serve before you can even come up for parole. I just want everything to be wonderful for you because I love you with all my heart. Oh, Ted, we've missed so much during our lifetime," I cried. Ted took my hands and held them tight, then he said tenderly, "Darling, there is plenty of time. Unless the law changes affecting my status, I'm going to be here for many more years. All I ask is that you please take care of yourself, so that when I am free, we'll be able to enjoy our time together. I need you just as you are. You don't have to build us a house and work so hard. When I get home, we will make a place for us to live together whether it's under an old oak tree or near a running stream." At that moment, the love of God united my Beloved and me. As the tears rolled down my cheeks, I said, "I love you so much, Ted, and have so little to give, only myself, for the rest of my life." "Darling, you are all I want and everything will be all right because we are together," Ted reassured me as he held me and kissed away my tears as we said our good-byes.

When I got back to Goodrich, I worked until dark and felt good when I lay down on my pallet with the windows and doors open now that new screens were on them. I woke up early the next morning and started getting things together for church and for the coming week. I felt quite pleased as I drove away, feeling good about the things that had been accomplished in such a short time.

The Lord moved again in my life the coming week when a man bought the travel trailer from me. I didn't ask anything for myself, all I wanted was the loan paid off. When he pulled the trailer out of the yard, I had my car packed and ready to go back to Goodrich. I followed him to the bank where we completed the paper work. I was so happy when I walked out of the bank and I praised the Lord for being so good to me. It just seemed as if everything was falling in place just the way the Lord had planned. After unloading the car the following morning, I started looking for a job at Livingston. I put an application in at the hospital first, then I went to the nursing homes in that area and filled out several applications. My heart was at the hospital at Jasper, even though I convinced myself that it would be the best to work closer to home and I found myself really hoping that I wouldn't get hired even if I had to drive the 65 miles to work. Every week, I worked my forty hours at Jasper, most of the time sleeping in an empty room at the hospital. Sometimes I slept at Isabella's or Mikie's, especially the night before I would be going back home. I would stuff all that I could in the little hatch back once a week and at the end of my shift I would head toward Goodrich. I had carried everything that I could in nine loads and Steve loaded the larger things in his pickup and brought them to me. I faced hard times during those days and I cried when it rained. I couldn't find enough pans to catch the water, which poured in from the kitchen ceiling. I was heartsick when the sheet rock started sagging in the kitchen ceiling and parts of it started falling.

"Lord, what can I do when I don't have the funds to get the roof fixed?" I would cry. Then one of my friends suggested that I apply for a loan from HUD, but they turned me down when I did. They said I made too much money as a nurse's aide. Then I turned to my boys for help. All of the children agreed to help so I bought the supplies we needed. One Saturday, they all came and all of the grownups worked while the small children played. As the men fixed the roof, the girls painted the house. It was a wonderful feeling when we finished and I looked at all my family had accomplished in only a few hours. I was so happy as I praised God not only for the work the children had done, but I was glad they had come to help me when I needed them.

I hadn't called upon the children for help much since Jacob had passed away. I did my best to manage alone whenever it was possible. When I did need their help, it made me feel like a beggar. I don't think they ever understood how alone and helpless I felt at times. How could they understand unless they had been through everything I had? Sometimes I had the feeling that they had decided that since I married Ted instead of someone who could take care of my needs that I didn't deserve their help, but whenever I was in dire need, it was wonderful when they all came together and helped me.

As time went by, I looked more and more to God to supply all my needs so that I wouldn't have to ask them for anything. During this time, I really learned how much God meant to me as my husband and my Father and I appreciated my Lord even more as we shared this sweet relationship together. Ted and I rejoiced in a special way on Sunday, July 21, 1991. I'll never forget that day as long as I live. After playing the piano for the worship service at Newton, I climbed into the car and headed toward Huntsville. It was an exciting day as I drove along, thinking how only one year ago I had driven this same highway on my wedding day. It was really a lovely meeting when I entered the visiting area. Ted stood with his arms ready to hold me hungrily and when he gathered me in his arms, he said happily, "Darling, I was baptized this morning at the Hope Chapel here in prison. God did a beautiful thing for you and me when He sent a Baptist minister to preach on our first wedding anniversary. You know how much I always wanted to follow Christ in baptism, Honey, and I feel wonderful. There were several others who were baptized too." "What a beautiful blessing," I cried happily, thanking God for such a lovely gift on this special occasion. Ted said excitedly, "Honey, I'll send my baptismal certificate to you for safe keeping, and one day we'll sit together at church, Darling," Ted said smiling happily. Ted was so excited as he added, "Sweetheart, we have such beautiful dreams and so very much to look forward to. Precious, we will be able to sit together in church like we haven't been able to. We've never been able to enjoy sitting on the porch holding hands and watch the sun go down or greet the early sunrise together. We are so grateful when we can walk hand in hand, the short distance from our table to the gate where we must part, and one of my favorite dreams is of us walking hand in hand down a country road at Newton in the springtime. These things that so many couples take for granted are our hopes and dreams which we are can't do because of the terrible thing I did, Precious, and I'm so sorry, Darling." Ted was holding my hands in his when I started to cry because his lovely dreams were mine and smiling through my tears, we placed our hopes and dreams in our Master's capable and loving hands while we prayed together. We have so much to be grateful for, even though our lives are different from others, but in Christ Jesus we have found happiness in spite of prison walls. Only God knows the depth of our love one for the other, because God planted that love in our hearts long ago. There aren't any words that I could use to describe the depth of our love. The Lord has showered so many of His blessings upon the two of us through His tender mercy. Ted was happy because the children had fixed the roof of our house. Ted felt in his heart that they would do more for me if we hadn't married, even though he was Jacob's brother. Isabella and Joyce seemed quite content with our marriage, but the Holy Spirit had dealt with both of them so that they were happy for us. He sent dreams and visions to Joyce and through them she received the comfort that our life together was the will of God. Isabella had also experienced doubts and had written Ted a letter begging him to let me go. Ted wrote to her and told her, "Isabella, your mother is free if she wants to be, but if she chooses to stay with me I won't ever send her away."

He included my writing about the Eternal Circle in the letter which told about true love that had no visible beginning or ending. This was the love we had for each other and separation would never stop us from loving each other. Only the good Lord above could have designed such a love in His own heart. After the letter, Isabella's fears subsided when she realized that God had truly brought us together.

My oldest son, Wayne never doubted from the beginning and he wrote Ted a letter saying, "I know your marriage was made in heaven because God ordained it." Wayne loved his Uncle Ted as much as he did his sisters and brothers. He wasn't ashamed of Ted because he was in prison. He teased me a lot and he would laugh and say, "Mamma, you've got it made I think. At least you don't have to worry about Ted. He has food to eat and a roof over his head. He has clothes to wear, even though they are the same as the other inmates. You don't have to worry about him running around on you and he's always easy to find. You can rest at night knowing Ted is sleeping too and everytime you go to Huntsville, he will be happy to see his Destiny. I'll just bet too, there are a lot of men everywhere that envy Ted because God has blessed him more than most by sending him a true and faithful wife and friend to make him happy in spite of prison. Don't ever hang your head in shame, Mamma. You did a wonderful thing when you responded to the call of God and gave your heart freely to Ted for Christ Jesus' sake." If only my other children had believed my testimony that God really did send me into Ted's life, I firmly believe they would not have suffered so many misgivings. Sam and Mark hadn't said very much yet, but I expected them to voice their opinion any day. It was a beautiful autumn morning when I sat down at the table on the front porch and started a letter to Ted. The whole world seemed to be at peace and the sound of the traffic from the highway nearby further enhanced the pleasant feeling of peace. As I started my letter, Sam and Karen drove into the driveway. I invited them to join me, but Karen stayed in the car. Sam walked up the steps, without saying a word until he stood opposite the table from me. I knew something was wrong by the look on his face. He was mad and I wondered if I had done something to cause his anger.

Sam got straight to the point immediately. I couldn't seem to move as he blurted out his cruel words to me, "Mamma, I know Daddy wasn't good to you and you suffered a lot, but I won't accept your marriage by proxy to Ted. I can't find it in the Bible anywhere where God approves of such a marriage. I won't accept Ted as my stepfather until you are married in the right way. The older kids knew Ted, I guess, but I didn't know him very well anyway." I couldn't understand why he had suddenly decided to come by the house mad and jump on me about Ted suddenly since we had already been married for some months. I was upset and hurt and told him, "Sam, I'm sorry you feel that way, but it won't change a thing. Our marriage by proxy is legal and binding and God has blessed our marriage. I can't force you to believe that God sent me to Ted or convince you that God let us know when it was time for us to marry."

Sam wasn't listening to anything I said or showed any regard for the way his words hurt me. He turned away quickly and walked across the porch. As he started to get into the car, I told him, "Sam, some day you are going to know the truth that it was God who directed my life and in spite of how much you kids hurt me, I'm determined to stand by the Lord and His will comes first just as sure as it ever did in the past, Son." They drove away and I went in the house and fell on my knees and cried out to God. "Father, I've known from the beginning that some or all of the children would turn on me because of Ted, but You know they just don't believe that You sent me and they think I've used that just to be with Ted. Oh, God, it's true that I've loved him for many years, but, Father, You know the truth. If only they believed then they wouldn't treat me in this way and instead of feeling shame because of what I've done, they would be proud that You counted me worthy to follow Your will. Oh, God, my Father, why won't they believe? Whether they believe or not though, Lord, I will continue to follow You until the end."

Mark was older than Sam was and he loved me. I suppose Sam loved me too, but we weren't as close as we had been through the hard times after he married Karen. Mark was preaching at a small mission a few miles from Cleveland. Since the mission wasn't far away, I would visit sometimes and play the piano for them. Although I was hesitant to invite Mark to go with me to visit with Ted, so it was a surprise when I finally asked him and he said that he wanted to see Ted again. `If only the other children would go too, they would feel differently about us,' I thought.

Mark seemed quite nervous as we walked toward the entrance of the prison. It was his first time to enter a prison so I understood how he felt. When we went into the visiting area and Mark saw Ted again after all those years, tears welled up in his eyes and as he sat down he said, "Ted, it's remarkable how much you favor Daddy." Ted fought back tears when Mark said this and in spite of the glass wall between us, we were a close knit family again. Ted told Mark how much he loved me and the way God had blessed our life together. "Your mother is a beautiful lady, Mark, and I'm sure she could have found a good husband in the free world, but she chose to be with me and when God sent her, she came to me. She's all I've got now, Mark, and she is the one that I've always loved. Our love story is a beautiful one and only the Lord could have united us," Ted told Mark. Mark's voice trembled as he turned toward me and said, "Ted, only God would have sent my mother here. He knows her so well and He knew that if He sent her she would go." His confession was sweet music to my ears, and only God could have revealed these things to my son. I felt such relief and a heavy burden had been lifted from my heart and I praised the Lord as I smiled happily. Mark said, "I don't understand God's wisdom in the choice He has made, but I do know my mother is a very strong woman and God knows best." "There isn't another woman on earth I could ever trust but her. I love her, Mark, and she is everything precious to me," Ted said proudly. Any amount of suffering on my part was worth it as I listened to Mark and Ted. The sweet presence of the Holy Spirit was wonderful and I felt so blessed and my joy was so wonderful as I listened to them. `Oh, can't you understand, my loved ones, that our lives are being lived for the glory of God,' I cried out in my soul. We joined together in prayer as Mark and I touched Ted's fingers through the wire barrier. It was such a sweet visit and we were all shaken when the time came for us to part. I felt sorry for Mark as we walked away and when we started back home, Mark said, "Mamma, there is a great ministry in prison and I would like to be a part of it someway. Mark realized there was a marvelous mystery surrounding our relationship and he also told me, "Mamma, I will be praying for you, but I have to leave you in the hands of God to work out His will in you." I replied, "Son, that is all that I ask of you and I'll be happy. I can't expect you to understand these things when I don't understand them myself. I just walk by faith and follow the call of my Father and I hope you do too. We can't see the end, but, Son, if I could, then where would faith come in?"

A short time later, I received a call from the Pharmacist at the hospital at Livingston. He wanted me to work part time in the pharmacy and said he would train me himself. I took the job, but I couldn't hold up to all the hours and I quit after a month or so and just worked at the hospital at Jasper. It seemed as if the whole world was crushing down on me and my problems seem to mount higher and higher while I lived at Goodrich. My life was such in turmoil as I tried to keep up with everything that I had to do. Besides my regular job at the hospital, I sold leather goods for some of the prisoners. When I would get my paycheck, I would send them the money for the things I had ordered and then collect the money to replace the money I had spent. Besides keeping up my home, I visited Ted each Saturday and on Sunday morning I packed my things and went to Newton to play for the church and start all over again. It became such a nightmare just to keep going that one morning after working too many hours I fought so hard to stay awake on my way home that I almost wrecked my car. When I finally made it home, I fell on my knees beside my bed and cried out to God to loose these chains and set me free because I couldn't take it anymore.

Winter was on the way and I was worried about heat for my little house. I bought another window unit in exchange of my air conditioner, which Sam installed, and it warmed the house very well. As winter set in, I had to cut the water off so the water lines wouldn't freeze before I started to Newton and it became aggravating. When I would come home in the middle of the night, I would have to turn the water back on again in the freezing weather. One day Isabella said, "Mamma, J. T. and Mikie have moved into their new house. Why don't you move back so you will be closer to your job and you can get more rest. Steve and I have talked it over and we decided that if you would agree we would trade houses with you. I don't think we'll have any trouble selling your house to a couple that needs an affordable home. It could be a nice place if someone would do a little work on it. We want you to move back to Newton where you are loved and there are people who want to help you. We are all so afraid that you are going to wind up in a bad car wreck, because you have to travel so far and most of the time you are half asleep." I was afraid to give up the security of my home and take another chance on Steve and Isabella keeping their word. I was afraid that someone else would come along and they would move me out again. I told her to let me think about it and I would let her know what I decided to do. It didn't take long to make my decision though. The little house needed a lot of repairs and none of the kids could help me because they said they had their own families to worry about and they simply didn't have the time so I had to go down in defeat and accept it as God's will. I had wanted to keep the little place because their Daddy had died there, but it didn't seem to bother them if I sold it or not.

When I finished my doubles that morning and I hurried to my car, I gasped in horror because a thief had stolen my best clothes and the small box of leather goods that I kept to sell for the inmates. I felt sick as I walked back to the nurses' station and told them what had happened while I was working. I should have locked the car up and not just take the key with me. I felt kind of stupid for being so careless and I told the ward clerk that I deserved to get robbed. It was kind of funny, but the thief didn't take everything, he left a bag that contained my underwear. I laughed and remarked, "At least he left my panties."

I woke up the following Sunday with the intentions of leaving early and as I relaxed drinking coffee, a soft gentle voice spoke to my heart, saying, `Destiny, your Bible was stolen too.' I thought, `Father, surely not the family

Bible!' I carried my Bible in the car with me all of the time and I ran to the car immediately to see if it was there. Tears streamed down my cheeks as I searched the car, but it wasn't there. Then I ran back in the house and searched everywhere, but I knew that I had lost one of my most cherished possessions which couldn't be replaced when it wasn't to be found. I broke down and sobbed as if a member of my family had died. "Oh, my God, this was a special Bible, not only because it was Your Word, but it held so many precious memories too. I had given it to Dad one Christmas many years ago. He had underlined some of the verses he had read and marked his signature of faith with a pencil with his trembling hand. Mom's recording of our family history was also written inside along with old markers she had accumulated over the years. It was filled with clippings about the prison as well. Father, who would want our Bible anyway with the name `QUINN' printed in large letters across the front cover? I'm sure the thief threw it in a ditch somewhere when he realized he had stolen a Bible anyway. It wouldn't be quite so bad if the thief read it, but he will just want to get rid of it as soon as possible." I cried all the way to Jasper and went by the Police station and filed a report about the theft, but they told me there was very little hope that my things would ever turn up. After I left the Police station, I went on to Sunday school. I felt lost without my friend, but I could use the new Bible the children had given Jacob. It wouldn't serve any good purpose just lying around collecting dust and I was sure he wouldn't mind if I used it. The Lord had convinced me that He wanted me to move back to Newton that Sunday morning and Isabella was thrilled when I told her my decision. Whatever lay ahead was in the hands of God and I would place my faith in His promise of grace. I learned that my Lord cared no matter what happened to me. He knew about my insecurities as well as my hopes and dreams. I guess I'll never know for sure whether it had been God's will for me to move back to Goodrich or not. At least the roof got fixed and I sold the travel trailer, so it wasn't really a total loss. "Father, guide me in paths of righteousness and help me find peace and contentment as I walk by faith and place my trust in You for the future," I prayed.

CHAPTER 8

GOD'S MERCY IS SUFFICIENT

After finishing my shift at the hospital, I headed toward Newton. The thought of going back home to Newton lifted my spirits. I wondered what I would find when I got there, since the house had been vacant for several weeks. I was pretty sure the house would be cold and damp and I didn't have any wood to build a fire with, but I decided to worry about that when I got there. As I entered the driveway I saw smoke rising from the chimney and a deep peace swept over me. I smiled to myself because Isabella had probably called Mikie and J.T. and told them that I was coming back home. J.T. had built a fire in the fireplace so I wouldn't walk into a cold house. I parked at the front of the house and walked across the porch. Upon opening the door, it was as though Jesus smiled and said joyfully, "Welcome home, my Destiny!" Tears filled my eyes as I walked inside and I cried, "Oh, Father, am I truly home at last?" Two chairs were placed near the fireplace. They were old and the upholstery was torn, but I didn't mind. Mikie and J.T. had left them there when they moved into their new house. Wood was stacked on the hearth as well and I thought, `What a wonderful homecoming the Lord and my friends have given me.' As I looked around the room, the sweet atmosphere caused me to rejoice in the Lord, thanking Him for supplying my every need and especially for good friends who were so thoughtful and kind.

The piano stood in its usual place and I ran my fingers across the notes, feeling so grateful to have my special friend that had been such a comfort to me when I played songs of adoration and praise to my Lord and King through the many lonely hours. My joy is in praising the Lord through music, especially when no one is around except the Holy Spirit and myself. No amount of earthly wealth could measure up to or replace this treasure. The peace of God surrounded my whole being as I felt His sweet presence in the room and I couldn't stop the tears of joy that flowed down my cheeks.

I continued praising God as I walked down the hall and opened the master bedroom door. A bed was made up with fresh linen on it and I knew that Mikie had prepared it just for me. Truly, my life thus far had been like a story book world, just like Snow White or any of the other characters I had read about as a child. I thought I could control my destiny, but in time I learned that God was molding me according to His plan. When I would try to accomplish something through my own ability and wisdom, I would fail miserably. With His gentle hand in mine, He would set me on the right path. Even though I didn't fully understand, I learned to accept His will. After seeing all the wonderful blessings God had prepared for my homecoming, I gathered my writing material and sat by the fire and started a letter to Ted.

"My Darling Ted," I wrote, "I am finally home at last. I just pray this will be the last move for me. There isn't much furniture, but, Darling, I don't need very much, just a chair to sit in and a place to sleep. I'm quite comfortable actually. When you consider the needs of one person, you come to the realization that you don't need all that much. You, of all people, can understand since you live in a two by four cell. You have a small bunk to sleep on and there is barely enough room to pass by your cellmate.

The Lord has provided me with a roomy place to live and all the necessary things I need to make me comfortable, but even with all these things, I long to be with you most of all. It's very pleasant just sitting here by the fire writing to you, feeling the presence of the Holy Spirit all around, even throughout the countryside.

Once in a while I glance out of the window and see J.T.'s cows grazing lazily on the green grass in the field nearby and I get the strangest feeling that this is a holy place. There are birds singing near my window and their lovely song adds even more beauty to the scene and tears of gratitude and praise start with the realization of how very much God loves me. I feel sure in my heart that I belong here and it's so good to be back home again in the valley God chose for me. Someday Darling, you will see it too, when the Lord sees fit to let you go free."

Ted and I met on our next visit he said, "Darling, I believe that God gave you a special place to live so it would be a blessing to you for being so faithful to Him all through the years. I also believe the Lord has provided this home for you so you will be comfortable through your old age, too." When I looked up at Ted and he saw that I didn't totally agree with him, he said, "Honey, you have lived in run down shacks all your life with Jacob and you never really had a nice home to live in that I know of. You have more money since he died and even though your paycheck is small, it's more than you had then because he wasted what he made. If I know anything of what you've suffered, I'm certain God does too, and it makes me very happy to know that God is blessing you." "Dearest, I know the Lord loves me and I love Him so very much, but who am I that God would go out of His way to bless me so abundantly as this," I cried? "The things He has done is like some fairy tale that leaves me breathless at times. He has filled my life with so much joy and peace since Jacob died that I keep thinking I'll wake up and find it is all just a dream. I just want to serve God in anyway He sees fit. I want to shout it to the whole world what a wonderful Lord He is," I said joyfully. Ted said, "Destiny, I'm so proud of you and all of your accomplishments. Most of all for knowing you are a Christian who loves the Lord. I love to hear your testimonies about the different people you have witnessed to. I'm ashamed that I haven't been a faithful witness the way the Lord wants me to be and I need to get off my duff and witness more for Christ myself." Ted twisted uncomfortably in his chair as he continued, "Who is going to listen to someone like me, Honey? I am in this prison for the worst possible crime that anyone can do." "But, Darling, don't you see, these inmates will listen to you," I said excitedly! "You can relate to their need for Christ much better than someone outside of the prison, Darling. They know that someone who hasn't been convicted of a crime and spent time in prison really can't understand, but you can, Honey. You were saved in this dreadful place, Precious. Why are you standing idle Ted when you are in a huge white field of lost souls ready for harvesting? I agree that you need to get off your duff and get busy while there is still time and don't be so lazy about it. I love you, my Darling. Let's both get busy for the Lord." "Amen," Ted remarked smiling, then he added, "All right, Mrs. Quinn," and we both laughed together. After our sweet visit I headed toward Goodrich. The thought of moving back to Newton was exciting, in spite of the fact that my little car couldn't carry very much at a time, the hope of settling down in that beautiful peaceful valley was exhilarating. When I got to Goodrich, I stuffed all I could into my car and headed down the highway toward Newton. `Lord, I must be patient,' I told myself anxiously. `It will take several trips to move all of my things to Newton,' I thought, expecting this move to be like my move to Goodrich in 1991.

When I went back to Goodrich the next time to gather as much as I could in the little hatch back, I looked out of the window and saw Steve and his Dad pulling up in their pickups. I ran outside excitedly, straight into my son-in-law's arms and he lifted me off my feet and swinging me around, he stated firmly, "This is the last time that I'm going to move you, Destiny. I'm taking you home to stay this time." Steve was laughing, but I wanted to cry, because I knew that I had done a lot of foolish things and I'd made a lot of mistakes, but in spite of all I had done my family loved me and went out of their way to let me know it.

The children didn't realize how much I didn't want to be a burden on them. I was trying to stand on my own feet so that wouldn't happen, but I had to learn that no one can stand alone without help. I didn't realize how much pride I had until Jacob died a pride that had been suppressed all those years of being dominated by him. Throughout our marriage I'd been forced to depend on others when I just wanted to lean on him when times got rough. All those years he would leave me with somebody to look after me when I was sick so he could leave on a truck and escape from his responsibilities. He always wanted somebody else to take care of me and tried to convince me that I couldn't make it on my own. He thought when he died the kids would have to take me in as if I were a helpless cripple. Then when he did die, they thought that I would just sit down and give up, but I fought against that idea with all of the determination that I could muster. Suddenly I had found the freedom that I'd always wanted and even though I made a lot of mistakes, I realized that I was only a young child in a new world, experiencing life for the very first time.

When I moved all of my things back to Newton I felt a true sense of belonging and security, believing with all my heart that God had fulfilled His promise. Most of all, I felt truly free without any fear that I didn't have a home to call my own and the heavy burden I had carried for so long was lifted. With this newfound freedom, I found the doors of opportunity to witness for Christ opening more and more at the hospital. There were times at night while I walked down the halls would hear the voice of a woman calling my name. "Destiny," she would say and I would look around startled and couldn't see anyone. When I would walk to the nurses' station and ask the ward clerk if someone had called for me, she would look puzzled and reply, "No one called for you, Destiny. You must be hearing things." It took a long time before I realized that when the angel called my name, there would be someone with whom I could witness to whether it was during the day or the middle of the night. Since I worked different shifts, these occasions came at varied times. Most of the time the Lord would open a door when I least expected it. I didn't deliberately begin a conversation with anyone about the Lord. However, my life had been a mixture of so many things that it was easy for the Holy Spirit to open a door which quickly led to a testimony that He wanted me to give to someone in need. One of the sweetest experiences that I had in witnessing to a patient took place in my early ministry at the hospital. There were two men who shared a semi-private room on West hall. I can't remember both of their names, but I remember one of them, because Anson had been in and out of the hospital recently and he had been my patient. Anson had just been admitted when I started my shift. He was in A bed and the other young man was in B bed. Since the lab technician was drawing blood and a nurse was starting an IV on Anson, I took the vital signs on the patient in B bed first. The young man began telling me how much God had blessed him for bringing him through his surgery. While we were rejoicing in the Lord, Anson spoke, "Mrs. Quinn, when you finish over there, would you come over here and tell me about Jesus?" I replied without hesitation, "Yes, I'll be happy to." The young man nodded and whispered, "Go and witness to him, Mrs. Quinn." I smiled and walked to Anson's bed and looked into his troubled eyes. My hands trembled as I took his hand in mine. Anson's face was taunt and strained from the pain he was suffering. As I stood by his bedside, I started to pray for the Holy Spirit to open our understanding and give me the right words to say. After we had prayer, I said, "The plan of salvation is simple, Anson. If you will invite Jesus into your heart, He will save your soul and forgive you of your sins. John 3:16 says, `For God so loved the world that He gave His only Son, that whosoever believeth in Him should not perish, but have everlasting life.' It sounds too simple, doesn't it, but salvation is a free gift. It can't be earned, Anson. In Ephesians 2:8, it says `For by grace we are saved through faith; and that not of ourselves: it is the gift of God: not of works, lest any man should boast.'" "Yes, I believe with all my heart, Mrs. Quinn," Anson cried.

Tears filled my eyes as he began telling me about his many trips to the hospital and how he believed this illness had been placed on him to bring him to the Lord. "I have a sweet wife and several children. They need me to get well so I can take care of my family properly. Without Christ, I am nothing but a hopeless man," he said sadly. I said, "Anson, the Lord can and will heal you if you will place your faith and trust in Him. Jesus can make you completely whole through the new birth, my friend. Now that you have accepted Christ by faith, you should immediately take your family to the Lord's house and bring them up to know Christ Jesus as their Savior too. I'm so sorry that I haven't witnessed to you before now, but all the other times that you were in the hospital, I just assumed that you were saved." Then I told him that I had to see about my other patients and

I left him smiling. Although Anson didn't tell me then that Jesus had entered into his heart, later that evening as I walked down the hall I heard the two men glorifying Jesus Christ.

Several days later, I was sitting in the nurses' report room, which is adjacent to the nurses' station. I was catching up on my paper work when I saw Anson walk by the nurses' station. I didn't think the doctor had discharged him yet, but he was headed toward the exit. The report room was full of nurses, some were working and some were on their break. I was startled by the reaction of some of the young nurses and I looked around to see why they were sitting with their mouth hanging open and staring at the nurses' station. As I watched, Anson came through the nurses' station into the break room and stood in front of me. You could have heard a pin drop when the handsome young man held out a single beautiful red rose and placed it in my hand. I could hear the young girls sighing in the background as Anson said in a husky voice, "Mrs. Quinn, I brought this rose to you, because you witnessed to me about Christ Jesus and I appreciate you so much." I smiled nervously because I'd never been rewarded for my testimony for Christ with a lovely gift of a beautiful red rose. Thank you for this lovely gift, Anson. I'll never forget you," I said shyly. As he walked away, one of the girls sighed as she said, "Oh, God, Anson is the handsomest man I've ever seen, and I almost fainted when I saw him walk into the break room. I wish I had known it, I would have told him about God."

Anson left the next day before I got back to work and I have never seen him since. Once the mission is completed, I seldom hear from them again, but there are a few who return and it is wonderful. We hug and rejoice in Christ because we now have an everlasting bond that no one can destroy.

Ted thought the event at the hospital was wonderful. He grinned proudly and said, "Destiny, Darling, you are a marvel. I am so glad you are mine, Honey. I think I'll just keep you around." Then laughing, Ted squeezed my hand and said, "I love you, Darling!" "I love you too, Baby," I said laughing with him.

Satan fights the ministry of Christ any way he can. He demonstrated his power one night at the hospital. In June of 1992, I was at the nurses' station along with the other nurses. We were waiting until report was over so we could go home. The call light came on in West 6, so I hurriedly went to see what the patient needed. When I entered the room, the patient asked, "Will you clean my false teeth before you go home?" I replied, "Sure I will," and I walked around his bed to the far side. He took the teeth out of his mouth and placed them in a small container and gave them to me.

Being in a hurry, I quickly turned and walked hastily toward the end of his bed. Without warning, my foot caught on the wheel at the foot of the bed. I lost all control of my footing and found myself plunging forward with such a powerful force that was more powerful than anything I had ever experienced before. My movements were completely out of control as I fell headlong toward the stone wall. There wasn't any doubt in my mind that my face would be crushed unless something miraculous happened to break my speed. All I could do was cry out to the Lord, "Oh, God, help me," and pictured in my mind what my fate was certain to be. I reached out for the bedside table that was over against the wall to my left. As I touched it with my hand, very suddenly another force took over. There was no doubt in my mind that there were two unseen forces in that room that night because in spite of the table some power stopped me instantly and I made a complete turn and then went uncontrollably backward slamming me under the table. My head hit the wall first and I lost consciousness for a moment. The impact of my head slamming against the wall made such a loud noise that it alarmed the patient and he called the doctor who happened to be at the nurses' station.

When I came to, I was looking up into a light that the doctor was using to look at my eyes. Then he turned to one of the nurses who had run in to see what all the racket was and he told her to help me back to the nurses' station and he left.

My friend, Belivia who was a nurse, helped me to my feet and I sat down in a chair still quite dazed while she cleaned the patient's teeth that I still had clutched in my hand. She said, "Destiny, it's a miracle that these teeth weren't broken." I replied, "Belivia, a greater miracle just took place here tonight than that."

When I got back to the nurses' station and sat down, I realized that I couldn't turn my head. My charge nurse wrote an incident report and called for a wheelchair and one of the security guards. When he got to the nurses' station, he took me to Dr. Joe's office. Dr. Joe was working late on some paper work. After Dr. Joe heard my story and examined my neck, he laughed. Then teasing me, he called me "Hard head." Then he said, "You must have a hard head to survive such a bang on your head and not even break the skin." Dr. Joe injected my neck with some medicine and told the security guard to take me back to the nurses' station. "Stay there for a while before you start home just in case you have a reaction to the medicine," Dr. Joe instructed.

Later the security guard helped me to my car and I drove home thinking, `God is so merciful.' My neck was numb when I went to bed. I had been through a terrible accident and was completely exhausted. I started to lie down, but all that I could do was cry out in agonizing pain because I had hurt my back as well as my neck. "Oh, God," I would cry, "My back hurts terribly. Help me, Father, what can I do? I can't even lie down on the bed." Somehow I made it through the night after forcing my body to lay down on the bed.

Isabella came early the next morning and helped me dress and get in the car and she took me to the doctor. He sent me to have some x-rays. Before I left, Dr. Joe injected my back and the medicine relieved most of my pain. He told me to come back on Friday because the x-ray results would be back by then. Even though Isabella wanted me to go home with her, I just wanted to go home so I could recover at my own pace. Since I didn't want to be dependent on my children during my period of recovery and also I wanted the freedom to be able to write Ted when I felt like it and I needed my peaceful valley and my own bed. Besides, I especially didn't want them to hear me cry out in all my pain as I forced myself to walk. All during this agonizing period of recuperation, I would cry out for God's mercy even when I would force myself to walk to the mail box. My legs were weak and would shake when I would stand up. Many times I would have to stop for a few minutes before making a few more steps. During this time, Jesus helped me bear the pain with His love and tender mercies when I felt like giving up. I felt that if I failed to exercise that I might lose the strength to stand and it took all my efforts not to give up. During the time when my pain would be so severe, Jesus was there and gave me the ability to continue and through His help, I became more determined that ever to keep exercising my legs. I would stay busy doing things with my hands, but I continued to write to Ted and play the piano. I worked especially hard on one special song that the Lord helped me learn which gave me great comfort. As I practiced on the piano, I would sing to Jesus, "God is my hiding place and I hide beneath Your Holy Wings seeking healing, Oh, my God." In agony I would cry, "Father, I know I am wounded, but draw me closer to You through this hard time."

When Friday morning came, I dressed to meet Dr. Joe and Isabella at his office. As I drove toward Jasper the highway was crowded, but the Lord performed such a beautiful miracle for me. After driving through the small settlement of Holly Springs in silence, I suddenly heard what sounded like a multitude of heavenly voices singing and it seemed as if God's heavenly choir was right there with me. "Oh, God." I cried as these voices came through the car windows. Every voice was in perfect harmony and not one voice overwhelmed another as they sang in unison, "You Are My Hiding Place." I drank in all the wondrous beauty while they sang and even rolled down the car window so I could hear them better and see if I could detect where this beautiful choir came from. As I met the cars heading in the opposite direction, I shouted out at them, "Oh, don't you hear the heavenly choir singing, too?" The lovely music continued until I reached the edge of town and I thought, `How wonderfully God has poured out His blessing upon me by opening the windows of heaven so that I might catch a glimpse of its beauty through the lovely music that I would one day be a part of myself.'

Thoughts of heaven raced through my mind as I joined in with the heavenly choir in the endless song that they sang. After they had completed the song of praise for our Lord and Redeemer, the choir would begin again without interruption. I thought happily, `This is what heaven is like. A constant praise to Jesus that never ends. I don't desire the golden crown that the Bible speaks of or to walk the streets of gold either. When God calls me home, my greatest joy will be to one day join the heavenly choir in praise to my Lord who shed His life's blood for the atonement of my sins.'

I was bubbling over with joy by the time I met Isabella just outside the main entrance to the hospital. I told her happily, "Don't worry, Isabella, everything is going to be all right because I just heard the most beautiful music in my life as I was coming to Jasper. Oh, I wish you had been with me and heard the heavenly choir singing and the glory of the Lord seemed to fill the whole country side." Isabella smiled and it seemed as though a burden had been lifted from her heart as she sighed. She walked by my side as she had for so many years, but today, she was anxious to find out the results of my tests.

As we entered the front entrance, we noticed a friend in the waiting area. She looked very sad as she told me that my friend, Gladys' son, had died in a car accident last night. The terrible news stunned and shocked me and my heart went out to Gladys. I told Isabella that I had to go to see Gladys and tell her about the beautiful experience I had on my way here today. "Surely, Isabella, the Lord sent a message through the beautiful music, letting me know that Gladys' son was safe in the arms of Christ Jesus." "Gladys told me how hard it had been to raise her family alone. They are grown now and she works to make her living in housekeeping at the hospital. She has joined me in the prison ministry and we've become very close since then, sometimes going together on the trips to Huntsville. She took over the sale of the leather goods for some of the inmates and it took a big burden off me when she agreed to do it. She has a tough exterior, but her heart is soft and kind and she tries to cover her heartache with jokes and cutting up. I love her, Isabella, and my heart is heavy. I pray that God will comfort her in the way that only He can." When we met with Dr. Joe in his office, he rubbed his stubby eyebrows as he looked over my chart. I was nervous and knew Isabella was as well. Finally, he told us that all the tests turned out fine except for the results of the CT Scan which revealed deterioration of my spine. "The lower part of your spine is deteriorating worst of all," he said. I had suspected that already and my greatest fear was that one day I wouldn't be able to work at the hospital anymore.

When we walked outside, I reassured my daughter that I would be all right, and the grace of God would see us through. "You know, Isabella, God has a mission for me to do right here in this hospital. As long as He needs me, I'll fill my place and in time I'll get back on my feet. Maybe the Lord wants me to rest and use some of the sick time that I've built up. Even laid up as I am, God can use my life, and it will give me more time to study His Word and write to Ted. God has a purpose for everything that He does so I'll listen for His still small voice to direct my path." Then we parted and Isabella left to go home, telling me to call her if I needed anything. I went to visit Gladys right away so I could tell her about the wonderful experience I had had on my way to Jasper. It was a sad time, but when I told her my story we held each other and cried tears of joy for the reassurance that her son was with the Lord. My heart ached to have Ted by my side, especially when I was sick. I ached for Ted's embrace in the middle of the many lonely nights when I lay sleepless and tossing about. Many times I cried out to God to send His grace when the troubles and trials of life became too overwhelming. While I lay sleepless, memories of the past would often rush to mind with thoughts of other sleepless nights when Jacob was away only God knew where. I fought against self pity for the many wrongs that I'd suffered in the past and now the Lord had sent me into much the same way of life. Then the Lord would remind me of the beauty He had brought into my life through Ted who loved me and suffered as much as I did. Neither Ted nor I had any idea that God would bring us together the way He did even though we had always had strong feelings for each other through the years. Many times we would question His wisdom in His decision to bring us where we were today and often sighed as we faced one another. Ted would often say, "Precious, I wonder what will ever become of us." Even though it was painful to make the trip to Huntsville, I went anyway. I needed Ted now more than even when I was sick. Together we would meet in perfect unity as the Holy Spirit blessed our sweet visits. "Jesus said in Matthew 18:20 `That where two or three are gathered together in His Name that there He would be in the midst of them," I told Ted. "We meet together seeking God's will in our lives, Darling, and we love Jesus with all our hearts. He will heal our sicknesses, Precious. Claim His promise, Destiny, that you will be healed," Ted cried as he caressed my hands lovingly.

There is healing power in the Holy Wings of our Father, and we find comfort there. God did heal me in His time so that I could return to work and to the ministry at the hospital. I knew that Satan would fight against the work of Christ anyway that he could. Even though I had been brought down, the Lord blessed me during those days in many wonderful ways. Ted and I grew closer together than we'd ever been before as we faced this crisis together. God had proved our faith, proving to old Satan that our marriage was indeed built on the `Rock of the Lord Jesus Christ.'

CHAPTER 9

MINISTRY OF HOPE

As I drew near the parking lot at the hospital, my mind was on the challenges which I would face shortly. Just as I started into the parking lot a familiar voice rang out, saying sharply, "Destiny Quinn," which took me by surprise. Even though I recognized the voice as that of my angel sent from God, I looked all around just to make sure that it was truly her. There was the usual hustle and bustle as the nurses looked for a place to park and my first thought was that maybe one of them had called out to me. It wasn't that I doubted God had sent her to me again, but I needed the reassurance that it truly was her. The words she spoke were very plain and clearly defined as if she sat next to me instead of coming through my window from the vacant lot across the street from the hospital. I had also learned not to be afraid when she would suddenly call out my name. There was always something the Lord wanted me to do; most often He had someone to whom I needed to witness.

This time I needed the comfort of the Holy Spirit myself as I walked across the parking lot and drew near the Emergency Room door. A strange white van was parked near the door and it disturbed me because I'd never seen it there before. I shuddered as I drew nearer and saw two guards leading a young man with prison clothes on toward the white van. Tears filled my eyes as I looked down at his feet where they had put shackles around his ankles and handcuffs on his wrists. The two guards held his arms as the prisoner took careful steps, walking slowly toward the white van. They opened the door back and helped the young convict inside. It was as if stark reality suddenly hit me for the first time since God sent me to Ted. My heart ached terribly and it took all the grace of God to help me keep my composure and not break down in tears when I saw the prisoner with handcuffs on his wrists and shackles around his ankles, hobbling along, stumbling at times to keep pace with the guards. `Oh, God,' I cried in my heart, `I couldn't bear to see Ted shackled like that and I pray I'll never have to see him that way. How could I bear the awful heartache, Father? I love him so much, but I'm faced with this reality of our life together through the eyes of the world and not just through eyes of faith. Who am I, my Father, that you would chose me to bear such a painful cross? The world looks down on us, but there are some that feel sorry for me, because by faith, I believed that You knew best when You sent me to love Ted even though he was in prison, someone the world considers to be the very scum of the earth because of what he had done. I am weak in my flesh and only through Your bountiful grace can I endure the dreadful pain of the shame that we can't escape as long as we live. It's hard to keep my chin up and separate the two different worlds I live in.' As I walk out here in the free world, I find myself alone except for the abiding Spirit of God who never leaves me without hope in my heart. I feel at home when I'm with Ted even though there are many guards everywhere and they watch our every move. There I can find peace and comfort for a short while and feel safe within the confines of barred doors because Ted is there. Once I leave his sweet presence, the reality returns of a different world with all of life's struggles waiting just outside those prison walls.

I was quite nervous and upset as I made my way down the hall after report. My friend, Gloria, listened as I poured out my heart to her on seeing the prisoner outside the Emergency Room entrance. Gloria, near tears said, "Destiny, I don't know how you bear the awful pain that you must endure." Gloria knew that I was going through heartbreaking times and so did my other friends who worked at the hospital. They were supportive and accepted me for myself, but I could tell if the Lord had sent them to a prisoner they would tell the Lord, `No, send somebody else.' The Lord wouldn't allow me to wallow in self pity for very long, however. He had a work for me to do so there wasn't much time for crying. Although I went about my duties with a heavy heart many times, He made me rejoice when He would open a door so that I could witness to someone in need. Sometimes the Holy Spirit would lead me to counsel with them, such as the young woman whose husband had died a few months prior to her being hospitalized.

The woman had been admitted into the hospital several times with high blood pressure and her doctor ran a number of tests to try to locate the reason why they couldn't get her blood pressure under control. As I walked from room to room taking vital signs, I could hear the doctor talking to the lady through the open door. As I passed by, I heard him say that her problem wasn't physical and my heart went out to her. I decided to wait until the doctor left before I took her vital signs so when I saw him walking down the hall I started to her room. When I walked through the door I saw my patient on her knees beside her bed. My heart was touched with compassion as she cried helplessly. Without hesitation, I ran into the room and fell on my knees beside the bed and prayed with her. After we prayed, I helped her to her feet and got her settled into bed, then pulled up a chair and sat holding her hand while she poured her heart out to me. "My husband died a few months ago and I can't seem to get my life under control. I feel so lost without him. He always made all the decisions and I don't know what to do anymore." I said, "Honey, I understand some of the struggles you are going through. My husband died a short time ago and he had made all the decisions too. We had been married thirty-nine years and when he died I thought my life was over. Then the Lord helped me understand that new beginnings can be beautiful. Stop and take a long look at your life. Are you working on a job that you like or would you like to try something else?" "I hate my job," she replied bitterly. "I always wanted to be a nurse, but I haven't been to nursing school." I smiled cheerfully and said, "My friend, why don't you follow your dreams. When Jacob died I found out the world was full of opportunities that were waiting just for me. You are free to discover a whole new life if you will place your faith in God and step out on faith, believing that God has opened a special door just for you." Her tears subsided and she smiled. I saw hope and excitement in her eyes as she hurriedly began gathering her belongings to leave the hospital. `To help others is my greatest joy, Father, and when I see their tears turn into a happy smile I feel rewarded,' I happily told myself.

There are several testimonies, which stand out in my mind, and some were things I had experienced myself. There is one that really stands out since this testimony was given to a young male truck driver just starting out. Late one evening, the nurses brought the young man to the floor on a stretcher and placed him in the Observation Unit. They hooked him up to the monitor so they could keep a close watch on his heart rhythm, but he was very excited about the adventure of being a new truck driver, so much so that he couldn't relax. As I entered the room and walked up to his bed, he began telling me how happy he was. "I went to truck driving school and learned how to drive a big rig," he stated gleefully. "I want to explore the country and see places I've never seen," he continued.

As he rambled on and on, my heart ached because Jacob had been so much like this man who was so restless as he lay on his bed. I resisted the still small voice that tugged at my heart thinking, `It's none of my business if this young man seeks all the same things Jacob did all those years.' The Holy Spirit kept troubling me, however, so much so that I began to tremble. My voice was weak and stammering as I spoke, asking him if he had a wife somewhere. He replied, "Yes, I do, and we have three small children. We have a home in California and I left them there to make this trip. When I get out of the hospital, I don't know where the company will send me."

I asked, "Do you mind if I tell you a story, Sir?" He replied, "No, I don't mind at all." Then I said, "This story is about another truck driver so very much like you. He had a wife and five children, and he too sought adventure and searched for what he thought he might find just over the next mountain. He loved trucks and the power that was underneath the hood of his truck. He drove powerful rigs that could haul heavy loads up high mountains and over treacherous terrain. Many times he left his small family to fend for themselves in a little tar paper shack. Many times problems arose that his wife couldn't handle, but he didn't know about them because there wasn't any way to contact him. He could always escape the responsibilities of home with the excuse that he had to make a living. The Lord was gracious to his wife, however, and carried her through the years by His grace. He gave his life for the trucking industry, Sir, and he drove a big rig for thirty-eight years. His health began deteriorating as the miles he had made took their toll and one night he came home and said, `The Lord saved my soul in North Dakota. I have parked the truck and I'll never drive one again. From this day forward, I'll live only for the Lord.' My family's prayer had been answered at last and we rejoiced when he was baptized. Two of our sons were ordained into the ministry and he had the pleasure of witnessing their ordination. Five grandchildren were saved that year and one son-in-law and God blessed him more than all the many discoveries he had found on the road. He cried every day during the last year that God granted to him, because he had missed out on the true beauty of life with his home and family which was his greatest treasure. He was sick that last year and I would grieve in my heart because he gave his life for trucks and the trucking industry. Not one of his truck driving friends came to visit him when he was sick and only two truck drivers came to his funeral. The License and Weight Officer who had given him so many overload tickets over the years was one of his pallbearers at his funeral. I'm telling you this true story because the Lord wanted me to, Sir. Now I have to clock out and go home, but I hope you will consider your course in life while you are young and think about the possibility of your life ending very much as Jacob's did."

I was quite apprehensive and disturbed when I left the hospital after work and drove back to Newton. I thought fearfully, `What if my testimony upsets the man and he gets worse during the night? I'm going to feel responsible if something bad happens to that young man. Besides the weight of guilt that I would carry, I could lose my job.'

As soon as I entered the hospital the following day, I heard my name on the intercom saying, "Destiny, you are needed in North 3." I walked to the nurses' station where Rosie, the ward clerk, sat. She said, "Destiny, there is someone who wants to see you immediately just as soon as you come in." Even though I was nervous, I braced myself for the worst. I knew the truck driver wanted to see me and I prayed that it would be good news.

My legs felt as heavy as weights as I walked to North 3. When I entered the room, I received a beautiful surprise. The young man was fully dressed and he sat on the side of his bed. He had a big smile on his face as he greeted me and he said, "Mrs. Quinn, I just had to see you before I leave. Your testimony has changed my life and I'm going home. I called the company and told them where the truck is. I'm going home to my family just as fast as a plane can take me there. I want to see my children grow up and be there for them. I realize where my treasure is now and I praise God that He sent you to me last night. I'll never forget you as long as I live, Mrs. Quinn. Thank you for your testimony which touched my heart and turned me around."

Tears of joy filled my eyes as he hugged me for the last time. "I'll be praying for you and the new beginning that you are starting today," I told him. The sweet Holy Spirit blessed my heart so. `Thank you, Father, for Your Divine guidance as I witness to so many,' I silently prayed as I walked to the report room. When I went back on the floor after report, the young man was gone, but I'll see him on the streets of glory someday. What a glorious reunion that will be!

It took time to grow in courage to testify about Ted, however. I never knew how people would react, nevertheless, when the Lord opened the door, I didn't run from my own fears. It was through those testimonies that I learned the great power of the Holy Spirit as my faith in God was being tried. Through these trials, God enlarged the testimony and I began to realize over the years that I had experienced something in my own life which related to what someone else was suffering at the moment.

My first encounter came quite unexpectedly when I couldn't avoid my testimony about Ted and where he was. While in the nurses' report room, the charge nurse assigned me a patient who had terminal cancer. All the nurses were afraid to take care of her because her husband was so hostile and was often belligerent to the nurses. He never left her side day or night and slept on the floor beside her bed. When the nurses went into her room, he watched their every move making them nervous and afraid because of his hateful attitude. I was tense and afraid when I went in to take her vital signs as he watched for something that he could complain about. There wasn't any doubt in my mind that he loved his wife and he knew she was going to die. It was as if he blamed everyone else for her condition and it seemed to me that he thought their suffering was unique. He stared at me with cold, piercing steel blue eyes and in his usual style, he tried to make me feel like I was lower than a worm which crawls on the ground. I just wanted to do my work and get out of the room when for some unknown reason the man asked me in harsh tones, "Are you married?" I caught my breath in surprise and thought to myself, `Why on earth did he ask me a question like that?' I realized that he took great pride in disturbing the nurses with questions that he could use to aggravate and torment them. At first I thought, `If I tell him about Ted he is just going to torment me with hateful accusations.' I couldn't lie though, because I would be ashamed and that would prove to the Lord that I was ashamed of him. Then I looked into his cold eyes which reflected so much animosity and said, "Yes, I'm married." He seemed to sense my fear and I'm sure he thought that he had found something that he could use to torment me with. He asked, "Why are you working when you are getting so near the age of retirement? Doesn't your husband have a job so you can stay at home?" My face flushed in anger at his statement as I told him that my husband was in prison. I've never experienced such a remarkable change on the face of any individual as I saw in his at that instant. Tears began streaming down his cheeks as the Holy Spirit cut him to the quick. All my fears subsided as I watched his cold steel exterior melt before my eyes as though he realized that someone else was suffering too.

Through his sobs he pleaded, "Oh, I'm so sorry that I taunted you with my hateful attitude. Please forgive me. You must carry such a heartache every day." I replied, "Yes, I do and my life is painful, but I also understand what you are going through, because I buried my husband, Jacob, Ted's brother just a year or so ago in 1989. I can forgive your attitude because I went through much of the same things you are going through when I learned that he wouldn't recover from his illness. I slept on the floor as well when he was in the hospital and I never left his side as you are doing." `Oh, my God,' I prayed in my heart, `there isn't much that I haven't experienced in one way or another. How can we relate to another's pain than to have walked in some of the same shoes with Christ carrying us, when we can't go on alone in our own strength.' Many times I had wondered why I had had to suffer all those years. Now I knew in my heart why and God uses my life for a testimony to reach others.

Ted and I would share these marvelous experiences together through letters and our visits. Sometimes I couldn't wait until the next morning to write. Very often I would prop up my pillows and write to him and often fell asleep with my glasses on and his letter in my lap. When we greeted each other on our sweet visits we always knew a blessing lay in store. Everything would come together when Ted would hold me in his arms. Such a beautiful and loving peace would surround us and give us the feeling of such sweet assurance that we both knew our love would endure the storms of life. Our folks couldn't have known the plan that God had in mind when they determined to keep us apart all those years. The Lord used them to carry out His plan when Ted and I were at family gatherings, and they made sure that we were never left alone, not knowing we would be used for His glory later. Sometimes Ted would say, "Precious, I wish we had spent more time together." "But Darling, don't you see that we would have spoiled God's plan if we had, because we couldn't have controlled our emotions," I told him wondering if he was right, but I knew better. "Our life is like a roller coaster with so many ups and downs. One minute we are crying and before we wipe away our tears, we are smiling again about something," Ted remarked as he reached over and brushed the hair back which the wind had blown in my eyes. His touch of tenderness was like a precious jewel which was of great value to Ted and me. His tiny expressive gestures made so many lovely memories.

Many times I would leave Ted with my heart aching. Many times it hurt so bad that I couldn't cry. I'd drive down the highway in silence for many miles before the tears would finally be released. Through these agonizing times, the Lord would send signs from heaven with a lovely rainbow and His glory would shine through sun rays through the broken clouds. Mysterious sights from Heaven would appear, not only in the sky, but also in nature itself and His wondrous creation. He showed me the true beauty which so few seek these days nor do they look up toward heaven in search of His beautiful face. Jesus placed a song in my heart while He healed my wounded spirit.

One Saturday after I left Ted and drew near Newton, the town was dark, except for the flashing lights of police cars. I watched carefully for a sign of life or some reason for such a commotion. As I crossed Caney Creek at the entrance of the town proper, suddenly the little town seemed to come alive with Christmas lights around the court house and square. People filled the streets with cameras and small children watched in awe as I did. I held my breath at all the beautiful sights I saw. "Oh, Father," I cried, "it's so beautiful. Just like a story book world and I'm a part of it. Our love story is more enhanced by the beauty of what seems an icy wonderland with the feeling of Christmas in the air."

My heart rejoiced as Christ lifted my spirit and hope filled my soul. Just when the world seemed at its darkest, the Shepherds and Wise Men saw a star which led them to where the Hope of all mankind lay in a manger at Bethlehem. The brilliant Christmas lights reminded me of the Savior's birth who was born of a virgin when the world least expected it. It had been prophesied many years before. Walking with Christ is the most beautiful life on earth. He promised to always be with us and never leave us alone. I missed my children since they seldom came to visit, except for Isabella and Steve, who had stood by me through the years. I had no desire to make the children feel obligated to visit me. I wanted them to enjoy their families and feel free without Mamma hanging on their coat tails. I turned all of my attentions toward the cause of Christ and to Ted, the one God chose for me to marry and love for the rest of my life.

The marvelous wonders that God has performed have been breathtaking through the witness which He gave to me. And to reveal great mysteries and wonders through things that I could see with my own eyes were so wonderful that I lived in a perpetual state of happiness most of the time. He proved His power time and time again to lift me up, as He gave me the incentive to continue on the path that He had placed me on. There were many God brought to me for my witness and I wonder sometimes what happened to them, because after the witness was given, they were usually discharged before I went to work the next day. At times I wonder what happened to the man who stood by his wife who had terminal cancer. His attitude changed toward the nurses for the remainder of the shift, but they were gone the next day when I got back to the hospital. I soon realized, however, that my mission was to witness for Christ and to place them in my Father's care afterwards. I would pour out my heart to Ted when I wrote to him and in writing I found comfort in the Holy Spirit. When problems came upon Ted and myself that we couldn't handle, I would fall on my knees and pray that God would hide us beneath His powerful wings as we placed our trust in Him for deliverance. The anointing power beneath His wings gave healing and renewed our hopes and He caused us to smile through the storms we faced in our lives.

CHAPTER 10

HONOR WITH RESPECT

Storm clouds began gathering over our lives when I received a message that Mark was in an accident. He had been cutting logs in the woods when a tree that had been lodged suddenly fell and the tree that he had cut brought them both down on top of him. He lay trapped between two trees which encased him on both sides. His helmet was crushed on his head and tree limbs covered him. He couldn't move except to cry out for help. He lay in terror knowing that any moment the driver of a huge tractor would come to the area where he was and him not knowing that he was underneath those trees could run over him. As the tractor came closer, he cried out for help and only through the amazing grace of God did the driver hear his cry. They rescued Mark and rejoiced knowing that God had performed an awesome miracle.

It made the workers realize how great God really is and they marveled as they witnessed first hand how God delivered His child. Only through God's mercy was Mark able to get their attention, and they trembled in fear of God when they saw the crushed helmet under Mark's head. His leg was broken so they were very careful when they handled him and carried him to the hospital. The doctor put his leg in a cast and sent him home to recover.

Mark was the pastor of a little Mission near Cleveland and I admired his faith when he told me that he had to continue preaching at the church even though he wore a cast from his toes to his hips. "Sunday is Mother's Day and I can't let my people down on such a special day, Mamma," he told me. I was so proud of him when I heard how he persevered. The men from the church loaded Mark into a van and carried him to church where he preached the Word of God in spite of his pain. I thought things were going well for Mark even though he was laid up with a broken leg, but Ted was worried about him. We talked about his condition on our next visit and Ted said, "Destiny, I'm burdened for Mark and I've been praying for him. Will you go by his house and see how he is before you go back to Newton?" I promised I would, but I couldn't imagine that he would have any serious problems. When I arrived at his house, everything was quiet. The place wasn't immaculate outside like it usually was, but with a broken leg he couldn't do anything about it. When I went in, I found Mark laying on the couch. "Where is Peggy," I asked? "She went off with some women to help the hurricane victims in Mississippi. She's been gone for days now. It's not the first time, however, she has been gone for weeks at a time before this," Mark told me. I couldn't believe Peggy would desert Mark at a time like this. I asked, "Son, how in the world do you manage?" He sighed, "I get by with Paul's help." I was bewildered at the way Peggy was treating Mark; she certainly wasn't a wife like the Lord wanted her to be. "Mark, you know I've never interfered in your marriage, but this is a terrible situation. You know a wife's first responsibility is to her family. It's certainly not to leave them in distress and go off for weeks on the pretense of doing God's will. I can't tell you what to do, but, Son, if it gets to be too much for you, come to Newton. I just want you to know there is a place where you would be welcome, at least you could stay there until you get back on your feet," I told him. "Thank you, Mamma, I appreciate your concern and if things don't get better, I may take you up on it," Mark smiled as he answered.

When I left and started home, I felt such a burden on my heart. I knew Mark and Peggy were having a few serious problems in their marriage even though he didn't tell me about them and I didn't really want to discuss them. I was very worried about the situation, but all that I could do was pray for them.

Things got worse for Mark as he recovered. In spite of his trying to preach and hold the little Mission together, Mark failed by giving too much attention to a young woman in the church. My heart ached for my son when the ministry at the Mission blew up in his face. He stayed at home until he recovered and was able to return to work. One day he called me and said that he and Peggy had separated. Even though it seemed inevitable, nevertheless, I was heartsick. Mark and Peggy had been married for almost twenty-five years. They had brought up three children whom I loved dearly. "Father, why does a marriage face a crisis when two people have been married for twenty-five years? One of our biggest problems happened around Jacob's and my twenty-fifth wedding anniversary. It seems that around that time the wife and husband look at each other and think that since the children were all gone either in school or married themselves. It is as if they see each other for the first time and then they think that they have lost all the romance in their lives. Instead of renewing the old flame that brought them together in the first place, they separate." Even as I talked to the Lord in prayer I knew that only God had the answer. Mark moved into the little house at Goodrich. He seemed quite happy when I went by there one Saturday after visiting Ted. He did a pretty good job of making it homey and comfortable. He didn't live there long, however. Mark and Peggy decided to get back together. I was so relieved and I prayed that they would sincerely work at making a go of their marriage because it wouldn't be easy after all the damage that had been done. I stayed away in the hope that they could work things out without any interference from me. After Mark moved out of the house, Isabella made a deal with Cindy, my granddaughter, and her husband, Jim, to buy the house at Goodrich. Since Isabella and Steve had traded houses with me they were free to make any sort of deal on the house they wanted. They decided to help the young couple out so they sold the little house to them and accepted a very small down payment with a promise to make some of the needed repairs on the house. Since they needed a place to live that was affordable, they would have an opportunity that very few young couples do. Since they were family I felt good about it, because I was sure they would honor and respect their Grandpa's memory since he had died here on that property.

My hopes for Mark and Peggy's marriage surviving vanished in a short while. One day I heard the clanging sound of an old junker driving up the driveway. I hurried out on the porch to see who it was and there was Mark in the driver's seat, grinning. Paul was with his Dad and Paul's two dogs were riding in the back of the old run down pickup. I fought back tears as I thought of this son who had been ordained to preach the Word of God. "Oh, God," I cried, "I know You love Mark, but look at him now, Father, he has nothing left of material value in this world." Mark said, "Mamma, will you take us in for a while?" "Of course, Son, welcome home," I replied. Paul jumped out of the pickup and turned his dogs loose and they raced around the yard happy to be free. "Well Mamma," he sighed, "I don't have much left to show from my life with Peggy, but I have peace and right now that's enough. Paul has stood by me through the troubles we've had. At least I have him and he wants to stay with me. We will have to start over, Mamma, and the first thing I have to do is to find a job." "Son, where is the new car that you bought recently?" I asked, puzzled that he wasn't driving it instead of the old pickup. He replied, "Peggy has it. She had the title put in her name so that old junker pickup is all the transportation that I have to get around in right now. At least she has a nice car to go where she pleases. She made sure the notes on the car were paid even if the other bills had to wait. I really believe she had it in her mind to leave all along, Mamma." I fought back tears as I went through their belongings. It broke my heart knowing Mark had been working in the woods in worn out cloth tennis shoes. They were full of holes and very thin. "Oh, God," I cried, "Mark has sacrificed so much for his family." It tore my heart out to see his clothes were torn and threadbare and so were Paul's. As I went through their things, I thought about the Parable of the Prodigal Son in the Bible. He, like Mark had done wrong, but when he came to himself he said, "I'll go back to my father's house and beg for forgiveness. If my father will let me be one of the hired servants I'll be very happy. At least they have plenty of food to eat while I'm tending these hogs and starving." The Prodigal Son didn't realize how much his father loved him until he saw him watching for his return. He was far away when his father saw him and he ran to meet him and embraced his son. He confessed, "Father, I have sinned against heaven and in your sight, and I am not worthy to be called your son." "Bring the best robe and put a ring on my son's hand and put shoes on his feet. Bring the fatted calf and kill it," his father commanded his servants. "Let us eat and be merry; for this, my son, was dead and is alive again, he was lost and now is found." "Lord, I'm sure Mark has made a lot of mistakes in his life, because none of us are perfect, but Father, I love my son too. It's so true that love covers a multitude of sins. I don't have much, but with your help we'll buy some clothes for Mark and Paul," I told my Lord.

"Let's go shopping," I exclaimed excitedly. "Bring that old junker and follow me to Lufkin!" The boys didn't waste any time getting in the old pickup and they were laughing excitedly. Isabella wasn't about to be left behind as she got under the steering wheel of my car. "Mark, follow us just in case that old junker quits running," I shouted. They followed close behind and I worried that we would have to stop along the way. We made it to Lufkin and I sighed in relief when we pulled up into the car lot. Truly, our God is marvelous and very merciful and I praised His Holy Name knowing He is our loving Father. I couldn't keep from crying when Mark and Paul sat down in the seat of Mark's new pickup because it was such a blessing to see the joy on both their faces. "Mark, meet us at the Western Store at Jasper," I shouted as they started backing out. "All right, Mamma, I love you," Mark exclaimed as they drove away.

When Isabella and I got to the Western Store, Mark and Paul were waiting near the entrance. Mark said, "Mamma, what are we doing here? I can't afford to buy anything, besides I don't even have a job yet." I smiled and said, "Let's go inside, Mark, and look around. We may just be celebrating Christmas early this year." It was such a thrill, watching Mark, Paul and Isabella shop for the items they needed. It was wonderful to see Mark's and Paul's faces beam with joy when they found the perfect pair of western boots and modeled them proudly. They picked out some jeans and western shirts to wear for Sunday, as well as some new work shoes for them both. I couldn't have been so generous though, if not for my credit card. It was a beautiful early Christmas for us all and I know it was the happiest Christmas that I had ever experienced before.

When we left there, we went to the grocery store and the boys picked out the food they liked to eat, then we all went home and had a feast.

"Thank you, Father, for the nice gifts we were able to purchase for Mark and Paul. If I have to work doubles to pay for these things, it's worth it, but Mark will have to pay for the pickup himself and keep insurance on it. They have the opportunity to start a new life now just like I did when Jacob died. You have blessed my life in so many ways. Will You extend that same sweet grace to my son, Father," I prayed later.

Mark had given up his home and everything of value that they had accumulated over the years to his wife. However, Mark had had two power saws and he had brought them with him. He found out right away that the pay was less in our area, but Mark took the first job that he could find. He took Paul along with him to teach him how to cut logs. Paul was almost seventeen and he had lost interest in school, most likely because there were so many problems at home. He had always been an insecure child. I hoped he would go back to school, especially since he was small for his age. I pleaded with him to start school in Newton, but he refused. He insisted on going with his Daddy.

As the Christmas season drew near, I worried about Mark and Paul. The holidays were especially hard for me because Ted was in prison, but my heart ached for the two of them knowing this would be their first Christmas without Peggy. I'm sure my concern about them made me lay aside my own pain for their sakes. Before they came to stay with me, my heart had ached so during the Christmas season that I couldn't bear to decorate a Christmas tree. Everytime I did, I became desperately lonely and depressed from the memory of past Christmases. "Oh, God," I cried out in agonizing despair, "I can't bear to hear the beautiful sound of the

Christmas carols being played everywhere I go. There are so many memories that I don't think I can endure this pain and loneliness any more, but I must try for their sakes and lean on You once more and wait for Your grace to carry me through this season of Your blessed Son's birth once again. I know that Your grace is always sufficient for my needs and has been more than sufficient since you sent me into Ted's life."

I knew that Mark and Paul were suffering as much as I was, but they put up an artificial tree that I had stored away. They decorated it beautifully with colorful lights and tinsel. They both seemed very happy in spite of all they had gone through.

All the children came home for Christmas that year too and it was a joyous occasion. After all the shrieks of joy when the kids opened their gifts, we had Christmas dinner and after Sam gave thanks to God for all His blessings that He had bestowed on our families, everyone filled their plates. After we had Christmas dinner and the table was cleared, Mark took out the Bible and placed it on the table. Everyone gathered around while Mark read from the Word of God. I enjoyed listening as my family discussed various subjects in the Bible. Each one had their view and Mark led the group. I learned some important points myself that day which impressed me deeply. Mark stated firmly, "The Word of God has all power. A testimony helps a lot of folks, but the Word of God is God speaking expressly to you. So if I speak, let it be through the Divine Word and the Holy Spirit convicts of sin with power piercing the heart of the lost."

As I looked around the table, a deep peace filled my heart. I thought, `Father, this is the happiest Christmas I've ever experienced. Look down on them with Your tender mercy, Lord, is my prayer. Some don't attend church faithfully any more, but through Your Divine Word, speak to their hearts and draw them closer to You before it is too late.' Several of the children made new commitments to Christ and others were given food for thought. At the end of the day, most of them went their separate ways. Before they left, however, they all gathered around the piano and sang the old songs of praise to the Lord. To have my family together was sweet and wonderful. `It's a shame that they don't come together more often,' I thought.

1994 was just around the corner, but I was working so many hours that it didn't take many doubles to wear me out. Even though I was worn out, I didn't neglect Ted. I continued to write to him every day. I told Mark and Paul that when they saw my bedroom door closed that it meant I would be writing to Ted and not to disturb me during that time. There were so many demands on my time in those days and the work at the hospital was like a nightmare at times.

It shouldn't have been a surprise when my back messed up again. Even though the doctor injected my back, it took at least two weeks to recover enough so that I could return to work. Though the pain was quite severe sometimes, I still made my trip to visit Ted every Saturday. My friends would just shake their heads, but I went anyway. They didn't understand how much I needed my husband. I would argue, "What if you were in my place and the man you loved was shut up in prison? What if you couldn't be with him except two hours each week? What if that was all you had and after you get there, he can only hold you in his arms for just one minute?"

In spite of all the objections of my friends and family, I made preparations to go to Huntsville in spite of my pain. Before I left Mark asked me, "Mamma, after you visit Ted, will you go by Cindy's and pick Paul up on your way home? It will save me a trip up there since they don't live very far from your usual route." I told him that I would, but if I had known what I'd find when I went by there, I probably wouldn't have gone. No one wants to be exposed to such terrible heartache and I am no different, much less faced with a situation which calls for a strong stand that you wish you didn't have to make.

Ted could tell that I was troubled during our visit, but I didn't know why unless the thought of going back to Goodrich would awaken old memories that I wanted to forget. "I'll be all right, Honey," I reassured Ted. "I'll just pick up Paul and not even get out of the car." Ted was still concerned even though I tried to reassure him, but he didn't want to be overly concerned. He said, "Darling, I'll be praying for you and especially for God to heal your back problems. Just do as you've said, stay in the car and let Paul get in and just drive away."

As I drove toward Goodrich I began to feel as if something terrible was about to happen and I couldn't shake this feeling. When I arrived, no one was there so I parked in the shade of a tree deciding to wait until they returned since they were expecting me. I tried hard to control the anger that was boiling up inside as I looked around at what once had been a tidy little cottage that I had taken such pride in and had kept it up.

Jacob and I had spent the sweetest moments here during the last year of his life and I tried to picture it the way it had been through all the clutter and shambles that lay everywhere. I cried, "Oh, Jacob, our granddaughter lives here now and the place is so run down. I feel so ashamed of the way it looks and it breaks my heart. They haven't tried to mend the porch where we used to sit and watch the sun set in the west on summer evenings. Dogs lie around on the front porch now and the place is infested with fleas. I can't imagine anyone living here under these conditions and especially our own flesh and blood, but I can't blame Cindy alone since Jim hasn't kept his promise to Isabella and Steve."

I tried to console myself with the thought that this place wasn't mine anymore. Steve and Isabella had sold it to them and it was really their problem now. While I waited for Cindy and Paul to come, I needed to go to the bathroom and thinking that the back door might be open, I decided to make my way around to the back since the front door was shut. My heart really ached when I reached the back porch which was sadly in need of repair so I made my way very carefully so that I wouldn't fall through as I stepped over the rotten pieces. `The door is open,' I thought as I pulled back the screen door and made my way to the bathroom.

As I started back to the car, I wondered how they could live here when there wasn't any room to get around. There was furniture stacked everywhere and there was only a trail to walk through the house. `Evidently, Peggy is storing her furniture here and selling her house,' I decided.

When I walked back through the door I had the strangest feeling that something was wrong, but I didn't know what it was. I returned to the car to wait for them to return home. As I did, I sighed in dismay, thinking, `I just want to get away from here so that I don't have to deal with whatever is bothering me so much.' As I sat in my car, it seemed as if some overpowering force came over me quite suddenly. It was so overpowering that all the reasoning I could think of to stay out of the house was unaffected. Whatever was wrong seemed more compelling so that I had no choice but to go back inside again. I tried to resist that force with all the strength I had, but my whole body began to tremble and I wondered what on earth it was that was so overwhelming that I had to check it out before I would have any peace. The tears began streaming down my face as I got back out of the car to check the house. I once more knew for certain now that it was the Holy Spirit who wanted me to go back in again and I knew I had no alternative but to follow His urgent call.

I stumbled blindly toward the back door again in complete submission as the voice urged me on. I was still sobbing out of control as I walked slowly toward the house and the terrible agony I was suffering was as though death was hovering just above me like some dark cloud. I cried out, "Oh, God, what can possibly be so bad that it makes me tremble with such fear." I knew that whatever it was would be something so devastating that I wouldn't want to cope with it. I knew the Lord would give me the strength I needed to face whatever it was as I walked back inside the house again. Immediately I found out what was wrong. The back door was missing. My first thought was that thieves would be able to enter and steal everything without any problem. That was just a passing thought, however, since the missing door led me to the area that the Holy Spirit wanted me to go.

I searched frantically throughout the house for the missing door which in my mind represented the many broken pieces from my life with Jacob. Still sobbing, I cried, "Father, I must find that door, but I can't find it anywhere. I struggled for many years to keep this house together and it continually kept falling apart. I have tried to mend the broken pieces of Jacob's and my life together as well as I could, even though my own ability to hold them together has failed miserably. We have lived in old farm houses and tar paper shacks, especially the one that Jacob built and we have known poverty, but we never lived in filth. Oh, God, I don't want Cindy to suffer like I have, but if Jim and Cindy don't do any better than they have here, she will."

God only knows how I suffered as I search frantically for that wooden door. I loved my granddaughter so much and yet at the same time I was feeling such anger for their lack of respect toward the ones who had offered them the chance to have a home. I couldn't find the door in the house, so I went back outside on the porch. When I started down the steps, I heard a strange sound coming from the back yard. "My God," I cried, "I hear a pig grunting close by. Oh, Father, surely they don't have a pig penned up right here in the city limits." I was unable to understand all the things that twisted my stomach into knots of fear for what I might find next. My steps slowed down as I was hesitant to go any further, but I walked carefully toward a make shift pen on toward the sound of the pig that I knew I would find when I looked inside. I cried even more as I looked down into a dry pen. The poor little pig didn't have any water in the water trough and the dirt was like powder. But the door I had so frantically searched for was inside. I tried to drag the door out, but it was too heavy with all the caked mud that had dried on it.

When I finally realized that all my efforts to pull the door out of the pen were useless, I tried to get my emotions under control so that I could cope with this situation. I really didn't know where to turn and my tears continued to fall as I looked over toward the area where Jacob had died. That memory of all the sorrow and heartache I had suffered when I found him kneeling with his head bowed in death seemed to rip out my heart so that it broke into a million pieces as I suffered from that memory of hopelessness and complete despair all over again. Rubble and junk was scattered everywhere over the area where Jacob's spirit had left this old world behind and joined the Lord to suffer pain no more.

I turned back toward the car once again grief stricken with sorrow in order that I could find a place to sit down. I cried out, "Oh, Jacob, what would you do if you were here today? You loved Cindy too and you often made hard decisions and even when I didn't agree with you, I stood by you. Sometimes those decisions had seemed so cruel, but when you stood up for the things you believed in for right and for honor, things always worked out right in the end. I don't know if I can handle all the things I've seen here today and I'm so afraid I'll make a terrible mistake. Should I just close my eyes and walk away as though I'd never been here? Should I stand the way you would have done even though Cindy is our grandchild and we love her?"

I desperately needed help and the only reasonable thing to do was to go to the truck stop that was nearby and call Steve and ask him for his advice. I called Steve from the truck stop and told him what I had found. I couldn't stop crying as I relived the horrible things, but Steve seemed to understand that what I had found made me distraught and unable to cope with the situation. He replied, "Destiny, you are there and you see what is going on and I don't. The place is still yours, so do what you think is best. There have been no papers or deeds signed on that property. Isabella and I made the agreement with you so that you would feel the security you needed to make your home in Newton. Whatever you decide, we will stand by you."

"Father, even Steve has deserted me now and left me to deal with the pain of making the decision that I wanted to avoid," I cried miserably. By the time I got back to the house, the kids had returned. They didn't know I had been there and thought I was just coming by to pick Paul up. Paul was sitting on the porch and he made his way toward the car. When he opened the door, he hesitated because he saw I was angry. He stepped back when I asked him where Jim was. He said that Jim wasn't there and went back toward the porch. I could see Cindy and her mother through the window so I told Paul to tell Cindy that I wanted to speak to her. I think she was trying to avoid me because she knew that I had already been there, but she didn't even speak or acknowledge me in any way. This was disturbing because she didn't intend to show me any respect since her mother was there, but it was not my fault that she and Mark had broken up. Paul called Cindy outside and she walked out on the porch. Then she came over to the car and I spoke to her through the window. I told her, "Cindy, I wanted to talk to Jim instead of you, but Paul said that he wasn't here, so I'm going to tell you what I have on my mind. You have broken your promise to Isabella by not keeping up the place. She let you move here with a very small down payment of only $60.00 and you've lived here for months and let the place run down. Why, Cindy, why? With just a little effort you could have had a home," I cried because my heart ached for her. The tears came to her eyes and I knew the shame she was suffering since I had been through much the same thing with her Grandpa. She started defending Jim and said, "Grandma, Jim has repaired what he could, but we don't have much money. I tried to get him to work on the house, but he wouldn't listen to me. I told Jim that one day you would come by when we least expected you and you would make us move out if he didn't repair some of the damage around here. He just ignored me, though." I said tearfully yet still filled with anger, "Cindy, if you can show me any improvements around here, I'll go." I knew she couldn't and she knew it too. She said that Jim had fixed the front porch, but it was sadly in need of repair with the same holes that had been there when I left some time back. Her excuses infuriated me even more and I told her that I wanted them to leave and take their things off my property today because I was going to have the house torn down so I wouldn't have to suffer anymore. I had tried to preserve the place where

Jacob had passed away. I heard my voice clearly and couldn't believe that I was saying those things to someone I dearly loved, but I knew someone had to stop the destruction and the lack of honor and respect they were showing for their grandparents. Cindy ran back into the house crying then. Peggy appeared at the door and shouted furiously, "Bitch, bitch, bitch!" I shouted back, "Curse me if you want to, but I meant what I said. Get this filth cleaned up and move off of this property today." Paul told me he wasn't coming with me, so I told him to get home the best way he could. Then I drove away filled with rage and sorrow because this situation could have been avoided if they had only lived up to their part of the bargain.

I was still angry so I went by Sam's house before I went home. He knew something was awfully wrong when he saw my face. He listened quietly as I told him my intentions concerning the house. I told him, "Sam, I want the house torn down so I won't have to suffer anymore with people moving in and destroying everything. This time the back door was taken off the hinges and used to build a makeshift pig pen. The porches are rotten and unsafe and Jim hasn't repaired anything the way he said he would. I told them to move out when I saw the terrible condition of the place. I realize that things can get disorganized and cluttered sometimes and with Peggy moving her things in there too, it would be impossible to have more than a trail through the little house, but I can't believe they are living there. They must be using it for storage. They also had that pig pen in the back yard and the place where Jacob died looks like a pig sty too. The little place is an eye sore to the community and I'm so ashamed that a member of my family doesn't have enough respect for their grandparents or for themselves to at least keep it cleaned up. All I've ever known since Jacob died and I moved away is people moving in the house and destroying it. I can't bear to go through this any more so if you will, tear it down. You can have anything you can salvage to use on your place." Sam said, "I'll tear it down if you're sure that is what you want. I need to build a shop for my tools and saws. There are other ways in which I can use the lumber on my house too and if your mind is made up, I'll do it." The little pig was still on my mind so I said, "Sam, will you go over there when Jim and Cindy move out and see if they took the pig with them or left it to starve." Somehow I felt sure that they would and when Sam went over, he found the pig still there without water or food, so he turned the little pig loose. He told me later that the little pig ran off into the woods. Sam saw for himself why I made the decision that I had.

There are so many things that happen that we can't understand. Some people might think of me as being cruel and think that I should have handled the matter with more patience and understanding. In time, though, I would be glad that I had taken such a firm stand even if it seemed as if my heart would break because of what I had had to do.

I was still distraught when I went by Steve and Isabella's on my way home. Evidently, they had called Mark and told him that I was coming by there to tell them the details of what had happened at Goodrich. He was very upset when I drove up without Paul, as he was worried about having to go get him himself. He asked, "Where is Paul, Mamma?" I replied, "Paul wouldn't come with me so I told him that he could get home the best way he could." Mark started grumbling at me for not making him get into the car. I shouted at him, "Mark, I've been through enough hell today and I've had about all I'm going to put up with. If you don't like what I've done, you can pack up your things and leave too. I'm sick and tired of my kids walking all over me. I won't allow any of you to run over me again!"

Mark straightened up quickly because he knew why I was so mad. He said, "Mamma, I warned Cindy and Jim about cleaning the place up. I told them that you might come by one day when they least expected you and when you saw the terrible mess that you would be furious and run them off. They kept promising that they would clean it up, but they didn't, so it just caught up with them. I just wish Paul had come with you. Now, I'll either have to go pick him up or get Jim to bring him home." I told him, "Mark, you treat Paul like he was a baby. He is almost eighteen years old and he will get home if he wants to. I'm not going to worry about him, I'm going home." Isabella and Steve agreed with my decision to make them move out, but they didn't say anything when I told them that Sam was going to tear the house down. They could see how upset I was, so they didn't interfere.

It was late that night when I heard a truck park on the road near the house. Jim and Paul came inside when Mark opened the door. He was afraid that the trouble would start again, but I didn't say anything. When things settled down, Paul found out that Grandma wasn't so bad after all and he also learned that she wouldn't let her family run over her even though his Grandpa wasn't alive to do just exactly what she had done.

After that, however, I tried to keep peace in my home as I remembered the terrible pain and heartache I had suffered as well as the heartache I had placed upon Mark and his children. I didn't mind the extra hours that I worked to help Mark with his car notes and insurance until he met a young woman that he gave a part of his paycheck to and then didn't pay his bills. I told him, "Mark, it's all right to help others, but it's not right to let your obligations be left up to me." I tried to reason with him now and then, but he didn't listen to my pleadings. Eventually, Paul didn't go to work with Mark either and I became quite upset because he just lay around on the couch after he finally got up around lunch. I hated to see him so lazy and it hurt me because I hadn't allowed my children to behave that way. When I mentioned it to Mark that Paul should find a job, possibly at a animal hospital because he loved animals, Mark became belligerent and said sternly, "Paul doesn't have to work if he doesn't want to." "But Paul is a young man now and he is no longer a child, Mark. He needs something to do other than watch TV and lay around the house," I told him. I just couldn't believe that Mark truly meant what he said. Mark reminded me that Paul had gone through a lot when he and Peggy were getting their divorce. Mark felt guilty and sorry for his son, but I still maintained that everyone needs something to keep their minds occupied.

Mark began taking more control of my home and I felt my freedom being threatened as time went by. I prayed for the answer which had to come soon since my patience was wearing thin.

One night at church the answer came through a visiting preacher from Arkansas whom the church had invited to speak. I was weary and heartsick as I sat on the pew and I listened intently to the story that the preacher told. It was about a mother eagle and her baby and he demonstrated how a mother does when she loves her son. So many times the actions of a mother seem cruel just like what I had done to Cindy and Jim, but it had hurt me far more than it had hurt them.

The mother eagle loved her baby and watched over his welfare giving him the nourishment he needed to grow and be strong. The young eagle had it made in his warm and protected nest enjoying the blessings of God through his parents. Then, as he grew older, his mother realized that it was time that her son got out on his own so that he would learn the ways of survival. She said, "Son, it's time for you to learn how to fly." But her son was quite content where he was. He pleaded, "Mother, I don't want to fly. Don't you love me anymore? Why should I leave my home anyway when I have everything an eagle could ask for in the safety of your nest, besides I'm so afraid that I can't fly and will fall to my death if I fall to the ground."

The mother eagle understood all of her son's fears, but she knew how important it was that he fly alone without her carrying him any more. In tears of pride, she shoved her son out from the security of her nest and then cried, "Son, just flap your wings and you'll sail up through the sky!" He was terrified feeling death was just a short distance away and frozen in fear, he couldn't navigate his wings as she had instructed him. He could see his fate was near as he viewed the stony earth just beneath his small feathered body. He covered his eyes and cried, "Oh, Mamma, it's too late, I'm sure every bone in my body is going to be broken when I fall on those big rocks. And you know that I can't stand the sight of blood," His fate was surely sealed, when suddenly, his mother swooped down and scooped her small son up with her strong and powerful wings and carried him back to his home and the safety of his mother. He was very happy and he bubbled with joy as he thought of all the blessings he had almost lost. He had it made he thought and with jubilation he shouted, "Gee, it's wonderful to be home and to escape from death. I don't want to fly anyway, it's much easier just to stay at home." But the mother eagle loved her son and told him that he would have to accomplish what he started. She told him, "Just flap your wings, Son, and you'll soar up to the heavens with pride in your accomplishments. Remember, you can do it and only you can. You'll be so proud and I will know I have done my very best in teaching you faith in God."

The young eagle thought his mother had surely lost her mind and must not love him or she wouldn't place his life in jeopardy again. He sputtered and pleaded as she forced him out of the nest into the brisk wind which blew through the high mountains so far above the earth. As before, he cried out in fear, "Mother, don't you love me any more? You are sending me to my death and you don't even care." He was falling swiftly when his mother's instructions came to his mind. Then he held out one wing and then the other and flapped them in the air. He exclaimed proudly, "Ha, ha, Mother, I can fly! See, Mother, I knew that I could fly all the time." He soared over the mountain tops with the greatest of ease and surveyed his surroundings with great pride at all that he discovered as he flew away from the safety of his mother's nest and her tender loving care.

I knew God had given me the answer to my prayers through the mother eagle and her son. Yet I lacked the courage to do as she had demonstrated, but the message was clear and I, too, would have to demonstrate my faith in God for the welfare of my family. Things didn't improve as the days wore on and I had come very near the breaking point when I went to visit Steve and seek his advise. As always, Steve didn't tell me what to do, but he always seemed to sense what my decision would be. I cried, "I can't take it any more, Steve. I hate to tell Mark that it is time for him and Paul to get out and start a new life on their own." Steve simply said, "Destiny, whatever you decide to do, we will stand by you." Steve and Isabella had always stood by me through all the many tests and trials that life seemed to throw at me and I needed their support as well as their understanding.

I was beside myself when I got home that day. Mark was relaxed in the rocker without a care in the world and Paul was on the couch watching television when I walked into the room and announced that it was time for them to get out on their own. I was crying, but I spoke firmly and as I spoke I couldn't believe the voice I heard was actually mine. Mark was stunned at first, then he stood up and said, "Mamma, you are right. Paul and I need to move out and start a new life on our own. I've been thinking about it lately myself, but I thought you needed us so I had put it off. We've been living with you for a year now and I appreciate all you've done to help us. We will pack up right now and find a place to stay." I told him, "Mark, you don't have to leave today. I just wanted to let you know my decision. Since it's the middle of the week, you can stay here until you find a place to live and move this weekend."

He got excited about the idea of starting a new life on their own, however, and began gathering their things together. It was such a great relief to have peace that I gave them various things of mine to help them get started. We excitedly chose pots and pans that they would need as well as linen and other things. It didn't take long for them to gather everything together either and they seemed so happy as they drove away. I watched them as they drove down the dusty road until they were out of sight. Although tears filled my eyes, I felt a great peace in my heart as well as pride for the son I adored.

They found an old house for rent near Jasper. Even though they had to work hard to make it livable, Mark told me later that he was glad I had brought things to a head and he was really happy now. I rejoiced in the Lord because I learned that His grace is wonderful. Many times we are afraid to trust in the Lord when it comes to our children because we are afraid of losing their love.

Everything went well for a while and Sam started tearing down the house at Goodrich. He built a work shop at his house and used the lumber to make some improvements to his house and he showed me the things he did when I went by to visit them. I was happy for them, but I became afraid again when Steve decided to put their house up for sale at Newton and then I decided that I had made a big mistake by having the little house at Goodrich torn down. It was far too late to even consider living there again. I told myself that maybe the Lord is punishing me for putting Cindy and Jim off of my property without any place to go. If I hadn't though, things wouldn't have improved. Maybe now things were better for Cindy, at least I had heard they were. No, I didn't really believe I was being punished because I had defended not only my honor, but also Jacob's and even my responsibility to my former neighbors.

I decided to go by the house anyway to see if there was any possibility I could rebuild without a lot of expense. I thought it was a good idea just in case I had no other alternative. When I got there I realized the impossibility of making a home here by myself. It had been a foolish idea in the first place, but I was so desperate. Sam advised me to sell it if I could and get rid of the worry the place had caused me and especially the high taxes that were due again. Only a shell remained of the house with clutter everywhere. I knew that it would take a long time to clean it up and the only time that I could work on it would be on the weekends. Insulation was in heaps on the floor and I carried away boxes of it, as well as other trash to the dump on my way home every Saturday. Week after week, I'd go visit with Ted and then go by the house and work. On my last trip to the dump there was a sign which stated, "No dumping after a certain date" which happened to be the same date. I couldn't help thinking that the Lord took care of every detail. Glory to His Name!

Isabella made a little for sale sign, which I carried with me on my final trip to Goodrich. I wanted to visit the place where Jacob died one last time before I left. As I walked around the house, my footsteps faltered. "It's going to be tough saying goodbye to any dream or any hope of making a home here to the memory of you, Jacob," I cried. "I'm Ted's wife now and somehow I must let go so we can build a new life together without the memory of you haunting me in the future. The only way that I can do this, Jacob, is to sell this place to strangers since our family didn't appreciate it. Goodbye Jacob, I'll see you again someday," and then I turned and walked away.

I gathered the few tools together and loaded them into the car and took the little for sale sign and a hammer to drive the stick into the ground. When I walked to the edge of the street to put the sign in place, a pickup pulled up and a man got out and walked toward me. I thought the man was simply curious or at least he seemed to be. To my complete surprise he asked, "Is this place for sale?" "Yes, it is," I replied. "I was going to put the for sale sign up before I left." Without looking at the house first, he asked, "How much are you asking for it?" I replied firmly, "I'll want three thousand dollars and last years taxes paid." "That sounds reasonable to me," he said and then he told me his reason for buying the property. "I want to buy it for my daughter, who lives in the Houston area. She has some children and she needs to get them out of the city. I believe her brothers will help rebuild the house for her."

"I'll be happy to sell the place to someone who needs a home. It's not very much to look at right now, but it was a nice home once," I told him. He said, "I have to work, but I'll send my daughter and my wife to meet you at the court house anytime. They will bring the money to pay you when the deed is ready." "Would Monday be too soon," I asked? He replied, "That will be fine." We shook hands and he left and I sat down in the car happy because it seemed so unreal that the man happened to come by at exactly the right time. Another thing seems unreal as well. The first time I sold this place I paid for Jacob's funeral. This time there will be just enough money to pay the IRS for the back taxes that Jacob owed when he died so we haven't done all that bad I guess, at least Jacob received his share even though he doesn't know it, I guess. There was no room for doubt that God had my life in full control. If I had ever doubted before, I would never be guilty of doubting my Lord anymore. I felt numb for a moment because the events of that day were so astounding and more like a miracle. "My Father," I prayed, "How wonderful You are. The beauty of Your grace is so marvelous, filled with mercy and goodness, far greater than this human mind can possibly fathom. Praise Your Holy Name for bringing peace to my heart. Now, Father, I can go home and write Ted and tell him that another chapter in our life together has ended and another hurdle is over. Our God reigns supreme forever more in our lives."

CHAPTER 11

PERSEVERANCE IN HARD TIMES

I believe everyone needs a sense of security. Something in this world that they can see, feel or touch, much as a child with his pacifier in his mouth or that special blanket which gives him a sense of security when he takes a nap. Grownups have these insecurities too, even children of God. Even though they know the Lord loves them and that He will supply all their needs, they still need something tangible that they can touch, feel or see. Some of these things could be a simple thing we scarcely notice which we take for granted every day. One of the most outstanding things that we need is the security of a home.

Fear filled my heart again when Steve put the house up for sale in Newton, even though he had promised that he and Isabella wouldn't leave me homeless. "We will build a small house for you on our land at Jasper so we'll be able to take care of you when you get old if we sell this place," Steve promised. I believed Steve would keep that promise, but the promise Jesus made years ago that this place would be my home some day, weighed heavily on my heart. My heart went out to Steve and Isabella, especially Steve. He'd worked so hard building this lovely home, not counting all the expense of the materials to build it with. His folks had helped him by cutting most of the lumber that he needed at the little sawmill that they had. They also helped Steve build their dream house.

When they built the house neither one knew that things would turn out the way it had. They hadn't lived in their new home but three years when an abrupt change took place. Before Jacob died, Steve and Isabella said that the company Steve worked for insisted that they move into the company house which was located on the company property. It didn't seem real and Steve tried to change their decision, but they insisted they move anyway. It was either that or lose his job, so Steve resigned himself to leave the home they loved.

They didn't want to rent the house, because renters wouldn't take care of it. They didn't want to sell it either since it was their home and they could move back when Steve retired. They also knew when they invited me to live there that my income would be too low to pay rent and that I couldn't raise the money to buy it even if they were willing to sell it. About all that I could do was to be a caretaker and even then I wouldn't be able to keep the place up the way they had.

Randall and Daniel weren't happy about leaving their schoolmates nor their grandparents. It was a giant leap for all of them, but Isabella was familiar with moving to another area since she had experienced moving from one school to another all during the time she was growing up. She told the boys, "It's not the end of the world. We'll be moving to a larger town, and you'll make new friends. I know it seems unlikely, but you'll be surprised at how quickly you'll adapt to the change. We'll find another church too and everything will be brand new. I don't want to give up our home either, but we must think positively."

I tried to comfort them in the only way that I could, by saying, "This is your home and one day you will be able to retire and move back. It will take time to adjust, but as strange as it may seem. One day you'll come back and realize things just aren't the same anymore." My heart went out to my children as they drove away and I'm sure they cried many times after they left their home behind. I noticed, however, in a very short time that their interests were in Jasper and the new friends they made. I don't understand the ways of God or why He decided this would be my home. Perhaps Steve resented the idea and he thought that God had used him for my sake. I'm sure he had some resentment in his heart and he voiced it by saying, "I'm going to sell the house, because I haven't benefited at all from it. I can't even build a house at Jasper which I intend to do if I sell this place. The only purpose it has served has been to furnish Mamma and Daddy a place to stay while they were building their new house and a place for you to live. It won't be a problem to relocate you, Destiny, and if we sell this place you won't have to worry."

It broke my heart and I cried day and night. If only I could stop this feeling of loss in my heart and feeling that my security blanket was being snatched away. I couldn't seem to get my priorities in order and accept the situation. Even though I understood how Steve felt in this matter, I still needed my security blanket and I simply didn't know how to deal with the uneasy feelings I was experiencing.

Steve's mother, Mikie, and I were best friends. One day she came to my house all upset. Mikie stated, "Destiny, I love my son with all my heart, but it hurts me to know that he is trying to sell this place. I told him, `Son, you promised Destiny that this would be her home, but in spite of his promise to take care of you, he broke his promise and I feel so ashamed. We both were crying by then and Mikie said, "If I had the money I would buy this place for you. I can't bear the thought of you moving away." "I'm heartbroken too, Mikie," I cried. "I know the Lord knows best, but I can't understand why the Lord would promise me a home here and then have it be taken away from me. I do understand Steve's view point, but it doesn't stop the terrible ache in my heart," I cried. "It's all in God's hands and God can stop it if it's His will. We'll pray that God will have His way. Trust in Him and wait patiently," my friend said.

Steve and Isabella put a for sale signs up at the entrance to the driveway and at the end of the road on 2626. I just moped around the house as I packed the things that I didn't need. Tears streamed down my face as I forced myself to wrap the glass items that I might never need again. I felt totally defeated even though no one came to look at the house.

Eventually, a nice elderly couple came by to look at it. They admired the well-built structure of the house, especially the lady, who thought it fit every dream she wanted in a house. Her husband said, "An acre just isn't enough land for my needs, because I need a workshop and room to park my trucks." He asked J.T. if any of the adjoining land was for sale and when J.T. told him no, they drove away disappointed. I felt sorry for them and for Steve too. I then realized this place wasn't going to sell that easily. I began to hope for the first time since Steve had the idea to sell the house. No other prospects came to look at it and my fears subsided. Finally Steve said, "I won't try to sell it again."

Ted was marvelous when I ran to him crying. He couldn't be with me through the trials I faced outside the prison, but his love for me was unyielding and sure. This year had been a very trying one for us both and when Ted dried my tears, he held me close as he comforted me saying often, "Precious, the Lord has everything in control. He has assured me that you are His and He will take care of you. Now, let me see your sweet smile, Darling. Everything will be all right." Ted was very strong and because he was, my confidence grew in the Lord.

Toward the end of one of our sweet visits, I told Ted that I had a longing to go visit my sister, Ellen. "Honey, I heard she bought the old homestead where I grew up. Since I've been through several trying experiences lately and thoughts of my childhood are coming back to me, maybe I need to go back to my roots so that I can get more established in my faith. I think it will be a good thing to do, don't you?" Ted kissed me goodbye and replied, "Baby, you are right, so go with my blessing."

When I left Huntsville, I took the Highway 75 exit, which was the closest route to Cleveland, where I had grown up and lived the majority of my life with Jacob. Although we had moved from place to place during our marriage, we would return to the little tar paper shack now and then until we sold it. We had lived in poverty as we raised our children, but my intentions were to go back even further in my past today, back to my childhood where I had grown up around the New Salem community.

As I entered the city limits of Cleveland, I marveled at how much it had expanded in growth. It was a small city now, but when I was a child it was just a dot on the map. The main attraction was the old Texas Theatre, where us kids went to the movies on Saturdays. It was just after World War ll before most of the folks in the outlying areas had electricity and the black and white films we saw on a huge screen at the theatre were a remarkable and fun thing for us kids to do.

My thoughts raced back in time when saloons were a common thing. Railroad tracks divided the town then as they do now. During that era, the saloons were across the tracks as Mamma had expressed to me when I was a small child and remembering Mamma's temper when she would hold my hand tightly as we walked down the wooden sidewalk one Saturday. On passing by a saloon, a drunk staggered out and bumped into Mamma almost knocking her off the sidewalk. She had given him a good tongue lashing, but he was so drunk that he didn't pay any attention and stumbled on his way. Cleveland had a constable; however, who carried a billy club. He would grunt as he gathered up the drunks and carried them off to the jail house. Every Saturday night, Grandmother Ray would plead with Daddy to bring Grandpa home, because she was sure that he was as drunk as a skunk by then and that Fred Bushell, the constable, would throw poor Grandpa in jail. Daddy always hated to look for him and once he found Grandpa, he had to force him to get on the back of his log truck so he could take him home. One Saturday night, Grandmother sent Daddy to pick Grandpa up and after Daddy found him and got him situated safely on the truck, Daddy started off and Grandpa got off at the first intersection and staggered back to the saloon. Daddy was furious when we arrived at Grandmother's house and Grandpa wasn't on the truck. He told Grandmother, "That's the last time that I will bring Papa home from a drunken spree." Grandpa suffered a stroke shortly after that and Grandmother didn't have to worry about Grandpa going to a saloon anymore. Eventually, the people in the town voted the town dry and the saloons closed.

On my way I passed by the new elementary school. The old school where I had attended school had been torn down many years ago, but I could still hear, in my mind, the sound of children playing during recess. The old school house had been several stories high and I could still hear the wooden steps creak as we climbed from floor to floor. I smiled remembering my introduction to classical music and the speeches of the principal and the superintendent in the huge auditorium every morning before we were dismissed to our classes. I'm thankful for the little education that I had even though it was only through the sixth grade which wasn't so unusual back then. Mamma had taken me out of school to help her with my sisters and my brother because of her poor health.

The New Salem Road turned off Farm Road 1010 which was located a couple of miles south of Cleveland. It had been a long time since I had driven down the road or visited the New Salem Church where I had attended and accepted Jesus who is so precious to me. Signs of progress were everywhere I looked and especially in this area. Where once nice wooden frame houses had been, brick homes lined the narrow highway now. I drove slowly since the area had changed so much and I watched frantically for the old landmarks which I remembered. I was close to tears as I searched for Mrs. Angel's house. If I could find it, I would know that the lane to the old home place wasn't far away. Finally I found it, but the area had changed there too. Creeping along I found a lane which I felt sure was the one I was searching for.

As I made my turn, I felt uneasy because nothing was familiar and it wasn't even a dirt lane anymore. It was a narrow black topped street now and looking at the surroundings, my first thought was, `Oh, Lord, I'm on the wrong road. Drive on for a ways and then if it's wrong, you can turn around and search until you find the right one.'

Things began to take shape, however, in spite of the changes over the years. When I saw the house that Grandmother's children had built for her before she died, I knew I was going right. The whole area had changed so much that I was heartsick and cried, as though my heart would break as I realized how quickly old landmarks from the past were disappearing. I hadn't considered that when I started out. The blacktop played out in an area where I had to make a sharp turn to the old homestead where I had grown up. It was a narrow lane that led to my sister's house. She didn't expect me so my visit would be a nice surprise and I hoped she would be at home.

As I drove up into her driveway, she came out to meet me. Ellen said excitedly, "What a surprise, Destiny, you are a welcome sight." When we went inside her house, we sat reminiscing about the past. She then took out some water color paintings she had done recently and my heart ached as Ellen's must have when she painted the old log cabin where our Grandparents had lived. I said, "Ellen, everything has changed so drastically. This area was so beautiful when we were kids. Now the pine sapling thicket has grown so dense that it doesn't even look like a farm ever existed here even though we know it did, but we can be very proud of our heritage."

My sister and I enjoyed such a sweet visit, but it was getting late so I told here goodbye. As I started to leave I said, "Maybe we can get together again soon."

As I drove away, my heart was weighed down in sorrow. "Oh, Father, it was so good to see my sister again, but I just can't seem to pull myself together after returning to the old place which holds so many wonderful memories. On my left, Grandmother who use to raise peas and corn. A fence was very near this lane that I am on. When Grandpa had his stroke, Grandmother did the work of two people. She not only plowed the field with a horse; she raised a vegetable garden. She also had a fruit orchard as well as the beautiful yard she kept up. You know, Father, during those days, there wasn't any such thing as a lawn mower," I told the Lord.

"Father," I continued in tears, "She raised my cousin, Blanch, just a year older than I am. When Grandmother was working in the field, Blanch and I would play dolls in the corn rows.

Most of the time the corn grew so tall that the summer breeze couldn't reach us. Many times when we would race to find her the sand burned our bare feet and then when we discovered the row she was plowing on, we would try to step in her footprints. The freshly turned earth was cool as we skipped along toward Grandmother's voice when she called out to her horse. When she reached the end of a row, sometimes she would just hesitate just long enough to reach into her apron pocket and take out a large handkerchief to wipe the sweat off her face. She always wore a long cotton dress that reached down to her ankles and a bonnet on her head to protect her fair skin from the sun."

As I continued reminiscing I told the Lord, "In the heat of the day, Blanch and I would run to Grandmother's house for a drink of cool well water. As we raced by the front porch, Grandpa would be sitting in a cane bottom chair in the shade. The stroke had left him weak on one side so he walked with a cane. He would smile as we hurriedly ran for the well, but by then we would be out of breath and couldn't talk.

Two little girls who weren't aware of any danger as we reached the big dug out well and lowered the heavy wooden bucket down into the water. We would stand on our tiptoes so we could see when the bucket was full and then four tiny hands would struggle with the rope which was too large to reach around and we would tug with all our strength to bring the heavy bucket to the top. Once we got it to the surface, Blanch would pull it out over the curb and we would drink until our little stomachs were full. Oh, I remember how good that water was," I stated, knowing God already knew all this.

"When Grandmother would come in from the field, we would help her with the chores. After the chores were all done, Grandmother would light the coal oil lamp and cook supper while Blanch and I took our baths in a #3 washtub. Everything would get real quiet when supper was over. Grandpa would retire to the living room and we would help Grandmother wash the dishes. Then she would take out the old family Bible and read exciting stories to us about all the different and interesting characters in the old Testament. I loved to hear her read the Bible and even though I was very small, those stories have stayed in my heart all these years. Even though I didn't know You as my Savior back then, Father, I never doubted any thing that Grandmother read. I believed then as now that Your Word is true."

I continued talking with the Lord and reminiscing about the past telling Him, "I am older now, my Lord, and I've been through a lot, but my Grandmother persevered through all those hard times with us. She didn't rest on Sunday either like so many do these days. When I spent Saturday night with Blanch, Grandmother would take us both to church every Sunday. We didn't have a car back then and we walked everywhere we needed to go. Grandmother would fix our breakfast and then would dress us neatly and place colorful ribbons in our hair. When we would start out the door, she would say, "Lonzo, we'll be back in a little while." Grandpa would reply, "All right, Ginnie, I'll be waiting for you." Then Blanch and I would skip along as we tried to keep up with her. Grandmother didn't want to be late, I'm sure, and the New Salem Baptist Church was quite a distance from the old home place."

When I drove onto the New Salem Road again, I felt as though I had passed back through a channel from another era. I didn't even understand why I had felt so compelled to return to the places of my childhood and it left me confused. It's possible, I told myself, that the Lord sent me back to remind me that others had persevered before me. My life with Ted required the same enduring and persevering faith.

My Grandmother was a unique example of this same abiding faith. I was convinced now that I could endure the many fiery trials with an even stronger determination and the will to work harder, not only for the Lord, but also for my beautiful marriage with Ted which God had ordained in heaven.

As I drew near Farm Road 1010, quite suddenly and compellingly, I felt led to go by my brother's house. There seemed to be such an urgency quite similar to the one that I'd experienced earlier as I left Ted at Huntsville. For some reason, it was as if for the entire day that the Holy spirit had full control of each turn in the road and that I was only a passenger. I couldn't imagine why I needed to go by my brother's house, thinking, `I really need to go home, Lord. I'm very tired after all the things that I've experienced today.' Very reluctantly, I followed the leading of the Holy Spirit. I decided that I would rest for a while when I got there before I started home to Newton.

I didn't have the opportunity to rest, however, because Pam, my sister-in-law, met me at the door. She exclaimed, "Destiny, I'm so glad that you came. I have some bad news and I hope you will go by the hospital and see Blanch before you go back home. She is hospitalized at the Cleveland hospital, and I'll go with you if you want me to. The doctor said that she was dying and she probably wouldn't make it through the night." Without hesitating, I replied, "Let's go Pam," and we hurriedly got into the car and started to Cleveland.

We drove toward Cleveland, Pam said, "Destiny, Joshua and I went to visit with Blanch and Joshua asked her if she knew Christ Jesus, as her Savior. Blanch was very weak, but she whispered and nodded her head, "No." Joshua explained the plan of salvation to her and he prayed that she would receive Christ as her Savior as he knelt by her bed.

We had to go home heartsick, because Blanch didn't acknowledge in any way that she had accepted Christ. Oh, I pray that somehow you can reach Blanch before she dies. Destiny, you may very well be her last hope in getting her to understand that her soul is in jeopardy."

Memories of my childhood came flooding back through my mind once again. I hadn't seen Blanch in years and at this moment I could see her as a child again. I could see her beautiful golden curly hair glistening in the sunlight, as she beckoned to me standing beside the fence row. "Destiny, come play dolls with me while Grandmother is plowing the corn." When Mamma said I could, we'd race breathlessly to an area in the field where we thought we were hidden from everyone. This was our own little world. Blanch had been my best friend and we shared everything. Playing school in the old log house when the weather was too bad to play outside. We walked together to meet the school bus through all types of weather. Sometimes our feet would be so frozen when it snowed, that Grandmother would put my feet in a pan of warm water to thaw them out before I walked on home. My heart was heavier than it had ever been and the thought that Blanch would die without Jesus broke my heart. "Father," I cried in the Holy Spirit, "Please have mercy on Blanch and myself. I can't bear the thought of her not meeting me in Heaven when I get there."

I fought to keep my composure as Pam and I entered the hospital. When we went into Blanch's room, she looked up at and smiled. "Oh, Destiny, you did come," she cried, and her lips trembled as she held out her hand and I took it and bent over and kissed her. Blanch whispered, as she strained to get her words out, "Oh, I'm so happy to see you again." Her beautiful blue eyes shone with joy, which I had always thought were the most beautiful eyes in all the world and they smiled happily again. I realized that she was heavily medicated, because her pain was so severe.

I was overcome with emotion and while I held her hand she drifted in and out of consciousness. `With the knowledge of all that Pam has told me, I must somehow appeal to her heart and in a conscious moment she has to hear my pleas for her to receive Christ Jesus as her Savior,' I thought anxiously.

I trembled in the Holy Spirit and realizing the time was running out for Blanch, I broke down in uncontrollable sobs. I cried with a loud voice in agony, "Oh, Blanch, meet me in heaven. I can't bear the thought of you going to hell." She opened her eyes and responded to my cries, letting me know that she was aware of the things I was saying to her. Then I spoke in a gentle voice of love and concern with questions in my mind that troubled me deeply, "Oh, Blanch, it's hard to believe that you haven't been saved all these years. What excuse can you give the Lord for neglecting so great a salvation? Don't you remember Grandmother teaching us the Word of God when we were small? In spite of her working in the fields all day long, she always read the Bible to us by lamplight at the kitchen table. She took us to Sunday School and Aunt Ruth taught us about Jesus in our Sunday School class. Oh, don't you remember? Aunt Ruth gave us pretty cards that had little stories on the back and pretty pictures on the front and we were so proud to show them off. We have such sweet memories to treasure, Honey."

Tears ran down my cheeks and my sobs wouldn't stop. I knew her soul hung in the balance and I felt this was her last opportunity to accept Christ as her Savior. Blanch was slipping away and her fight to stay awake seemed hopeless, so I asked her daughter to join me in prayer, and I fell down on my knees beside her bed and groaning in sorrow, I poured my heart out to God. After I prayed, I knew that I had done what God had sent me to do. Now it was in God's powerful hands to decide the fate of my beloved Blanch. She didn't respond in any way to let me know that she had accepted Christ. So I kissed her again and said, "I love you, Blanch,". After saying a few words to her daughter about God's love for her through these heart breaking times, I said, "I pray that your mother was saved today. We may never know until we reach heaven ourselves, but through this experience we should draw even closer to the Lord and realize the need to witness to a lost and dying world." I hugged her daughter and left feeling sad all the way home.

I learned a valuable lesson that day that I'll never forget. When the Holy Spirit leads you into strange places we don't understand, it's not always to teach you a certain thing, instead it's very possible that these are preparations for a designed mission He has in mind. He took me to another age and time in memory showing me how through the passage of time the surface of things, such as land and homes do change. But the true values we are taught by those who persevered for the cause of Christ will forever be a beacon of hope for the ones they leave behind. Blanch died the next day and she was buried at Liberty. Joshua presided at her funeral with a short message from God's Word and we went our separate ways. If my beloved Blanch accepted Jesus as her Savior, our Father carried her to heavenly heights beneath His Holy Wings of love.

CHAPTER 12

THE VISION

On our next visit Ted held me in his arms as long as he could and then led me to a chair. We sat in silence for a moment. Ted said tenderly, "Darling, I think that we should pray right now." He reached across the table and took my hands in his. Ted began praying humbly for mercy toward us both. I listened carefully to Ted's prayer, which was moving and beautiful. Even though our marriage wasn't a normal one, we were together in God's presence and Ted was the head of our family. For two hours, this became our home, and I looked to him for comfort as his wife with him as the leader, and I'm sure the Lord was pleased with our marriage of faith. I drew strength from this man, whom I loved and God had blessed him with wisdom and patience to accept His will in the unusual relationship we shared.

My heart was so troubled when Blanch died. Many times I'd witnessed to others, but it had never left me grieving like this even when they left suddenly and I didn't know the results of my witness. This time, however, the witness for Christ was given to someone very dear to my heart. This time a life was slipping away as she drifted in and out of consciousness. No other witness had left me so drained and I really needed Ted to lean on as well as my Lord.

Ted responded wonderfully and I knew God's grace worked through him. This was my first experience of witnessing by the bedside of someone dying and the effect on my heart was devastating. Ted told me that I had to realize that God had sent me to Blanch in His own time and He had prepared me for the witness. "Precious, God knew what He was doing. Don't grieve now, because you have more things to do for Jesus. You must put this behind you and go on." I felt a lot better when I went home because the Lord gave me peace and the work for Christ took first priority over everything.

One morning in the fall of 1994 my sister, Brittany, called. I hadn't seen Brittany in quite a while so it was a wonderful surprise to hear her voice again. After we had talked a while, Brittany said, "Destiny, I had a special reason for calling you today. Even though it's wonderful to hear your voice again, I felt so led by the Lord to tell you about my experience that I couldn't put it out of my mind. I don't know how you feel about dreams or if you believe they have any effect on your future. Normally, I seldom dream anything of value, but this one was very disturbing, to say the least. It was concerning you and maybe, when I explain the experience that I had, you can explain what it's all about." Before she started telling me about her dream, I started trembling. The Holy Spirit seemed to tell me, "Listen carefully to Brittany, Destiny, because the Lord has a message for you alone." I held the telephone tightly and told Brittany to go on with her dream. She began the dream in the way that she had witnessed it and this is the testimony that she gave.

"I was apart, as though suspended, in a strange location. I saw a platform in the center of an enormous crowd of people. As far as I could see, there were people surrounding the small platform, Destiny. I saw the President of the United States along with his wife seated on the front row. I saw you standing on the platform and a man in a beige colored suit stood beside you. You were speaking, but I couldn't hear you. I could see your lips moving and even though I couldn't hear a word you said, evidently the audience could, because they focused their full attention on you."

Brittany was silent a moment, then she said, "Destiny, it was such an awesome dream. The silence was so great that you could have heard a pin drop and I asked myself, `Why can't I hear my sister speaking? Everyone else seemed to be able to hear her and evidently, they were very interested in everything she has to say.' Destiny, do you know what the dream means? Am I going to lose my hearing, do you think?"

Suddenly the revelation became very clear and so many things that had bothered me since Ted came into my life were no longer a mystery. I replied, "No, Brittany, you aren't going to lose your hearing. This dream applies to me. In spite of my feeling so inadequate to write a book, your dream tells me that I will. You didn't hear a sound since certainly most readers read silently. I hope that if the Lord is calling me to write, I will have an enormous audience. I hope the book holds their interest so greatly that it will get their full attention in just the way you described. I have no doubt the Lord has called me to write since He has been dealing with me in that area for quite a while now, but He hasn't let me know what He wants me to write about yet."

I continued saying, "You may not know it, but I wrote two short stories for the town paper. You see, I've felt the call to write before now and I truly hoped with all my heart that those two short stories would be sufficient for the Lord. However, the Lord sent you the dream to confirm His will for me to write through you. I'm sure that is why the Holy Spirit wouldn't let you rest until you told me about your dream." Brittany giggled, and exclaimed, "Just think, my sister is going to be a famous author." We both laughed at ourselves and I wondered how such a thing could really happen.

I don't know why most Christians think the Lord calls us into a special ministry or service when we are feeling our best and everything seems perfect. I should have known the Lord didn't always work that way, especially since the Holy Spirit had awakened me three times with a shout in the middle of the night in 1991. He called me at a time when my time was completely filled with things to do and His booming voice rang throughout the little travel trailer, "GET UP, GET BUSY!" I was so startled that I jumped straight up in my bed and couldn't imagine what was going on. He did that three times and once I was fully awake, then the Lord shouted the same command as I sat on the side of my bed.

I wasn't exactly up to all that noise in the middle of the night. I was exhausted and needed rest, because I had another full day ahead on Mother's Day. In spite of my irritation and lack of understanding, I finally realized that the loud command came from God. It had been over three years between that experience and Brittany's dream. How long does the Lord take to reveal His whole desire? God knows that I tried everything I thought could be the answer. I got in a hurry I guess and made a lot of hasty decisions. I drove myself hard thinking that I was fulfilling His call. I'm sure, however, that each learning experience was for training toward His main purpose. God would teach me through real experiences.

My busy schedule became too much for me because my health was deteriorating. The injuries that I had suffered when I fell in West 6 started affecting me on a regular basis. Eventually, the damage affected my neck as well. On December 11, 1994, I awoke with a terrible pain in my neck. I didn't know exactly whether I'd slept wrong or if complications were beginning to show up from my fall. The pain was so severe, but somehow I managed to dress and I started to Jasper deciding to go to the Emergency Room. It was also Sunday morning and I knew the church would be expecting me, but I told myself that I couldn't play that today because I couldn't bear the pain. When I approached the street to the church, I said, "Father, if You will give me the strength, I'll go by the church first and play the piano and get me some help later." I turned down the street, trusting the Lord would grant my prayer and played for the church that morning. No one seemed to notice that I was suffering and my Pastor seemed surprised when I told him that I was going to the Emergency Room as I went out the door.

Isabella met me at the Emergency Room and after Dr. Joe treated my neck, he turned to Isabella and said, "Daughter, take your Mamma home with you." I felt so bad that I consented to go with her, however, I didn't want to be a hindrance and keep them from attending the evening worship service. Isabella told Steve that she thought it would be best if she stayed with me, and that he should take Randall and Daniel with him to church. When they left, Isabella decided to do some Christmas baking. I told her, "I think that I'll just lie down for a while and rest."

I went into the living room and stretched out on the couch. As I watched the colorful Christmas lights twinkle and listened to the beautiful Christmas carols playing softly in the background, a sweet peace filled the room and I drifted off to sleep or at least I thought I did. Suddenly I found myself in the strangest place and I looked around at the setting in amazement. It was as though I'd been transported back to another age, to a location deep in a wooded area. I didn't recognize the location or the wooden frame house where I found myself. However, I recognized the little rocking chair that I was sitting in as being my favorite chair. I rocked contentedly as I looked around the room, but wondered how the chair had gotten there. I didn't understand and just sat thinking; `This old room hasn't been lived in for many years.' Spider webs with dust tags hung from the ceiling and the corners. A make shift cabinet was on my left which was sadly in need of repair. The floors were thick with dust as well and I thought to myself, `Well, if I'm to live here, it will take an awful lot of work to make it livable. I don't understand why I'm here though. I'll just wait a while before I worry about it,' I decided.

I leaned my head back and relaxed, rocking back and forth for a short time, when I suddenly became aware that something lying directly at my feet. In stunned surprise, I glanced down and saw an old wooden chest on the floor. As I looked, I gasped in wonder and delight and said in surprise, "Where did this come from?" I thought in wide-eyed wonder, `This is the most mysterious event that I have ever witnessed. Now all of a sudden this old chest has appeared out of nowhere. It wasn't here before and, Lord, it doesn't even have any dust on the lid which is very odd.' As I examined the old chest, it seemed to have been built with the same type of lumber that the walls and the floors were made of, but the old chest looked so much older, almost like it was petrified, I decided. I ran my fingers across the smooth grain of the wood and it felt like satin to the touch. As I sat musing about this wondrous mystery, thoughts of another age went through my mind. I thought about pirates with hidden treasures and I even thought about the era when soldiers wore armor. I smiled, thinking, `I'm being so silly, there couldn't be a pirate's treasure here in this old chest. Besides, there isn't even a lock on it to keep nosy people from seeing what it contains.'

`Now, Destiny, all you are going to find in this old chest will probably be just a hammer or maybe a handsaw and it's probably so rusty by now that it will fall apart if you disturb it. Some old carpenter probably built this old house, and he probably died without anyone left to claim it,' I told myself smiling.

`It won't hurt anything to just take a peek,' I thought mischievously. Then I lifted the lid back ever so slowly, and as I did my heart raced madly as I gazed down at the unbelievable contents in the old chest. I couldn't believe my eyes and my hands began to tremble, because I knew immediately that I was looking down on a holy treasure and not pirates' gold nor anything from this old world. The old chest was at least four feet long and about eighteen inches wide and at least two feet deep. It was filled to the top with gold-colored broken pieces of metal. I assumed this metal had once been armor that a soldier had worn in battle many years ago. Then I thought, `Lord, that soldier must have fought a lot of battles for his armor to be so broken. Evidently, he had been a faithful warrior, both tried and true to have such honor bestowed on him that You would guard it with a two-edged sword.' The broken pieces were square; some appeared to be four inches wide and some six inches. I sat frozen as I stared down, unable to comprehend the awesomeness of this discovery and I trembled in fear as I gazed at the two-edged sword which lay threateningly across the top of the broken pieces of metal. I could easily see that the marvelous sword was from God and the two edges of the blade appeared to have been sharpened recently, and I could clearly see the slanted lines where it had been filed to perfection. As I looked down at the cold steel, I realized that it was ready to be used in battle. The beautiful sword was made of silver and it lay the full length of the chest with very little room for anyone to disturb the broken pieces which seemed to be guarding the holy treasure of God. I noticed the fine detailed work that only a master craftsman could have designed on the magnificent silver handle. I marveled at its' beauty as the sunlight streamed through the old dusty window and sent golden streams of light spreading upward as it touched the mysterious treasure. I sat very still and trembled in fear knowing all of these things were from God.

The silence was suddenly interrupted when I began to cry, as though the Holy Spirit spoke to my heart and said, "The broken pieces lying in the old wooden chest isn't the armor of an old soldier at all, Destiny, it's the broken pieces of your own life." As I realized the truth, I felt desperately helpless and cried out to God in anguish, "Oh, please, Father, help me mend these broken pieces. I know they look so uneven and the edges aren't even smooth, but if only I had some thread or glue with me, there is a possibility that I could fit these broken pieces together like a puzzle myself."

I realized how dangerous it would be if I tried to remove any of the broken pieces from the chest, but I was determined to try even knowing the sword could very easily slice my fingers. `I can't just sit here and stare at the contents in the chest without at least trying to make them join together,' I thought. `But Destiny, you may be defying the Lord if you try to retrieve any of the pieces from beneath the sword that you know very well is guarding the treasure of the Lord.' "Don't you understand, whether your life is broken or whole, it belongs to God and He has the power to use your life as He chooses," the voice in my heart spoke warningly. "But, I must try," I cried in despair, as I reached down near the edge of the chest and retrieved two pieces near the edge.

I sighed in relief as I leaned back in my chair and held the broken pieces gently in my hands. `That's strange,' I thought. `I could see the oil on the pieces of metal as well as the two-edged sword, which had more oil on it than the pieces. But I just assumed it was there to protect it from rust and decay, but these pieces feel like satin to the touch and I didn't think they would feel that way.' As I examined the broken pieces, I soon realized how hopeless it was as I tried to fit them together like a puzzle. Tears began trickling down my cheeks as I realized how defective the pieces of metal were. There were bubble-like formations near the center and on the edges as if they had been through extreme heat. The pieces became slippery between my fingers because of the fine oil and my teardrops which mingled together as I sighed hopelessly in despair. I had tried to fix the broken pieces of my life, but I had failed miserably. I just slumped over in my chair and sobbed, as I realized that only God could perform such a miracle as this.

The old room was as silent as a tomb except for my sobs, which seemed unrelentingly as I cried out to God in agony and distress, "Oh, my God, won't You mend these broken pieces together for me. I tried and failed, so will You please have mercy on me. I don't even understand why I'm in this strange old house. What does all this mean anyway? Father, I know that I have made a lot of mistakes in my life, especially during my life with Jacob, but You forgave all my sins and those of Jacob's when he was saved just before he died. The broken pieces of my life are so many, Father, and I don't understand why. I've been faithful to Your cause for so many years, walked through the fires of hell, gave up my only true love for the love of my children and for Jacob in honor and respect for my Lord. The only true happiness that Jacob and I ever shared out of all our years together was the last year after he accepted Jesus as his Savior. One year seems so little, compared to thirty-nine years of walking in fear with only You to stand faithfully by my side. Oh, my God, I don't want to remember my life the way it was with so few happy times to rejoice about. Don't You see, I just want to blot out the past from my mind, and enjoy the freedom to worship You the way that I always longed to do."

Broken Pieces of Beauty

I placed the broken pieces on my lap, feeling totally and utterly helpless. `I don't know what to do now,' I thought in dismay as I leaned back in the chair and gave in to the hopeless feelings in my heart. I decided the whole experience seemed more like a horrible nightmare and I hoped that I'd wake up soon and find that was all it really was.

As time passed ever so slowly, I thought wistfully, `Lord, when will this nightmare end?' My sobs pierced the silence in the old empty room and my heart wouldn't stop hurting because of the broken pieces lying in the old wooden chest and no hope left of their ever being mended. Then suddenly, I had the eerie feeling that someone else was in the room. It was such an overpowering feeling as I became more aware that it was the very presence of Jesus Himself who was standing nearby. Then turning to my right, I held my breath as I caught a glimpse of Jesus' sweet and precious feet. I began wiping away the tears from my eyes so that I could see Him better. I sat very still and held my breath as the mist which blocked my view vanished gradually where my Savior stood. I was too afraid to even breathe and my heart was pounding so hard that every heartbeat sounded more like the beating of a drum. Tears of joy filled my eyes as I beheld the Son of God, thinking how unworthy I was to even be in His holy presence. As I looked into His glorious face I felt limp and I didn't know what to say to the King of Glory. I just wanted to fall on my face at His precious feet and tell Him how very much He had meant to me all through the years. But I couldn't seem to move as I sat in complete awe at the realization that Christ would love me so much that He would leave His throne in heaven in answer to my prayer.

It just seemed as if it wasn't His will that I worship Him on my knees and I had the strongest impression that He came for a much more important reason. `Perhaps He has come to mend the broken pieces of my life,' I thought hopefully. But I knew those broken pieces were from this world, and yet, I just couldn't seem to let go of a past that was so filled with heartache and regret which really didn't have to be that way. It was too late to undo what had happened in the past and there was no more opportunity to say I'm sorry when you draw your last breath. I couldn't bear the pain from seeing the pieces of my life which were so broken and somehow I thought they must be made whole.

I cried out, "Why don't You speak, oh, precious Jesus? Don't You feel my pain and the awful heartache that I'm suffering? Why are You standing so still and unmoving as though Your eyes seem to question me," "Oh, why don't you trust in Me, Destiny? In spite of all the suffering that you have been through, there is much more work to do."

His dark brown eyes seemed to pierce my very soul as His steady gaze never wavered to the right or left. Although they revealed love and compassion, I saw His Divine Authority and power to use my life for His glory as He chose. He really is the Lily of the Valley, the Bright and Morning Star and the beautiful Rose of Sharon, far more beautiful than anyone could describe.

I thought about the suffering He went through as He gave His life on the cross at Mount Calvary. As I did, I looked carefully on His forehead to see if there were any scars there from the crown of thorns which had dug deep into His flesh that cruel men had placed on his sweet head in mockery and shame on His way to Golgatha's Hill. There wasn't any evidence of the suffering He went through on that horrible day on the face of our Lord. His skin was as smooth as a tiny baby and I marveled, praising God for Jesus, the Son of God who had been willing to offer Himself up as the perfect atonement for all our sins.

Broken Pieces of Beauty

The sunlight streamed through the dirty window pane and streams of golden light danced upon the strands of His soft brown curls that nestled upon the shoulders of the Lord, while some lay ever so lovely around His handsome face. While on His way to Mount Calvary, the angry mob pulled parts of His beautiful hair out by the roots, and they had plucked out His beard as well. My Lord was clean shaven today, and I couldn't detect any sign of the harsh brutality that He suffered that dark day in history.

I couldn't see His strong back where the King of Glory had been beaten so severely with a whip they call the `cat of nine tails.' The razor sharp metal on the ends of the leather thongs dug deep into the flesh of the Son of God and ripped out His blessed flesh. He was cut into ribbons while the Holy and innocent blood of Jesus ran down His body and spilled upon the ground. He was beaten so badly that He wasn't recognizable, yet here He stood tall and straight and I knew there weren't any scars on His back either. Still, He had carried the old wooden cross on His bleeding back and shoulders up the path to Mount Calvary and He had suffered more than any man out of love for us all so that we might be saved by only trusting in His Holy and righteous Name.

Our Lord wore a fine white linen garment. It was as white as freshly fallen snow, with a rich brown silk robe draped over His shoulders that lay gently in folds down His side and was almost the length of His white linen garment that reached the top of His ankles. "How beautiful You are, Oh, my Lord and Redeemer!"

His lovely sweet feet were so precious to me and as I looked down at them, I just wanted to fall down on my knees and worship my King. Oh, how much He must have loved the whole world when He carried the rugged cross up the steep hill to die for all our sins. His feet were so beautiful and slim and there weren't any bruises or scars on His lovely feet now from the rocky paths and hot desert sands that He walked on. Many times He walked to a secluded place to pray to His Father, who He longed to be with though knowing His mission had to be completed. Everywhere He went, He healed the sick and taught multitudes of people about a better way that offered hope to as many as believed before His death on Mount Calvary. There weren't any visible signs on His precious feet from the huge spike the angry mob drove through His tender flesh. Then after nailing the hands and feet of our Lord to an old rugged cross, cruel men raised Him above the earth and dropped the old cross into a hole they had prepared for our Lord, Jesus Christ, the Savior of the whole world.

His blood had run down His sweet face and down His body, and His sweet hands bled from the huge spikes that were driven through His innocent hands that had gently blessed little children. His tender hands and feet bore the weight of His precious body on the cross as He hung suspended between heaven and earth.

His ministry wasn't finished though as He hung there in shame. One more soul repented of his sins and even through everything He was suffering in such terrible agony, He promised the thief on another cross that believed on His Name. He told him, "Today, shalt thou be with me in paradise."

What a sad and mournful day it was as Love hung on the old rugged cross for sinners like you and me. Yet, Jesus could have called ten thousand angels to set Him free. But if He had, we would all die in our sins, without any hope of spending eternity in heaven with Him. No, no one took His life; Jesus gave His life's blood that we might go free. When He died, they thought they were rid of Jesus forever, but Praise God, He arose victorious over death and the grave and reigns by the right hand of God, His Father, making intercession for you and me. Now He reigns forever, the KING of GLORY!

`Oh what a wondrous Savior,' I thought, as I looked down at the broken pieces in my hands. `All that Jesus would need to do is speak and all these pieces would be mended immediately, but He doesn't seem to care, He just stands there, not moving a muscle or blinking His eyes, just watching every move I make,' and tears of frustration started falling again.

I continued crying until there weren't any more tears to cry and I just wanted to die. I kept waiting for some response from the Lord as I sat slumped in my chair. I was getting more and more irritated as I glanced toward Him now and then since nothing had changed. There was complete silence now and neither of us spoke nor moved. I thought, `Well, Destiny, you might as well relax. At least Christ is here and no matter how much time goes by, you don't have anything to worry about. You know you could be imagining this whole thing and Jesus is only a figment of your imagination. Oh, Lord, have I started seeing things that aren't real? After all, He hasn't moved or spoken since He came, only His eyes that watch every move that I make.'

Out of the corner of my eye, I saw Jesus start to move and I quickly turned my head to see. The Lord held His hands out to me with His palms open. I was so happy that I started to get up from my chair thinking, `Jesus is going to comfort me,' but I stopped short when I realized that He was showing me His hands. He wasn't inviting me into His arms. As I looked closer at His hands, I realized His hands were Ted's and not the nail-scarred hands that I expected to see. He looked down at me with pity in His eyes. Then I began to weep because of my love for Ted and not for my own selfish desires.

My selfish heart melted as I looked at Jesus' hands and saw that they were really Ted's gentle hands. Tears of love began falling down my cheeks and the broken pieces of the past didn't matter anymore as I thought of Ted and the beautiful life we had shared. I realized that Jesus really wanted me to trust Him the same way that I trusted Ted. Suddenly the present became so important to me that I bowed my head and let the warm tears of healing flow and they cleansed my heart and soul.

I was content now to sit quietly with my Lord nearby, when suddenly Jesus started walking in my direction. I held my breath as I looked down at His feet, which were suspended a few inches above the old dirty floor. I got so excited and thought, `Oh, God, Jesus is really going to comfort me now since I've humbled myself the way I should have from the start.' Then I looked at His eyes and I knew instantly that the Lord didn't have that in mind. Now His eyes didn't show any compassion for me at this time, they seemed to be filled with righteous indignation and I became so afraid then that He would take my life because of the way that I had doubted Him. Jesus didn't look my way at all and it was as if I weren't even there as He approached the old wooden chest. I thought happily, `Maybe Jesus is going to mend the broken pieces before He leaves. Even though He doesn't seem concerned about them really, He might do it just because I had asked Him to.' I was afraid to even breathe as He approached the chest near my feet, thinking, `I don't dare blink my eyes or I might miss the marvelous miracle that I'm about to witness.' I've never seen such a look of determination in anyone's eyes as I saw in the eyes of my Lord as He bent over and lifted up the two-edged Sword with His right hand. As He straightened up, He turned around and walked for a couple of steps with His back to me. I was so completely awestruck that I watched in amazement as the King of Glory turned ever so slightly to His left and lifted the Sword up high and started rising upward. As He rose He disappeared gradually in the same manner that He came, this time carrying the Sword of God with Him.

I awoke immediately and didn't know where I was. I became very frightened and began to tremble as I prayed, "Father, where am I? I don't recognize this house, Lord." As I looked around the room, my mind started to clear and the sweet aroma of cookies baking filled the room where I lay. It had been such an awesome experience to have seen Christ Jesus and actually talk to Him, even though He didn't speak a word throughout my beautiful dream. I felt different somehow and knew that I had changed, because I truly had an encounter with the Lord. I didn't know how to explain what had happened to the children since I had seen the Lord and the thought of me dying entered my mind too.

It took quite a bit of effort to gather my emotions before I could even try to explain to Isabella and Steve about this awesome and mysterious experience when I lay down to rest for a while on the couch. I needed their help and understanding more than I ever had and prayed that the children would believe that this experience had been more than just a dream. I hoped they wouldn't just slough it off and tell me that I had most likely experienced such a dream because I had been ill. I was still dazed when I went to the dining room and sat down at the table.

Isabella said, "Mamma, are you feeling any better since you rested for a while?" I replied, "Honey, I'm not sure how I feel really. I had the most mysterious dream that I have ever had." She listened quietly as I told her my story while still in a daze and unable to understand all the things that I had witnessed. When I finished, she said, "That was quite an experience, Mamma. Evidently you had a vision instead of just an ordinary dream. I didn't realize you were sleeping because I could hear you talking to someone. I just assumed that you were talking about the TV program." "Can you explain the meaning of my dream, Isabella?" I asked. "No, Mamma, I can't, but maybe Steve can help you when he gets home. I think the broken pieces represent your past, and the two-edged sword is often referred to as the Word of God. The Holy Spirit will reveal it to you in time," she replied. When Steve came home and we told him about the dream, he said much the same thing as Isabella did. The kids didn't realize that Christ had come to visit their home that Christmas season.

I couldn't get the dream out of my mind and I cried every time I thought about my encounter with Christ. The dream had been so vivid and hasn't faded with time. He was so beautiful and after the experience, I loved Him even more than I had before. I longed to see Him again and grew homesick for heaven. I realized that I had a mission to do for His sake, however, and there wasn't any doubt now what it was. He had called me verbally in May of 1991 and then sent my sister a vision confirming His will that I write a book. Now he had shown Himself to me and also what I would write about and I didn't have any more excuses to offer such as, I don't know what You want me to do.

It had been hard to step out on faith when he sent me to Ted, but this time His call would require even more faith and trust in God than it had then. I cried over and over, "Lord, I can't," besides my lack of education and the lack of knowledge to even begin a book, I didn't want to relive the past with all the pain and heartache I had suffered through those hard times. I rebelled and felt sorry for myself believing that the Lord wouldn't put me through such heartache and despair again. I felt so alone, as if Jesus had thrown me to the wolves into a even stranger world than the prison which I knew nothing about. At least there, I had Ted and his love, but this time I would have only the Holy Spirit to guide the things I wrote.

I cried out, "Oh, God, my family will suffer from this because they only know bits and pieces that happened during my life with Jacob. They will think that I'm just striking out at their Daddy and he's not here to defend himself. It just doesn't feel like it's right for me to do this either, Father, because what family wants their dirty linen strung out for all the world to see and wag their heads in disbelief. You are asking me to lay my pride aside to do something that seems more than I can bear. How much more can I bear, as You require more and more sacrifices from me? This time I know I'll surely die because I can't believe that I can possibly bear the terrible strain, but I know I have to surrender in time just as I did when You sent me to Ted, but please, Father, not yet, at least not until I'm better prepared. Oh, please let me go, Jesus, what possible good can come from all this heartache and misery from my life of poverty and shame."

One day as I walked through one of the major department stores at Jasper and saw books of every description stacked along the aisles, I almost broke down in tears. My heart ached terribly and I felt ill wondering why the Lord wanted me to write a book to be added to a display such as this. `Don't You see, Father, if I write like You want me to, the book will just get placed on a shelf and no one will be interested in it. Why would You put me through that?' I continually complained. I walked to the car with a heavy heart and drove to Isabella's house to visit with her that day. When I got there she was gone, but I knew she would return shortly since she was expecting me so I went outside and sat on the carport. My heart ached as I looked up at the white fluffy clouds drifting by. They looked so peaceful as I scanned the heavens in search of my Lord, as if I could suddenly see His sweet face again.

"Jesus, my Savior, I know You are up there somewhere. Please have mercy on me and heal my broken spirit. I don't understand the course You are leading me on or why all this heartache is mine to suffer," then Jesus whispered, `Go inside and get the Word of God and you will find the answer there."

I hurried into the house and got Isabella's Bible and went back outside. As I held the Word of God lovingly, I prayed that He would bless His Word. Then I opened the Bible gently and looked down at the scripture. Tears started falling as I could see Jesus again in the vision as I read in the Song of Solomon, Chapter 2:1, in the King James version, "I Am the Rose of Sharon, and the lily of the valleys." I knew Jesus was the bright and morning star also, and God gave me peace like I had never experienced before. Still I resisted the Lord until July of 1995. Even after I almost died with an infection that landed me in the hospital and I lost a lot of work because of all my pure stubbornness. The time came, however, that I tossed and turned many sleepless nights unable to find rest or peace. I would talk to Ted about it, but he wasn't much help. He would tell me that he felt certain the Lord had called me to write and I would change the subject immediately. "We both know God brought us together for a greater purpose than just to bring two people together who had loved each other for years," he would say.

One night after tossing all night long without sleep, I sat on the edge of my bed that morning and promised the Lord that I would write for Jesus' sake. I had been so miserable and now I became very frightened because I had no idea of how to begin such a work. Many times I would cry out as I had in the vision, "Oh, God, my Father, I'm not capable of writing correctly with so little education. When I read what I've written, it sounds so immature, and when I try to correct it, it only gets worse. I feel so much like Moses did when You sent him on a mission and then You sent Aaron to help him. I need help too, Father." The Lord heard my cry and sent Mona Cook to help me in this work. She has been a soul sister to me and she has met all of the requirements the Lord needed. Throughout this ministry, Mona found something which had been missing in her life as the Holy Spirit entered her life in such a way that this work became as important to her as it had been to me. We worked side by side as the Lord dealt with us both to the point of her sharing my pain as I had done all those years. Mona and I both realized that this task would be difficult, but, Glory to God, we know it is all for Jesus' sake. May God bless everyone who reads this story with an open heart and mind.

CHAPTER 13

QUEST FOR HAPPINESS

I couldn't escape the heartache from the past no matter how much I tried. One of the reasons why I couldn't was because Ted was a part of the past. Somewhere buried deep in my heart lay the memories of my love for him which the Holy Spirit had kept in reserve until Jacob died and was revealed in God's own time. Without Ted, God's plan wouldn't have come about. No other man could take his place and even though he was in prison, this was included in God's plan too. When Satan takes full control of someone's life, then that person has no control over what he does. This is what happened when Ted committed such a terrible crime. Satan was probably so happy because he thought this would make Ted unfit for God's service, especially someone who is locked away in prison. Satan didn't know that God can use anyone, even the most vile person on earth, because when Jesus saves that person's soul it doesn't matter what he has done because Jesus forgives you of your sins. He didn't seem to realize that he actually placed Ted in a field of lost souls so that he would find Christ himself and begin a ministry for Christ Jesus' sake.

At the same time that Ted was placed in confinement, old Satan threw me into a prison too, and my prison was a truck.

Now, as I begin the writing which God has placed on my heart, I must go back in time, back to the hopelessness, poverty and pain, but Jesus was always there helping me to bear all my suffering.

I met Jacob Quinn in 1949. He was 17 and I was 16 years old. We were just two kids really, but I had a six month old son by a previous marriage which had failed miserably. Even at 17, Jacob was a strong man with strong muscles from manual labor. He loved my son, Wayne, and that influenced me most of all, I'm sure. Eventually, we married on May 31, 1949 at a small church in south Texas where his parents, Sid and Kate lived.

Jacob was the oldest of four children. Carol, his only sister was 15 years old. He had two younger brothers, Ted and Luke. Ted was 9 and Luke was 4.

I was the oldest of six children and my parent's names were Johnny and Emily Ray. I had four sisters and one brother, Joshua. My sister's names were Sandra, Ellen, Brittany and Heather. We grew up at Cleveland, Texas, about 45 miles north of Houston. Kids got married young in those days and we thought very little about it. We weren't old enough to raise a family, but we were blessed with a baby girl, Joyce, who was born on our first wedding anniversary. We didn't think much about dragging our small family from pillar to post, moving at the blink of an eye if the idea occurred to Jacob.

We were living in a small two-room house just down the lane from my parent's house when Mark was born on August 11, 1952. Mark was fourteen months old when Timothy was born. When I was pregnant with Timothy the doctor planned to tie my tubes so I wouldn't have more children, but he was born early and it didn't happen. Everything possible went wrong and our baby died. We went through a very trying experience as Jacob made the funeral arrangements and I watched my family gathering from my hospital bed just across the street. I couldn't handle the loss of our baby and it wasn't long before I had to get help. Jacob was off on the truck, only God knows where and Daddy had to put me in the hospital for a good while. It was there that I found help from my doctor when he suggested that I take up a hobby or something apart from my daily routine. I knew he was giving me sound advice and I wasn't willing to give up on life even though our baby had died. Jacob found a way of escape from our problems by working for a truck line that sent him away from home for several weeks at a time. I didn't want to escape from our problems; I wanted to get well so I could make a better life for my family so if a hobby would help, then I was willing to try.

Music came to mind instantly at the doctor's suggestion and a small ray of hope lit up in my heart, turning my sadness into joy. I had taken piano lessons for a few months when I was young, but Daddy made me stop, because I wasn't showing any progress and I had lost interest after a short time. I did remember the lines and spaces my teacher had drilled into my mind and I remembered her last words to me before I left. She said, "Destiny, you can learn to play the piano if you try. You know the roots of music and the things I've taught you are planted in your mind, so if you should decide to try again just remember that you can." With renewed hope in my heart, I went to work on music when I got home from the hospital. Mamma had a piano at her house and I walked down the lane to her house everyday and she watched after the children while the Lord and I sat together on the piano stool as He taught me how He wanted me to play. Music filled my life and the poverty conditions that we endured didn't get me down anymore. God placed a song in my heart as I cooked our meals on the little iron cook stove and washed baby diapers by hand. I wasn't saved at the time, but I knew that Christ was with me, teaching me a beautiful way of life which He would use for His glory. Our lives didn't change much until we built the little tar paper shack. One day Daddy told Jacob that he could pick out a place to build us a house anywhere on the 365 acres of land that he owned. We were excited about the opportunity to have our very own home. Of course, Jacob chose a spot quite a ways from the main road, never once considering the fact that it would be hard to get electricity. He wanted to build our house in a secluded area, but I didn't realize at the time why.

One cold morning in February 1955, as I stood by an open fire, Jacob and Daddy laid the foundation for our house. The kids ran and played, not noticing the cold north wind and neither did I, because we were happy. We were going to have a home and it would have three rooms instead of just two which we were used to. We didn't have enough money to buy the windows, so Jacob tacked tar paper over the openings until we could afford them and we moved into the little tar paper shack which Jacob built.

The wind blew through the cracks in the floor and blew my dress up. The wooden floor felt warm to my bare feet though. I knew it would be a while before we could afford to cover the floor with linoleum. I took cardboard and tacked it over the cracks on the walls to make the house warmer. Pam, my sister-in-law and I pieced quilt tops, using toe sacks, instead of the soft cotton filling that most folks use in their quilts, and we sewed them together on her sewing machine. They were warm anyway and no one knew the difference. Gradually, our family found comfort and warmth in the little tar paper shack and we were very happy. It was pitch black at night with the tarpaper tacked down. One night Jacob scared me half to death. I heard something scratching near my bed and reached out for him, but he wasn't there. I froze in fear, unable to speak or move. Finally, I called out to him in a shaky voice, and he mumbled, "I'm trying to find the window." He'd been drinking earlier in the evening and I was relieved that everything was all right, so I laughed and rolled over and went back to sleep.

We had our ups and downs like most young couples I knew, but they weren't so serious back then. In time, however, it got tougher and we kept having children which we couldn't afford. Jacob wanted another girl. He said that Joyce had told him she wanted a baby sister. I became pregnant again in 1956 and Jacob beamed with happiness. It seemed as if our life was getting better. He worked on a steady job driving a truck. He was home with us at night then and helped with all the chores, especially keeping plenty of wood for the tin heater and the little iron cook stove.

During these times, Jacob dug a well, making the curb out of the lumber they cut at Daddy's sawmill. The well was such a from blessing for me because I didn't have to carry buckets of water from the gully to wash our clothes with anymore. We didn't have the modern conveniences that most folks enjoyed, but I was grateful to God for what we did have.

Our hard times didn't really begin until Christ came into my life. When God saved me from my sins, He filled my life with the greatest joy I'd ever known. Jacob and I had attended church when it was convenient, but we weren't faithful. My parents had brought me up in the New Salem Missionary Baptist Church. I was baptized when I was a small child, but I hadn't truly received Jesus as my Savior or His pardon for my sins, until the Holy Spirit made me realize that I was lost that Sunday morning.

Jacob went to church with us that morning. The small church was filled to capacity so we had to sit on the back pew. I was in one of those self sanctified moods as I watched all the hypocrites around me, especially my brother-in-law who sat with my sister on a pew in front of us. I had such a haughty attitude when our pastor called for an invitation. I thought, `I know that man must have the longest finger in the world and he is pointing it right in my direction. Why is he doing that when he must know that I'm a good Christian? He has to be the bravest man on earth to stand there so boldly and point his finger toward the crowd as though he were so righteous that he could bring judgement down on all of us if we didn't make a decision right now.' "Make your election sure," the preacher stated firmly, as his voice boomed threateningly throughout the little church house.

I shrugged my shoulders when my sister ran down the isle crying, thinking, `Well, I'll bet she's going to rededicate her life again like she does every Sunday morning. I'll bet she does it to impress her husband, but he just stands there clinging to the back of the bench in front of him until his knuckles turn white. Why are you being so stubborn?' I thought angrily.

Suddenly, it was as if I could see the fires of hell as the Holy Spirit spoke to me saying, "You're not any better off than he is." I broke down and asked God to forgive me of my sins as I ran down the isle and joined my sister, who had also been saved that day. We held each other while tears of joy streamed down our cheeks. What a glorious Lord's day it was!

Many others were saved during those days when Brother Fuller pastored the church. Some were like my sister and I who had been baptized when they were young, but they had never experienced the new birth. I was six months pregnant when I was baptized and a new life began for me.

On Thanksgiving day, November 29, 1956, the family gathered at Mamma's house to celebrate the holiday. A big cold front blew in while we were eating supper and as soon as we cleaned up the kitchen we went home. My labor started when I went to bed and Jacob rushed me to the hospital and the doctor performed a Cesarean section immediately. We didn't get the little girl, but we were blessed with a beautiful baby boy whom we named Sam. Jacob carried us home seven days later and his mother came and helped us out for a few days. This was the happiest time in all of our marriage and the future looked so bright and promising.

It wasn't very long until I became pregnant again and I started having problems right away. Since I had so many problems my doctor sent me to a Specialist in Houston in hopes that our baby would have a better chance to live and be healthy. I needed corrective surgery, but it would have to wait until a later date. My labor started early this time too and the doctor did a Cesarean on me again. We were so happy when the doctor said, "It's a girl!" She was born on February 19, 1958 and we named her Isabella. Joyce was so happy, she finally had a baby sister and she spoiled her terribly when we carried her home nine days later.

Jacob became discouraged as our family grew and he changed jobs a lot. We were doing the best we could, but the cares of this world became harder on both of us. It didn't help our situation when the doctor told me that I needed corrective surgery as soon as possible, but I was already pregnant again and it would have to wait until our baby was born.

I was confined to bed during most of this pregnancy and my parents carried me to their house to live so they could take care of me and also see after the children. The strain was awful on everyone and I cried a lot, because I had placed such a burden on my parents.

I told my family doctor that I wanted him to take my case, because I didn't want to be sent to a strange doctor this time. He set the date to perform the Cesarean and he called in another doctor to help him with the procedure.

Jacob admitted me into the hospital and I had a Cesarean section and our small baby boy was born on July 16, 1959 and we named him Corbett Ray. When I started coming out from under the anesthetic, I could hear the doctor talking to Jacob. He said, "Jacob, Destiny may have a year to live, but I can't even promise you that she will live that long if she doesn't have corrective surgery very soon. She won't have to worry about getting pregnant again though, because we tied her tubes to prevent that." The doctor hurried to my bedside when I turned my head toward him and I asked him if our baby was all right and he replied, "I'm afraid that your small son isn't going to make it, Destiny. If he survives now, he can't live more than a couple of years. If he lives that long he will be an invalid, Honey. I'm so sorry that I have to tell you all these things, but you have to know."

I cried helplessly, "I don't want to go home without our baby. I just can't bear to lose another child." I had known my doctor since I was a small child and he had been a friend of our family as well as our family physician. His voice trembled as he spoke, "Destiny, you have other children who need you terribly. Your battles have only begun, Honey. I can't emphasize enough how much you need corrective surgery without delay. If you don't, you won't live to bring up the other children. You must think about their welfare, Destiny."

Jacob looked so worn and weary as he sat in a chair in the corner of the room. He seemed so distant and far away while I sobbed and prayed. I knew the doctor was right so I placed our baby in God's loving hands. Corbett Ray only lived ten hours, then he died and Jacob made all the funeral arrangements for our son. He was buried next to his brother, Timothy, on July 17, 1959. I had the sweet assurance that I would see our baby's in heaven someday, and I could cuddle them in my arms, but Jacob was lost and even though he didn't say it, I believed that he was angry at God and blamed Him for all of our problems.

You would think that after all we'd been through together that Jacob and I would have reached out to each other. But we didn't seem to be able to communicate anymore. We had never communicated very well in the past and lately it had grown even worse. He went to work during the week when he had a job and then went to the bars on Saturday nights, sometimes waking up in jail on Sunday morning with a hangover. This pattern never seemed to vary much from the way we had always lived. He sought release from all his problems with whiskey and beer while I turned more and more to the Lord.

God's Word was the one true friend that never let me down. When Jacob wasn't home, I slept with the kids in their bedroom. I would place the oil lamp on a table by the bed and read God's Word to them until they fell asleep. I would read about the great men of faith in the Old Testament, such as Abraham and Moses, and I taught them about Jesus, and all He had suffered on the cross for our sins, which stirred up their interest and they asked questions far into the night.

Many times some of their friends would spend the night and they would get as excited as my kids did when they heard stories in the Bible that they hadn't heard before. Since we didn't have electricity there wasn't any other distractions, such as television or radio, and this was a new experience for them. My baby sister, Heather was saved during that time and she testified that through these teachings the Lord touched her heart.

Those were precious times that I'll never forget, sweet times of perfect peace and Jesus was always there protecting us. Those times helped me through all the heartaches and despair. At the very mention of God's name Jacob would get very upset, so we tried very hard to be careful and not say anything about God around him because of Jacob's outbursts of temper. The children and I lived in fear when Jacob was at home because we dare not upset him. Jacob resisted everything that was of God.

During this time, Jacob became very bitter against the church and that was when the great battle started. I wondered if he would deny me the one sweet beauty that I so looked forward to each week. I'm not really sure how Jacob felt because he wouldn't ever talk about it and I wondered if he knew himself. He seemed to have a need to completely control and dominate every move that we made.

The church meant so much to me and it was there that I found peace. On Sunday mornings, I went to a place where I could walk away from all the problems at home and serve God at the piano and hear our pastor bring a message from the Lord.

Finally, things came to a head one Sunday morning when Jacob made up his mind that one way or another he would stop me from going to church. He simply didn't like the idea of sharing his family with the Lord, especially his wife. He wasn't about to let God come first in my life and if he decided that he wanted me to stay at home with him, then I'd better do it or suffer the consequences. Ordinarily, I didn't defy Jacob in anything, but when I gave my heart to Christ He became my life and His need took priority over Jacob and everyone or anything.

That particular Sunday morning, Jacob ranted and raved. He was sick and tired of his wife being faithful to the church. He had worked hard all week and this was his day off and he simply wasn't going to stand for his wife and kids to go traipsing off to church and leave him there all alone. He wouldn't let us use the car to go to church anymore, so Daddy carried us. Jacob knew my parents would soon be by to pick us up, so he began using abusive language and threats to kill me if I went anyway.

Somehow I got the children and myself ready even though I trembled as Jacob stood over me cursing and defying God. My heart raced madly, but I told myself that my faith was being tried to see how much I trusted in the Lord for my life, which was laid at the cross when Jesus saved my soul. I must follow Jesus and be faithful to Him and He will preserve my life if it's His will. He would take care of this situation and all I had to do was obey Him and He would stand between me and Jacob's fury. Jacob stood in the doorway shouting abusive threats as he cursed me for going against his wishes, but we climbed into Daddy's car anyway. Mamma and Daddy didn't say anything because they were astonished to see Jacob behave in such a violent way. They knew that I was already hurting enough without them voicing any opinion and causing me further pain. I fought back tears of shame because my folks had been exposed to such vile behavior, as well as the children, who had been quiet through the entire ordeal, because they were afraid of their Daddy.

I was afraid too, and my hands trembled as I sat down on the piano stool and began playing the piano. Somehow I made it through the music and then sat on a pew with my children. The memory of Jacob's threats ran through my mind and I thought about the kids witnessing such horrible things. I prayed that God would hold us up through the terrible heartaches that my children and I had to suffer as long as Jacob rejected the Lord.

I couldn't hold back my tears when our pastor began his sermon. He didn't know about my problems so I knew the message was sent from God to give me strength and courage. The text he used was from Matthew 10:36-39. As he read the verses, tears streamed down my face because I loved Jesus more than anyone. Jesus stated that a man's foes would be in his own household. Then He said that if we love father or mother more than Him, we weren't worthy of Him. If we loved son or daughter more than Him, we weren't worthy of Him either. He that taketh not his cross and followeth Him is not worthy of Him as well. My heart broke and I sobbed as our pastor read this verse, "He that findeth his life shall lose it; and he that loseth his life for my sake shall find it." I had placed my life in my Father's hands that day, not knowing whether I would live or die when we got home and faced Jacob's anger, but I knew if I died I would find my life again in Christ Jesus. When I made the decision to follow Jesus no matter what the cost, I made a commitment to be faithful to His cause until death.

Daddy was afraid for us to go home, but I told him that I refused to run away from Jacob. Reluctantly, Daddy drove up to the house and we got out. When he drove away, I noticed that our car had a flat tire. `Well, I guess that stopped Jacob from leaving,' I thought. Everything was quiet and I noticed the front door was shut. I asked myself, `What if he's standing behind that door and he'll catch us off guard if we just walk into the house like we normally do?'

I held Isabella tightly as I walked up the steps and the other children followed closely behind. I took a deep breath as I took hold of the door knob and turned it ever so slowly and then opening the door back, I stared in amazement at the tough individual that had threatened to take my life. Instead the Lord had shown him that He was God and that I belonged to Him. If there was going to be any punishment handed out, then Jesus would be the one to do it and not Jacob through abuse and jealous rage. Even though I realized that he must be suffering terrible pain as he lay on the couch with his hands hanging over a large pan which caught the blood that dripped from his crushed hands. He wasn't cursing now, but I couldn't feel sorry for him. I was rejoicing in my soul knowing that God had delivered me from Jacob's cruel threatening hands. He lay quietly, as if he had been completely conquered by the Lord.

The kids rushed to him when they saw the blood. They cried, "Oh, Daddy, how did you get hurt like that?" They fussed over him, but I walked on by as if he weren't even there and set Isabella in her little highchair and started dinner as if nothing had happened. Later, when Jacob called me, I went to the living room. He said, "I fully intended to hurt you for going against me and I intended to go to that church to carry out my threats, but I had a flat on the car and the only spare I could use was on the steel trailer. When I jacked it up to take the tire off, the jack gave way and the trailer trapped my hands. I got it off finally with my head somehow."

Jacob was blinded to what God had done for us both that day because it could have been a lot different. I praised the Lord for delivering me out of Jacob's hands, but he never once thought about how God gave him the strength with his head and neck to get that heavy steel trailer off of his hands. He knew God had trapped him so he couldn't do any bodily harm to me. He never once said, `I'm sorry for what I said to you or for the terror I put you through.' When he did anything bad he would just pass it off as if it had never happened. He closed his mind and went on his selfish way without ever regarding God or anyone else.

A day later, one of his friends came by our house searching for his wife. She had run away in the woods to escape his threats because she had gone to church. "What should I do, Jacob? My wife has changed so much! All I hear when I get home is something about God or the church she goes to. She leaves me at home to fend for myself and goes on off to church in spite of my objections. When I made it clear that I wasn't going to put up with it, she ran away and now I can't find her."

Jacob squirmed in his chair and I could see he was uncomfortable barely raising his head. He said, "If your wife is living for God, you had better leave her alone. That's all I can tell you." Jacob didn't tell his friend about his experience recently, but I rejoiced just listening to them. Later, his friend accepted Christ and he and his wife went to church together. Our lives didn't change though. Jacob just became more cautious and devious. He began using other methods to get back at me. Jacob did fear God now so he didn't threaten me concerning the church, but he tried to break my spirit in many other ways while I tried to keep a smile on my face. He made life very rough for me by being careless about simple things such as not cutting wood for the winter.

Many times I gathered limbs that usually burned quickly. Most of the time, Jacob would burn it up before he went to work in the morning. Sometimes the house would be so cold when I got the kids up for school that I'd have to go into the woods and search for more limbs to get the house warm. Sometimes my sister-in-law, Pam, and I would go down in the woods and search for pine after a big rain. Both of us wore rubber flip-flops and wore dresses since a woman didn't wear pants in those days. When we walked through the water and mud, the flip-flops slapped mud up on our dresses. We laughed just like a couple of silly kids, though. Our objective was to get the rich pine and it was much easier to work the pine stumps loose after a big rain. Pam and I tried to make chores fun and we would laugh at everything.

One night, Jacob and I had an awful fight because he had promised to cut some wood when he got home from work. Before he went to work he told me, "You just stay with your Mamma today so the kids will be warm." I should have known he was lying to me, but I did as he told me to. If I had known the way things would turn out, I would have stayed at home and managed to gather the wood we needed. When Jacob came home that night, he had changed his mind. He had never intended to keep his promise to cut the wood and bring the kids home to a warm house. So when he got home, he was in a very foul mood and sleepy. When I reminded him of his promise, he began threatening to slap me. When we pulled into the driveway, he was still threatening. I felt like the whole world was falling in on me when he started out of the car on my side. `You had better get ready to stand on your feet and fight him,' I told myself.

Jacob made the mistake of thinking he had things under control, but when he stuck his head out on my side of the car, I let him have it with Isabella's glass baby bottle. The force of it sent his head back against the rim of the door and cut a gash on his temple. I was furious, completely out of control and ready to fight the biggest man who had decided he could abuse me again. He turned to the kids who were still waiting to get out of the car and said, "Stay in the car, we are going to leave and go to Mother's house." He bent over the seat and I was fighting mad. He was always threatening to leave, so I kicked him as hard as I could and he landed back up in the car. I leaned over the hood of the car with Isabella still in my arms and passed out. When I came to, I was still standing on my feet and ready to fight again. Jacob was so surprised that I had acted that way that he thought I was having a nervous breakdown and decided he had better get some help, so he sent the older kids to my parents' house.

The kids were afraid of the dark, but they ran all the way to Mamma's house. When they got there, they fell in the door crying and they all blurted their story out at the same time. Daddy asked, "Is your mother hurt?" "No, Grandpa, but Daddy is. Mamma hit him with a bottle and it cut a big gash on his head. They were fussing and Mamma got so mad she kicked him back up in the car when Daddy told her we were going to live at Grandma Quinn's house." Daddy asked, "Did Jacob hit your mother?" "No, Grandpa," Joyce replied. Daddy laughed then and he told the kids to go to bed that everything was going to be all right. Daddy got the kids settled in bed, then chuckling, he remarked, "Well, it's about time Destiny took up for herself," and then he went to bed too.

The next day at church everyone knew about the fight and teased me, looking at me to see if I had any bruises. I felt awful, but being meek hadn't changed Jacob's ways or the man that I so wanted to be proud of. I loved Jacob and was determined to live with him. At the time, it didn't seem as if anything I did helped, but when I look back, I realize now that it did. Jacob learned that God would stand between us when I was faithful to the Lord. He also found out that I could lose my temper and fight back.

I tried to keep peace for the children's sake and I took a lot because I didn't want them to see it if he decided to hit me in front of them. It was the only way I knew to protect them from violence. I really didn't want them to grow up thinking that it was all right to abuse others. I suppose it became a way of life for them though since many such encounters with Jacob didn't seem to bother them. They must have thought that every family lived the way we did. Many, many times it took only a little thing to set him off.

When he was at home, the tension would become almost unbearable.

CHAPTER 14

SACRIFICIAL LOVE

In the Spring of 1960, Jacob decided to go to Fort Worth and look for a job. I am sure that he could have found one nearer home, but he was just looking for any excuse to get away from us. His parents were living at Fort Worth then and his mother found him a job at a feed mill, so he packed his clothes and left us to fend for ourselves. He promised to send for us as soon as he got a paycheck. He also told us that he would look for an apartment. In the meantime he would send money home to feed the kids. My spirits lifted, hoping things would get better, but during the weeks ahead it was more like a bad dream. Weeks went by without a word from Jacob and we struggled to survive. I worked some at Daddy's sawmill and did ironing for Mamma. The church gave us groceries to help us. Still, I didn't hear anything from Jacob and I became more and more angry and hurt.

After several weeks went by, I went to Mamma's house and called Jacob's mother, not understanding why Jacob hadn't even bothered to call. She was irritated when she heard my voice. I could hear Jacob's voice laughing in the background. Mom said, "Jacob told me he had left you so why are you calling here?" I was petrified for a moment, then I exploded. "Put Jacob on the phone immediately," I shouted. I was furious because he was still laughing when she handed the receiver to him. When I got through with Jacob, he was ready to move us to Fort Worth. I'm sure he'd rather have lived a happy-go-lucky life without the responsibilities of a family, but I didn't intend to let him get away with it.

Daddy heard my explosive temper when I was talking to Jacob and he told me, "Destiny, I thought you had more pride than that. Are you going to force Jacob to move you, when it looks as if he wants to get rid of you?" I replied, "Well, Daddy, pride won't feed the kids. My health has broken down from child bearing and I didn't have these children all by myself!" I was really furious at Jacob and if he'd been there right then, I would have hit him with whatever I could have gotten my hands on. I would probably die soon so what did I have to lose. It didn't take Jacob long to find an apartment either. Mom couldn't believe he had just walked out on us without any reason. She seemed really disappointed at him for telling her such a bald faced lie. She wasn't as hurt and disappointed as I was, however. I needed him as much as the kids did, but he didn't seem to care about anybody but himself.

It was kind of exciting to move into an apartment. We had running water and other modern conveniences that we didn't have in the little tar paper shack. My hope for things to be at peace didn't last long though. I should have known Jacob wouldn't keep a job that would allow him to be at home at night. A week didn't pass before he left one morning and it was weeks before he showed up again. Mom came over every day accusing me of knowing where he was, saying we had probably had a big fight and I wasn't telling her. That simply wasn't true. I was as dumbfounded as she was. Surely Jacob could have picked up the phone and at least called his mother, but Jacob's thoughts were always just for himself. Mom reported him to the Missing Person's Bureau and the officer in charge said Jacob would probably show up soon. They were right, he did, with the excuse that he'd been working and he wanted to know what the fuss was all about. Jacob said, "Destiny, you should have known I was working. I went on a cattle truck when an opening suddenly became available." Mom ranted and raved, but he just ignored her. She cried because he was so selfish, but he didn't seem to care. Jacob always thought that everyone should be happy with whatever he wanted. Whether he came home drunk as a skunk or had spent the night in jail, it should be fine and not say anything about it. I really didn't know what to say so I kept my mouth shut just to keep peace. Now that he had a job and brought a little money home, we were supposed to be satisfied. Jacob was like that, but he had been brought up that way.

The first thing I noticed when I visited his parents for the first time was Jacob's sister, Carol, and his mother waiting on the men of the house hand and foot. In spite of the fact that the men were placed on a pedestal, Mom was still the dominating force in their house. She tried to dominate our life after we were married, but it didn't work. Jacob listened to her when he wanted to, but when her ideas didn't match his, he just ignored her. I tried to tell her some of the things Jacob had done, but she wouldn't believe me. She wouldn't believe that he could be like that, so I stopped telling her anything and she found it out for herself.

Spring was almost gone and I was getting weaker. I knew I didn't have very long to live if I didn't have surgery soon. Many times I would look out the kitchen window and cry out to God, "Father, I don't want to die and leave my children behind. No one will love them like I do. No one seems to be concerned or believe the doctor's report, but You know that it is true." When I told Mom she would just make light of it as if it didn't matter to her whether I lived or died. She would insist that she had been in far worse conditions than I was and she hadn't died. Jacob wouldn't even discuss it. He seems to think that by ignoring the problem, it would disappear. I felt so alone and I tried not to think about it. I didn't mention it to Jacob anymore. I knew then that he didn't care.

It must have been late in June when Jacob's brother, Ted came home from the Navy. I had regarded Ted as a boy all these years, but he was a man now. He had only been nine when I married Jacob and he had grown up with the kids. They would play cops and robbers just like other kids. Ted visited our home a lot and stayed for weeks. He always seemed happy when he visited us, even though we couldn't afford to buy many things to entertain our children, but they had a good time nevertheless.

I watched Ted grow into a teenager and didn't really notice the special attention he always gave me and I would just laugh it off, telling myself that he was just a silly kid. I ignored it when Ted brought several of his friends by our house to meet his pretty sister-in-law one day while we lived at Port Lavaca, Texas.

He was only sixteen then and had a great imagination, I decided. I didn't have time to worry about Ted since I had a large family to take care of. I hoped that strange attraction he'd had for me when he was a teenager was over and I could relax when he was around. Jacob was very proud of his younger brother who was a man now. Ted came to our house when he got home. Jacob listened excitedly when Ted told him some of his exciting experiences in the Navy. Ted had been all over the Pacific and he had a lot of interesting stories to tell. Ted adored Jacob and always regarded him as a John Wayne type of man and there was no doubt in my mind that Ted loved Jacob and Ted loved me too.

Jacob wasn't home very much though. Most of the time he would tell me to pack his suitcase while he took a bath and he'd leave us again. There were many times that he was in such a hurry to leave that he wouldn't stay long enough to sit down and share a meal with us. I would hold back the tears when he would insist that he just had to go and me crying my heart out and begging him to find a job that wouldn't take him so far away from home. My heart ached when Jacob would kiss me goodbye and rush out the door. "I need you Jacob," I cried, "Please, spare some time for us." He would ignore me, never responding to my cry. Ted became important to me as time went by. He never failed to come by the house every day, even for a little while. The kids would watch for Ted every day and when they would see him coming, they would run up the sidewalk to meet him. They would chatter away as they walked toward the house and Ted became very important to them also. Ted seemed quite content and happy just to be with the kids and myself. I wondered from time to time why he had rather be with us than with his friends, especially in the evenings. He enjoyed the old movies on television and I watched some of them with him, but I was very busy taking care of five children.

It seemed as if I had always known there were special feelings between us, but I just closed my eyes to the truth. I told myself that it was just a childhood crush, but Ted should have been over it by then. After all he was a grown man and besides, who in the world would want a woman like myself with five kids hanging on her dress tail constantly needing attention? Isabella and Sam were still in diapers and it seemed as if I didn't have time for anyone else, not even for myself. With so little time for myself, I looked terrible with stringy hair and a cheap cotton dress. `What could Ted possibly find so appealing about me,' I would ask myself? It was very hard for me to understand even though I tried. Ted didn't care what I looked like on the outside at all. He would disregard my feeling so tired after a long day which often left me moody and irritable. Actually I needed him more than I wanted to believe, but I never tried to impress Ted. In fact, I figured my stringy hair and foul moods would only drive him away, but he still came to the house with a sweet smile and I would invite him in. One night Ted was watching television and it was late. The kids were in bed, but I was straightening up the house before I went to bed myself. Ted said, "Destiny, come here a minute." I walked near the couch where he was sitting and Ted reached out for my hand and pulled me down into his lap. He held me gently in his arms and kissed me tenderly. It took me by surprise, but I didn't resist him. I really needed affection from anyone who truly cared and I knew that Ted was the only one who really loved me through those years, even though he was younger than I was. In spite of our age difference, he loved me anyway. Ted had never tried to hide how he felt about me, but I refused to admit it to myself or to him that I loved him. Now I realized that I couldn't ignore it anymore, but I didn't want to bring this shame on my family or on my Lord. Someone had to be strong in this situation and I realized that he would never be where I was concerned. I pushed him back as I rose to my feet, muttering tearfully, "Ted, this is wrong." I was really shaken by what had happened, but the truth was out in the open now and I didn't know what to do. Ted went home then, but I knew in my heart that it wasn't over.

I needed Ted more than he knew, but I could die at anytime and I didn't want to meet Jesus with this sin on my conscience. "Father, I don't understand why this has happened. No matter how Ted and I feel about each other we are bound to suffer. I know Jacob doesn't love me and he treats me like an old worn out shoe that he can kick around, but he is still my husband and the father of our children. I know that I love You, but I feel so forsaken and alone and only Ted seems to care about me anymore. Please help us through these trying times when I'm too weak to fight anymore. I need You most of all, my God," I cried.

It was around the tenth of July when Mom came to my house. I knew she was mad when she slammed the car door and stormed in the front door. She was furious as she glared at me and then she said, "Destiny, your Daddy called today. He said that your doctor had called him and asked about you. He asked if you had made any arrangements to have the corrective surgery that you needed. Your Daddy told him that you hadn't and the doctor warned him again that you could die anytime without any warning. Destiny, I didn't know how seriously ill you were. I got real mad at your Daddy when he started threatening Jacob. He said if he didn't get help for you without delay that he was going to take things out of Jacob's hands. If he fooled around and let you die, he would wish he'd never been born. I called the office where Jacob works and they are bringing him back to Fort Worth. I've never heard your Daddy threaten anyone before, but he means business, Destiny."

Jacob came home reluctantly and wanted to get tough, but Mom told him that he should take me to a Specialist for an examination before he made a fool of himself. One of Jacob's friends recommended a Specialist who had performed extensive surgery on his wife, so Jacob called the clinic and they set up an appointment for me to see the doctor. After examining me, the doctor told us that I needed surgery right away. Jacob would have time for one more short trip so he left and I started making preparations to enter the hospital. Mamma and my sister, Heather, volunteered to come and take care of the children for a few days and I was very excited about seeing my mother and sister again. That alone lifted my spirits.

I was alone on the morning I was to be admitted. I hadn't heard Ted come in so I was quite surprised when I came out of the bathroom after my bath and walked straight into his arms. My hair was wet and I was partially dressed, but nothing seemed to matter. He just held me gently in his arms and it was as if this was where I was meant to be. He just held me and kissed me tenderly and I felt safe in his arms. A sweet peace swept over me and Ted must have felt it too. We both seemed to know this may very well be the last time we would be able to hold each other like this so I just melted into his embrace and he whispered softly, "You're so sweet, Destiny." For a moment, any guilt I had washed away and Ted kissed me and I knew then that I would always love him forever.

Reality returned suddenly when the kids came rushing through the door. Mamma and Heather came shortly and then Jacob came home too and took me to the hospital. I was thankful that the Lord had answered my prayer and I was finally getting help. Of course, Jacob took charge of everything. I had the feeling that he just wanted to get this thing over with so he could be back on the road again. Even though my life had been in a turmoil lately, God gave me peace before they carried me to surgery and I wasn't afraid. I knew that I could die on the operating table, but I had placed my life in God's very capable and powerful hands. The next thing I knew, Jacob was standing over me and I was in my room. He looked tired and I knew that he was glad that I was going to be all right. `This ordeal has interrupted our lives, but only for a short while, Jacob,' I thought as he sat down in a chair beside my bed. Everything was hazy and disoriented, but I looked around for Ted, certain that he would be nearby. He sat in a chair near the foot of my bed. He smiled and said, "How are you feeling, Destiny?" I smiled back and replied, "I'm doing all right." Then I drifted off to sleep again.

I'm not sure what day it was when Jacob told me, "Destiny, you seem to be doing all right, so I'll go back to work. Ted will see after you while I'm gone and Mother will be in and out too." "It's all right, Jacob," I said, "I'll be fine." He bent over and kissed me goodbye and walked away. I fought back tears as I listened to Jacob's footsteps as he walked down the hall.

It was very nice to wake up from a nap and see Ted waiting patiently. I couldn't understand why this handsome young man with the whole world at his fingertips who could have any girl he wanted, I guess, but he chose to sit by the bed of a woman that he couldn't have no matter how much he wanted her. `Surely, Father, Ted must know how hopeless a young man's dreams can be when he stubbornly won't let go and only allows his heart to control his emotions. I love him, Father, because he loves me, even though he hasn't told me so, but when you truly love each other you don't have to say the words.' On my last day in the hospital, a nurse came into the room and told Ted that she needed to weigh me. The scales were located quite a distance away, and Ted told her, "I'll walk with Destiny down the hall to the scales and get her weight for you." She told him it would be all right, but walk slowly because she is still very weak.

Ted took me by the hand and gently helped me to my feet, then just like two lovers; we strolled slowly down the hallway hand in hand, which was our first time to walk together. His hand was soft in mine as he held it tenderly. Although it wasn't very far to the scales, I found myself wishing our walk together would last forever. On the way we met some of Ted's friends. One of them asked Ted who I was and he replied proudly, "This is my wife, Destiny." The young man said, "It's nice to meet you, Mrs. Quinn." I looked up at Ted in surprise and I thought, `Why did he do that when he knows I'm not his wife.' I didn't say anything, but I knew in my heart that Ted was pretending too. I felt loved and wanted and was happier than I'd ever been. I'd never really known the true beauty of love or how very sweet it could be until then.

Sharp reality brought us back into the real world when we saw Mom standing at the end of the hall watching us. I also knew by the look on her face that she knew we loved each other, but how could we hide something so wonderful? I was sure that she would tell Jacob about her suspicions when he came home and he would break up this love affair very quickly. I could understand how she felt having her daughter-in-law mixed up with both of her sons. I knew that she would blame me for everything that had happened too. Mom took me to her house when I left the hospital. Lord, I just wanted to go to my apartment. She had her suspicions about Ted and I and the picture in her mind was ugly and distorted. She became a tyrant and Ted stayed away from home, except to sleep and bathe and then he would disappear. When Jacob came in from his trip, Mom stormed and screamed at him, "I don't want Destiny in my house. She's just no good and I don't want to be around her!"

She was determined to make my life a living hell and blamed everything on me. Mom and Dad took Jacob to the side and filled his head with wicked ideas of how to force me to confess that I had been sleeping with Ted. Dad told him that I would probably lie out of it and he would have to trick me into telling the truth. Although, I don't know what they thought they would accomplish if I had been the worst harlot on the face of the earth and I confessed it to Jacob. They knew Jacob had driven me into Ted's arms. They also knew they wouldn't be able to stop Ted from seeing me. He was a grown man and they couldn't just send him to bed without his supper to punish him. They could warn him and even threaten him to stay away from me, but Ted had a mind of his own, and no one could stop him, but me.

I'll never forget my first night back at the apartment. Jacob held me in a grip with a knife to my throat. He shouted, "Tell me the truth, or I'll cut your throat." I was calm for some reason as if I didn't care. I'd rather die than to live in the living hell that Jacob put me through. Jacob had not been a saint, but he never thought anything about that, or the fact that if he had treated me like a wife, then Ted couldn't have come between us.

All Jacob thought about was that his pride had been hurt. He wanted me to beg for my life, but I wouldn't. I said, "Jacob, you don't have to threaten me. If you had asked, I would have told you the truth. Ted and I are not having a cheap love affair. Ted showed me the affection that I needed, which you wouldn't give. I do love the kids and I have loved you too. I know you'll punish me for what has happened, but I haven't been as bad as you think, whether you believe or not."

Jacob ranted on and on, threatening to kill Ted if he ever came over to our house again. "I'll find out if you let him in, Destiny, and I'll make you sorry if you think you can sneak around and I won't find out." He didn't stick around to see if I was being faithful. He packed his suitcase and left on another trip.

My heart was torn apart every night, because Ted came night after night begging me to let him in. He would knock on the door time and time again, pleading, "Please open the door and let me in. Oh please, Destiny, I want to see you and the kids." It broke my heart, but I was so afraid. I was sure that if I let him in Jacob would find out and the kids wouldn't lie if he asked them if Ted had been there. It was tearing me apart and I cried silently to the Lord, "Oh,

Father, if only I could see him just one more time and feel his arms around me." But in my mind I could see him being beaten and even worse, so I had to tell him, "Please Ted, I can't open the door for you. Jacob has threatened to kill us both and he may be hiding in the bushes and watching to see what we'll do."

I was so afraid and I knew that Mom had my neighbors spying on us just across the street. Ted was persistent and he wouldn't leave. The kids wanted to let Ted come in, but they remembered Jacob's threats that he would whip them if they did, so they were quiet. Ted didn't give up though; he walked around the house and knocked on my window pleading with me to let him in. My heart ached terribly, but I asked him to please forget about me and go home. Eventually, Ted would walk away and I would cry until I would fall asleep from exhaustion.

Night after night he came and begged me to listen to him, but I sent him away. When Ted would give up and leave, I could still hear his voice calling out to me and I would cry until my pillow was wet with tears. I knew that Ted was hurting as bad as I was and I felt so sorry that I was the one who was hurting him most of all. Mom and Dad threatened Ted and told him to stay away from me, but they couldn't understand that Ted really did love me. They thought Ted was having some sort of fantasy about me that would pass if they could keep us apart. They didn't realize that Ted had loved me for many years, even though I was his brother's wife.

In spite of how we felt about each other, I had to consider the children first. Ted was young and in time he would meet a beautiful girl, start his own family and would forget me. My greatest fear was that someday he would hate me for what had happened and may regret that he had ever known me. I was so torn apart as crazy thoughts ran through my mind, but I had to pull myself together somehow and do the right thing.

It wasn't long until Jacob decided to move back to the little tar paper shack at Cleveland. Before we moved, Dad came over to our house. He told the kids goodbye and we sat down and talked about the situation. I started to cry, because my heart was broken. I didn't need a lecture about the terrible things I had done to hurt his family or how unfit I was now to raise the kids.

Dad said gently, "Destiny, I do understand how you feel and I know you have been terribly hurt. I know the way Jacob has mistreated you over the years. I've seen him come in after being gone for weeks and not even kiss you hello. He's treated you like a doormat and like a servant. I knew if he kept it up, one day a man would come along and see how lovely you are and would sweep you off your feet, but I didn't know that man would be Ted. Jacob doesn't deserve a wife like you, but Honey, you must be strong for our family's sake. I don't say that what you and Ted have done is right or wrong, but I'm caught in the middle. I love you and both of my sons. When you move back to Cleveland, Ted will get over his feelings about you. He is still very young and he doesn't know what love really is all about." Dad held me in his arms while I cried my heart out, then we said our good-byes and he left.

Jacob had only one thought in mind and that was to make me suffer for my crime. When we moved back home he couldn't wait to tell my folks what a terrible tramp I'd been, and he made me feel so small and ashamed. I felt dirty and he reveled in my misery. Every time he found an opening, he reminded me that I was a fallen woman. It was as if he had thought of me in that respect for a long time and because of Ted he was convinced of it now. He was bitter because his mother had told him all these years that I wasn't any good and she was right. He hated me, but he wouldn't let me go. He would keep me around so he could punish me for wounding his pride.

First, Jacob told my parents what Ted and I did. He made it all sound so terrible and I felt such shame, not so much for what Ted and I had done, but for the way Jacob presented everything. He got a surprise when he accused me to my parents, however, because Daddy started laughing at him. Jacob couldn't believe it and his mouth hung open when Daddy looked him in the eye and said, "Well, Jacob, you deserve what you got. I don't know how Destiny has lived with you this long. You'd better thank God that she didn't run off with Ted, then you would have five kids to raise all by yourself. You'd better be glad that it was your brother too, or your story could have been a lot different."

Mamma had been sitting quietly while Daddy was speaking. When he finished she said, "Jacob, Ted has loved Destiny all these years. Everyone knew it because you could feel it when they were together, even though they didn't seem to know it themselves. If you adored Destiny the way that Ted has, then you wouldn't be treating her with the disrespect that you are doing right now." Jacob was even more furious and he stalked out of the house. I was so happy that my parents stood up for me at a crucial time when I felt so unloved and unhappy.

Jesus became my all in all during those days. He was my peace and comfort. My folks knew the suffering that I had been going through and they carried me to church in spite of Jacob's objections. He would grit his teeth when I was getting the kids dressed for church. He was afraid to hurt me though, since the Lord had brought him down by cutting his hands up with a steel trailer. Jacob had gotten away with a lot when we lived at Fort Worth, but the church was the Lord's business and that was a different story, also I had been out of the Lord's will then. I realized the protecting hand of God had been on me all of the time. If I would serve Him, He would fight my battles and stand between Satan and me.

CHAPTER 15

GOD'S ENDLESS MERCY

The Lord was the Light of my life and the church meant so much to me. The Lord was my peace and the church was a haven of rest from the bitter hatred and revenge Jacob took out on me.

Jacob was cutting logs for Daddy when God intervened again. Abuse can take place for a while and if the one abused has all of their trust in God, He will bring judgement down in His own time. One day when they were cutting trees near a narrow blacktop, one large tree fell across the road. My brother slowed the traffic down so Jacob could cut it up and they could clear the road. The power saw was running wide open and it made a loud noise. Jacob didn't hear the approaching car and apparently the driver had her attention on her neighbor's yard. My brother tried to flag her down, but she was evidently so absorbed with what she looking at that she didn't see him or hear the roaring sound of the power saw. Suddenly she found herself crashing through tree limbs and pine straw and she ran her car over Jacob, then upon the realization that she had run him down she became so terrified that she put her car in reverse and then backed over him. Everything became chaotic as Daddy and my brother got an ambulance to the scene and when the ambulance got there they carried Jacob to the hospital at Cleveland. I was at Mamma's house when a car drove in and let Jacob out. We were terrified when Jacob stumbled in the door and sat down on the couch. He was vomiting up blood and holding his head and we all knew something terrible had happened to him. He was in considerable pain and his speech was incoherent as I asked him what had happened. All that he would mumble was, "Go and get me some clean clothes." Pam and I ran all the way to our house, which was quite a distance, terrified and wondering what had happened to Jacob. Pam exclaimed, "Destiny, Jacob is so bloody and skinned up he looks like he has been in a bad car wreck. I wonder where Joshua and your Dad are? They were all together when they left this morning." "Maybe Jacob can tell us when we get back, Pam. I just wish that we had a car. I know it must be a mile to Mamma's and we're already out of breath," I replied. I gathered a suit of clothes for Jacob and we ran back to Mamma's as fast as our legs could carry us. When we got back, Jacob cried out in pain while we cleaned him up and helped him get fresh clothes on. He was in a terrible condition, but we finally learned that Joshua and Daddy were all right. "He didn't know where they were," he said. The hospital called right away and the nurse told me to bring him back to the hospital immediately. He was hurt pretty bad, but he was so concerned about his beat up clothes that he slipped out of the hospital and everyone was looking for him. Daddy and Joshua had been waiting for Jacob in the lobby while he was getting his X-rays and he was so disoriented that he walked out another door and asked a friend to drive him home so he could get cleaned up.

A neighbor carried us to the hospital and the nurses put him to bed. Then the doctor came and told us an ambulance was coming to carry him to Houston. The X-rays revealed that he had a seven inch skull fracture and Jacob would need specialized care. The doctor told me that I could go with Jacob in the ambulance and Pam said, "Destiny, I'll go with you." I was grateful that she did, because I was so afraid and nervous. The rain was pouring down when they loaded Jacob in the ambulance. The driver failed to latch the stretcher securely and our nightmare began. It was an old type ambulance and next to impossible to get the driver's attention. When I tried, Jacob would start raving and cursing, telling me to leave the driver alone. The stretcher was completely out of control as it rolled here and there and I don't know what I would have done if Pam had not been there to help.

It stormed all of the way to the Methodist Hospital and Pam and I gave completely out trying to keep Jacob, stretcher and all from rolling out of the ambulance and dumping him out on the highway. If Jacob hadn't been hurt, I would have let him go just to see where that stretcher would wind up, because I was sick and tired of his filthy language. It was a nightmare and when we finally backed up to the Emergency Room Entrance, Pam and I both breathed a deep sigh of relief.

Sometimes it is best not knowing much about medicine and I didn't realize how serious Jacob's condition was. The doctors were constantly checking his eyes with a pin light. They told me that Jacob didn't have any broken bones and except for the skull fracture and lacerations all over his body, he was in a pretty good shape and he was a lucky man. It was really a miracle that he hadn't been hurt worse. God was good to us and Jacob was tough and I never once thought that he wouldn't get well.

Through the days ahead, I sat by his bed, not leaving him because he would get beside himself if I even went to the cafeteria. I usually dozed in a straight chair until one kind nurse brought an old wooden wheelchair for me to rest in which was a little better. Jacob improved day by day from his terrible accident. One night a nurse took me to a room that had an empty bed. She told me I could rest there until six o'clock. Since I was completely exhausted, I slept like a baby and thanked the kind nurses and the good Lord for all their kindnesses toward me.

God's tender love and care always amazes me. He not only healed Jacob; He also blessed us through the church. They gave us a love offering and some of the church members offered to sit up with Jacob while I went home to get some rest. However, Jacob got so upset if I left the room that I didn't go, so Pam brought fresh clothes to the hospital and I managed all right during those times. We witnessed the loving care of God again before we left the hospital. I knew that Jacob's bill would be expensive and I didn't know how we would be able to pay it. When the doctor came in and told Jacob that he could go home that morning, I asked him how much money we would need to pay our bill. He told me some small figure, which I don't remember, but I was relieved and happy because we didn't have any money and we'd have to borrow the money from Daddy to pay our bill when he came to carry us home.

Daddy's face turned red when I told him how much our bill was. He looked puzzled, but he didn't say anything. I'm sure he thought that I had misunderstood. On our way out, I walked up to the nurses' station and asked to see the bookkeeper. When I told her the amount the doctor had said we owed, she became very agitated and began arguing with me. Jacob's doctor was sitting a few feet away and he got up and walked over to the bookkeeper. He told her, "That is the amount that I quoted to her." Daddy was embarrassed, not believing what he had heard, but he took the money out of his billfold and handed it to the bookkeeper and she took the money reluctantly. She just couldn't seem to understand that God was able to touch the heart of anyone like that. God had miraculously took care of us again and I praised Him for all He had done.

The little tarpaper shack really looked good as we pulled into the driveway. It was a wonderful feeling to have all of our family together again. The kids ran into our arms and they chattered away as we went into the house. Even though we hadn't been gone very long, it seemed like we had been gone for such a long time.

I couldn't understand how Jacob could ignore the mercy God had shown toward him. He had almost been killed, but he didn't give the glory to God for saving his life. His attitude improved a lot in the days ahead when he realized that I would work just as hard as he did to make enough money to buy food for the table. He began to see me in a different light as I peeled poles by his side. It was a very strenuous job for a weak woman like myself, who had just gone through major surgery only a few weeks ago. He stopped badgering me about Ted and for the first time in a very long time we had peace in our lives.

It's strange to me though, that every time something happened to Jacob, then Ted was also going through a bad situation. While Jacob was in the hospital, Ted was in the hospital at Fort Worth with a broken jaw from fighting. Jacob was disappointed when Mom didn't come to see him when he was in the hospital. She told me that she couldn't leave Ted and I was glad that she had stayed away. We tried to put the past behind us and we started going to church together and both our interests changed for the better, which was a step in the right direction, I decided hopefully. It wasn't long before we received the message that Ted was getting married and I felt a heavy burden being lifted from my heart and I could tell that Jacob was relieved too.

Jacob almost received Christ Jesus as his Savior one night at church. I'll never forget how our family were all lined up on the same pew, when he suddenly rose to his feet, almost knocking Mark down, who was leaning over the pew in front of him snoozing. Jacob ran up the aisle with tears streaming down his cheeks and took the pastor's hand. It took him by surprise and he stammered as he turned to face the congregation and tell us that Jacob had come asking for prayer. I was so disappointed when the preacher just stood there as if stunned and didn't know what to do. I was absolutely heartsick when he didn't kneel down and pray with Jacob and I felt terrible not knowing what to do. I felt such a sense of urgency to do something, but I seemed to be paralyzed as I waited for someone else to make a move. I was so hurt and ashamed for not speaking up and was so afraid Jacob would believe that no one cared for him or his soul. I was terrified at the thought that this opportunity might never come again, while hot tears began streaming down my face. "Oh, God, forgive me," I cried. "Please save Jacob before we leave the church tonight." But Jacob didn't accept Christ that night. If he did, he didn't let anyone know.

I had never seen Jacob happier than when Wayne started playing football on the `Pee Dinker' team. Wayne was so short and small and his uniforms so large that he got lost in them. Jacob would get so excited when Wayne made a touchdown. It was so funny to see him play because he was so small, but he was quick and when the defense thought they had him he would spurt out and run down the field as hard as his two short legs could carry him. Jacob thought he was the greatest football player in the world and you would think he was playing on a big college team to hear them talk.

He took an interest in the boys playing baseball too and he took such pride in his family those days that he just didn't seem like the same man I had married. I took an interest too and rooted for the home team, yelling and screaming until my throat would burn like fire. Finally, we were a complete family with the same interests that other families enjoy.

There were times, however, when Jacob would go off with his friends on Saturday night. I learned to live with it, but I didn't approve of it or learn to like it. One Saturday morning, Jacob was looking for an excuse to leave the house to meet his drinking buddies, so he asked the kids if they wanted to go to the movies. Of course they did. They were just too excited to heed my warning as they hurriedly dressed. "I know you're excited, but what will you do if your Daddy drops you off and he runs off with his friends? How will you get home if he pulls a stunt like that? He's been known to get drunk and get thrown in jail every Saturday night lately, in fact. I don't have a car to pick you up if you get stranded," I warned. They went anyway and didn't heed my warning.

I really became worried when darkness set in. I sat by the heater and kept a warm fire in case the kids would be cold when they got home. I thanked God that Sam and Isabella were too small to be influenced by their Daddy's foolishness. They were sleeping soundly, safe and warm in their beds and I was grateful.

Somewhere around midnight I heard the kids running across the yard. Then they burst in through the front door, all of them trying to get inside at the same time, wide-eyed and frightened, each one babbling complaints about their Daddy. I sighed in relief that my kids had made it safely home even though they had gone through a bad experience. I couldn't help laughing even though they were furious. Joyce wasn't laughing, her eyes blazed with anger as she shouted, "I'll never be guilty of going off with Daddy anymore. We saw the same old show so many times I know it by heart. I just can't believe Daddy would do this to us. Mamma, he didn't watch the movie very long before one of his buddies came by and asked Daddy if he wanted to party. Of course Daddy was all for that, so he told us to stay there until he came back for us. We watched that movie all day long and finally about ten o'clock tonight he came back, but he had been drinking. He gave Wayne some money and he called a taxi to take us home."

The boys looked up at their big sister, who had fought several battles for them. Every word was like the gospel to them and they depended on her to see that Jacob got a good tongue lashing from me because he had treated them so badly. Joyce had her hands on her hips. She was so mad as her outburst continued, "Well, Mamma, a taxi picked us up and started home with us and Wayne was so afraid that we wouldn't have enough money to pay the taxi driver to bring us all the way home, that he told him to let us out at the cattle guard. Mamma, it was so dark and I know we ran as hard as we could for at least a mile and it's all Daddy's fault. He didn't have to run off and leave us and go out on a party!" She fumed and fussed, but I laughed until tears streamed down my cheeks. "Thank You, Father, for bringing the children safely back home. They have learned from experience which is always the best teacher. Thank You for that too," I prayed in gratitude.

When Jacob went out on the town with his friends he usually woke up in jail, then he would drag in on Sunday morning as meek as a lamb. Evidently, he put some money back to pay himself out of jail, because I had never bailed him out and I promised him that I never would. While he would sit sheepishly by a warm fire, with his head splitting from a hangover, I would get the kids and myself ready for church. I had sort of gotten accustomed to this way of life which I knew that only God could change. So Jacob chose the pleasures of darkness and I chose to serve Christ, the Light of the world.

One day Jacob met a man from Hallettsville, Texas, which is located about 100 miles west of Houston. The fast talking man flashed his money around like he was rich and he convinced Jacob that he could make a lot of money if he would move his family to Hallettville and drive his cattle truck. Jacob had been driving a truck, but he got tired of barely getting by, so he sold the little tarpaper shack for $500 and loaded our belongings into a cattle trailer and we set out for Hallettsville.

We found an old farmhouse for rent and we moved in. It was a beautiful place that set on a high hill surrounded by green pasture land. We had usually lived where there were a lot of trees, but there weren't many around Halletsville. It was terribly cold with only a big fireplace in the living room for heat. As time went by, Jacob's job wasn't what he'd hoped for as his paychecks got smaller and smaller until there wasn't any money coming in. His boss's wife was supposed to bring some money to me every week while Jacob was hauling cattle to other states, but his boss blew what they made and we had to suffer so he could live like a king.

Jacob wouldn't listen to me when I told him what they were doing, but it wasn't long before I didn't have enough flour to make bread and a little gravy for the kids and I cried out to God to intervene. Jacob came home that day and I showed him the bare cabinets and refrigerator. He got terribly upset with his high rolling boss, but all that he could do was quit his job and go to work for a reputable truck line in town. The church that the children and I had been attending helped us out some. Jacob never got the money owed him from his former employer, but I hoped he had learned his lesson well. The man went broke and left that area owing debts, but God came in our time of need and we didn't have to suffer very long.

One night Sam became so ill that it scared me, so I started looking for another house to rent in town. I found a nice big rambling house near the school and by the time Jacob came in from his trip, we had most of our things moved. I thought he would get upset about me making the decision to move without consulting him first, but he just laughed about it. He liked the location that I had chosen and he was surprised that we had moved so much of our stuff without his help. He didn't seem to mind moving the heavy things with the boys to help him. In fact, we all laughed and cut up just like normal families do when they are happy. We still drove to New Home and attended the little Baptist Church that we had discovered one day when we first moved to the area. We'd made a lot of sweet friends at the church and I played the piano. No matter where we moved, God always had a spot open for me at the piano, it seemed. Jacob would have preferred that I not go to church at all. He wanted my full attention and didn't like the idea of sharing me with the Lord. He didn't rebel against the Lord this time, however, and he went with us to church when he was home. He actually seemed very happy and invited some of our new friends to our home often.

I took in sewing too, which helped take up the slack when we were running short between paychecks. The boys mowed yards to make their own spending money too. There was always laughter in the old rambling house and such a peaceful atmosphere all of the time. I know the way we lived then was more like the American dream of family life. We had a taste of what it meant when we lived at Hallettsville for a while with the kids running in and out, grabbing a freshly baked cookie just out of the oven and running out the back door to play with their friends. There were football and baseball games, proms and teenagers coming by, new girl friends and birthday parties at a moment's notice sometimes, even Wayne was taking too long to comb his hair with the bathroom door locked in the only bathroom in the house.

The big rambling house was the nicest home we'd ever lived in and the kids wanted to live there for the rest of their lives, but Jacob would get restless sooner or later and destroy their hopes and dreams just like he had always ruined mine. I didn't want to believe that God wanted us to move from place to place, but it seemed to be our destiny. Jacob wasn't happy anywhere very long and we lived on the edge, always hoping that we could live a normal life, but it never happened.

Jacob began getting restless when Mark took his physical to play football. His coach notified us that the doctor said that Mark had two heart murmurs and with our permission he would set up an appointment for him with a Cardiologist at San Antonio, which we agreed to and took him there. After the Cardiologist examined Mark, he told us he believed Mark had at one time suffered rheumatic fever. He said he could have had it when he had a sore throat when he was very young. Jacob told the doctor had had rheumatic fever and was paralyzed for a while when he was quite young. The doctor had told him that he probably wouldn't live to be 25 years old. "You know rheumatic fever scars the heart and there's no telling how badly your heart is scarred right now. I'm going to recommend that Mark give up sports. After all, there is more to life than sports and contact sports are a bit too much." Mark was terribly disappointed and so was Jacob. Jacob understood how Mark felt since he had to quit playing baseball and running track, and his doctor had made the same recommendation to his coach when he was going to school. Jacob quit school shortly afterwards because he had lost interest.

The kids were really disappointed when Jacob decided to move again. He quit his job at Hallettsville and we moved to Splendora, Texas, and he cut logs for Joshua for a while. In the meantime, Jacob's parents sold their house at Fort Worth and moved to Mississippi on their daughter's place.

We didn't stay at Splendora very long before we were on the move again. This time we moved to West Columbia, where Jacob thought he would get rich for sure this time by cutting cross ties for a living.

Mark came down with rheumatic fever shortly after we moved there and Jacob took him to the same doctor at Cleveland that had treated him for rheumatic fever when he was young. Mark stayed with my parents for a few days so he could be near the doctor in case something went wrong. We went to see him the coming weekend and Daddy said, "Jacob, why don't you build another house somewhere here on the land so we can help you take care of Mark? We can cut the logs and bring them to the sawmill and cut enough lumber to build a nice house this time. It's time that you were settling down and make a home for your family, instead of dragging them around and living like gypsies." I held my breath, hoping Jacob's answer would be `yes, I will,' and I got so excited when he told Daddy that he would. It was hard for Joyce to lcavc West Columbia though. She had met a nice young man, Gentry, who lived in a trailer park near the apartment where we lived. They were in love and she didn't want to go, but Gentry promised that he would come to see her on weekends. She was all right then, but Joyce had changed. She didn't take an interest in us building a new house; she just wanted to be with Gentry and nothing else.

At least, something beautiful had happened during our moving around. Joyce had met her true love and they may never have met otherwise. We moved in with my parents until we could move into our new home. We all helped at the sawmill when Jacob and Daddy brought the logs to the mill. It was such a time of hope for a better life and I couldn't really believe my dreams were actually coming true. A lot of men from the church came and helped lay the foundation and dry it in one Saturday. Gradually our home took shape and we moved in. We built this house near the blacktop, instead of so far back into the woods that we couldn't get electricity. One of the first things I bought for our new home was an old piano which made my dreams complete and I was happier than I had ever been.

Things started changing in our lives soon after we moved into our new home. Joyce married Gentry and later, Mark married Peggy. Shortly after Mark got married, Wayne got married too. He married Cindy and our family grew. Our first grandchild, Michael, was born in August to Mark and Peggy. Wayne and Cindy had a little boy, Kevin, born in December of the same year. Jacob and I were ecstatically happy and we turned our attention toward our growing family.

Mark and Wayne received their draft notices in January though, and things got hectic for a while. Wayne went into the Army and Mark joined the Marines, and Peggy joined Mark in California, and Cindy lived with her parents while Wayne was in Vietnam.

Cindy didn't bring Kevin to visit much and we were heartsick about it. We didn't get to see Michael either, since he was living with his parents in California. Our lives were changing so drastically in such a short time. One minute we had our family together and then suddenly, Sam and Isabella were all we had at home.

Jacob went back to work for a truck line after we got settled in our new home and he practically lived on a truck lately. When he was home, he just lay on the couch and slept. He was always too tired to do anything else. I turned most of my attention to fixing up the house and stayed very busy.

What I didn't realize was that the reason our lives was running smoothly was because the Lord's work had been put aside to devote my time to other things. Things had taken priority and Jacob liked that. Things don't hold the interest of a child of God very long, however. Even though Jacob seemed content right now he could change in an instant. Our marriage didn't have the strong foundation that was built on Christ Jesus and our house was divided. Storm clouds were gathering over the horizon and without that much needed strong foundation, the waves would dash against our home and in spite of all I could do, I would have to stand helplessly by when it came crashing down. My temporary false peace made me spiritually weak and I wasn't prepared when the storm came so that it caught me unaware, and everyday I would yearn to serve Christ in the church as soon as things were in order.

CHAPTER 16

NO AVENUE OF ESCAPE

My wonderful peace came to an abrupt halt one morning when I answered the telephone. Fear gripped my heart when I heard Mom on the other end of the line saying, "Destiny, I want you to go look at Grandpa Quinn's old house and see if it's livable. If it can be repaired, the boys can help us fix it up so we can move there. I can't take Mississippi anymore and we need a place to live. Tell Jacob I'm going to need his help too. He will have to come and drive our car to Cleveland, because we aren't able to drive that far." I told her that I would look at the house and see what kind of shape it was in. I knew our lives were about to change drastically because she had already made up her mind to move to Cleveland regardless of what condition the house was in.

I went over and looked at the the place and the house was terribly run down. I thought, `Mom can't fix this old house, even the foundation is bad.' I called her that night and I told her what I'd found, but she insisted on moving anyway so Jacob went to Mississippi and drove their car to Cleveland.

Mom seemed so happy about moving to Cleveland that I thought, `Maybe her attitude has changed toward me since we haven't been around each other for quite a while. Maybe she won't interfere in our lives this time, since she will have her mind occupied with getting the old house livable.'

Everything was peaceful while we helped Mom and Dad get settled. There wasn't any reason for trouble as long as I went along with whatever Jacob and his folks wanted.

Mom always took Jacob's side against me when I became too involved in church activities. There wasn't much said if we only attended church now and then, but when the children and I were faithful a battle always started. Mom didn't approve of us attending the Baptist Church anyway. She thought we were all hypocrites, even though Dad was saved while they were attending a Baptist Church when they were living in Mississippi. I was ecstatically happy when she told me about it, especially since Dad was getting old and he had lived for Satan many years.

Because they had attended the Baptist Church, I hoped that she would understand why I loved the church so much. She had brought her children up in the Assembly of God Church and we attended their church when we were visiting with them. It was her right to believe what she wanted to, but she would rant and rave because I stayed true to the church where I found Jesus and He saved my soul. Many times Mom would shout, "You'll never make a Baptist out of Jacob!" I wouldn't say anything back to her when she would storm out in rage like that. I would think to myself though, `I don't want to make Jacob anything. I knew that only God could with the convicting power of the Holy Spirit and Jacob would have to make his own choice.'

Things began to happen when I saw a strange car pull into the driveway shortly after we got Jacob's parents settled. I recognized my visitor immediately and invited him in. He was the pastor of a Baptist Church in town and even though I'd never attended the church I knew the pastor and some of the members who attended the church. We talked for a while before he told me, "Mrs. Quinn, we need a piano player and one of the members recommended you. They said that you might be interested if you're not attending another church regularly. I hope you can help us out." It was an answer to my prayers and I replied excitedly, "Yes,

I'll be happy to. I have been out of church so much lately and I can't wait to get started back, so I'll be there Sunday morning." He was very happy when he left and I was on the mountaintop.

I knew our world would turn upside down now that I had made a commitment to the Lord, but I was more determined than ever to live for Christ this time even though I knew another battle with Jacob would start. Isabella and Sam were teenagers and they needed to get involved in church activities as well.

Our lives began changing so fast that Jacob couldn't have stopped it had he tried. Like a ball rolling down a steep hill, God set our hearts on fire. It caught Jacob off guard and he didn't know how to handle a situation that he didn't want any part of. There was just too much excitement going on around the house when he came home and all because of some church up town. Once, all he had to worry about was stopping me from serving the Lord, but now Isabella and Sam were involved in church and he had three to contend with. He always wanted all the attention and he seemed to hate the Lord, all because Christ had brought so much happiness in our lives, something he wasn't capable of and this made him more furious than ever. He especially despised coming home and finding us gathered around the piano and having a wonderful time rejoicing in the Lord. Because we did not want to aggravate him with our music, we would wait until he was gone. I always felt uneasy when I would sit down on the piano stool even when he was gone. If I heard any sound resembling his truck driving up, I would tense up in fear.

Sam and Isabella didn't experience the same fears that I did, but they knew that the least little thing would set their daddy off so it put them on edge too. He wanted me to feel guilty as if I was committing a terrible sin and as if I was cheating on him, not with Ted this time, but with someone that he couldn't fight against because he knew he couldn't win.

Jacob seemed to stay angry about something and he always found something hateful to say. His eyes would blaze with anger whenever the church or even the Lord's name was mentioned. With him being so full of hatred for anything to do with God, it forced me to serve Christ in fear and because I was so afraid, I didn't study the Bible when he was around. Since I taught a Sunday school class, it was necessary that I study my Bible, so when Jacob was home, I would sneak around to study. That was the most painful heartache of all. Only by the grace of God was I able to carry on during this time, what with Jacob fighting against my serving the Lord, but when his mother added fuel to the fire with her snide remarks about my reasons for going to church, his hatred for God got even worse. It was especially hard during Revivals and Bible School which demanded so much more of my time.

Our life was one great battleground and I had to face his look of sheer hatred more and more as time went by. The battle grew even worse when Mom fed Jacob's jealousy by filling his head with her suspicions that I had a boyfriend at church and I was only using the church to be with him. Jacob wouldn't go to church to see why I loved the church so much that I would be willing to bear the persecution that he put me through since I had accepted Christ as my Savior. I think he was afraid to go, afraid because he didn't want to find out whether or not he was terribly wrong. He'd rather believe the worst in me, as if he enjoyed the hate that kept him in a constant turmoil, instead of the beautiful peace that Jesus would give to him if he would only allow Him to come into his heart.

Since the Lord had taught Jacob not to abuse me with threats of taking my life or beating me when he got both hands pinned between the steel trailer and the wheel, so he used other devious methods to bring me to my knees. He thought he had found the perfect answer when he invited my Grandmother into our home to live. I'm sure he thought his little scheme would work since my Grandmother was almost ninety years old and blind, but she could see better than he thought and she didn't have to be led around. His idea had been to give me more to do at home and then I would have to give up my work at church. If indeed this was what he thought, then Jacob made a terrible mistake. My Grandmother, whom we all called Granny, brought sunshine into all our lives, not only into my home, but also into the church. She made every step that I did and never complained. When it was time to get dressed for church, she was happy. It was such a blessing to have her with me and it was my joy to fix her beautiful snow white hair and dress her up in pretty dresses with new shoes on her feet. It was my privilege to be an important part of her life and she was a blessing to the church as well.

Isabella shared her bedroom with Granny and they became the best of friends. When Isabella went on a date, Granny would sit up until she came home. Granny and Isabella listened to music together and they talked about Isabella's boyfriends. It was hard to tell who was the youngest because Granny became a young girl in her mind when she and Isabella shared the sweetest friendship while she lived at our house.

It was very hard to hide my fears while Granny lived with us and I had hoped that Jacob wouldn't be so suspicious of me since she was with me constantly. She was a witness that I'd been faithful to him, but I couldn't shake my fears, especially when we went to church. The only time that I didn't experience fear was during the church service, but when I walked out the door to go to my car, that terrible fear came rushing back and surrounded me. I would try very hard to put it out of my mind by making conversation, but my mind would race as my heart beat madly all the while thinking, `Father, what will I face when we get home? Oh, God, don't let Jacob be there. I don't want to have a confrontation with him. If he gets mad enough, Father, he's not going to regard Granny's feelings, or anyone else's.' I lived in a perpetual state of fear and felt like I was walking on the very edge of a bottomless pit. If I made one faltering step, I would plunge to my death. This fear never left, even when everything seemed peaceful around the house. There were times when my family laughed and cut up and no one would have ever suspected that everything could change in the blink of an eye with no warning.

To add to all my heartache, Ted moved his family to Cleveland too. They rented a house right across the street from his mother, and that really added fuel to the fire. One Sunday, Jacob invited his parents and Ted's family, as well as our family, to our house for Sunday dinner. Everyone seemed at peace and it was a good feeling. It made me happy when Mom asked me to play the piano after we had cleared the table. Jacob fussed a little, but she told him that he could go outside if he didn't want to hear us sing. It had been such a long time since I felt that relaxed as I played the piano in our home, but it was different when Mom made the suggestion that everyone gather around the piano to sing.

In spite of the peaceful atmosphere, I had an uneasy feeling and there was an undercurrent of pretense on Jacob's part. I saw it in his face when Mom took a picture of Ted and Jacob together. From the way Jacob looked, I knew that at any moment he could throw one of his temper tantrums. Because I knew I couldn't trust Jacob to behave while the family was there, my nerves were so taught with the fear of what he would do at any moment. Ted was oblivious to all that was happening and just laughed innocently as he placed his arm on his brother's shoulder. He didn't know that Jacob still resented him for the things that had happened in Fort Worth.

When I was standing at the kitchen cabinet, Ted came over and stood close to me. This didn't help me a bit because the whole family was there. I really don't know how to describe how I really felt because the cloud which seemed to surround us and set Ted and I apart from the rest when we were together, no matter how many people were around us. The force that surrounded us had such power that it took all of my strength not to burst into tears and reach out to him. I trembled as I tried to control my emotions and found myself struggling to shake off the feeling of how much we truly loved each other. `Lord, we can't love each other. Don't You see how hopeless it is? We have commitments to our families and it's a sin to want to be in the arms of another man. Help me, Jesus, I didn't tell myself to love Ted and these feelings that I resist must have come from Satan to torment me. I can't believe that You placed this type of love in our hearts when it seems so wrong. I can't understand why I can't forget Ted and put him out of my mind completely,' I prayed in my heart.

I was so afraid that I couldn't restrain myself and when Ted walked away, I began to relax, but I was still shaking and prayed that no one there had noticed, most of all Ted. I was relieved when they all went home and I placed my feelings for Ted back in that little isolated corner of my heart that no one could touch or destroy as I had done so many times in the past.

One day Jacob wanted us to go with him to visit his mother. When we got there, she was sitting on the front porch and we joined her. Ted and his wife came over too. I had been to the beauty shop earlier so my hair looked nice. Mom just couldn't pass up an opportunity to embarrass me and try to make me look like a tramp in Ted's eyes if she could find a way. She glared at me and said, "Well, Destiny, you've got your hair all fixed up. Who is your boyfriend now? I always know when you're running around because you start fixing up like that." I looked at Jacob and he seemed stunned, but he smiled like he always had when she made snide remarks to me. Ted looked pale and hurt when I looked at him. Jacob deserved any answer that I might give to his mother because he knew she despised me, but he seemed to get some sore of thrill from the way she treated me. I turned to Mom and looked at her defiantly and said, "Well, just which one of my boyfriends do you have in mind, because I certainly have more than just one?"

My answer took her completely by surprise, and when she noticed that Destiny wasn't crying anymore, she certainly wasn't going to hang her head in shame just because her mother-in-law and her husband had wicked thoughts about her, she became flustered and was embarrassed herself. When Jacob laughed and told her that she really put her foot in her mouth this time, she was the one who was ready to cry. Ted sighed in relief and he and his wife started laughing too. Ted said, "I wish Pauline was more like you, Destiny." Then I thought about how little Mom cared for me and had no respect for my aged Grandmother who never left my side. When I remarked, "Mom, I don't know why you people think that I have a boyfriend anyway, especially with Granny making every step that I do and she can tell you that I have much better things to do." Mom twisted her mouth and blurted out, "What's to keep your Granny from having a boyfriend too?" With that ridiculous suggestion, I was ready to leave. Hate eats away at a person and they seem to enjoy feeding that hatred, but hate can and will destroy you in time.

Later I was told that Ted and Pauline had trouble when they went to their house. Ted was very upset with his mother because she accused me of having a boyfriend. Pauline asked him why he was so mad since it wasn't any of his business how his mother treated me. He told her that his mother always treated me that way when he was around because she wanted him to hate me. But Ted told his wife, "That won't ever happen, no matter how hard they try, no one will ever be able to make Destiny look bad in my eyes." It was a wonderful feeling to know that Ted still cared for me. Ted and I had that special love for each other which no family member or anyone could destroy in a lifetime. The terrible strain I was under surfaced in Sunday School class one Sunday morning and I started crying. "I just can't take much more of this pressure," I cried. "Jacob is so full of hate and every time I look at him, I can see the fury building up. He needs Christ, but I can't reach him. It's as though I face Satan every time I look into his eyes. I feel so much fear and the only thing that keeps him from destroying me is his fear of God." Donna put her arms around me and said, "Destiny, I'll go witness to Jacob. I'm not afraid of him." "But Donna, you have never met Jacob and you don't know how bad things really are," I warned. "Don't worry, Destiny, I've never met a person that I couldn't witness to about the Lord." She was so confident that I thought, `Maybe the Lord is sending her to witness to Jacob. She's so sweet that not even Jacob could be cruel to her. Bless her heart, she's been crippled all of her life, at least since I've known her and that's been since we went to school together.' "Thank you, Donna, if anyone can touch Jacob's heart it would be you," I told her weeping.

Donna kept her promise and came to visit one day when he was home. I was nervous and could see that Donna was too. As we sat at the kitchen table, Jacob walked by and he ignored us because he knew she was a member of the church. I suppose he had suspected why she had come, because he glared at us both and I held my breath in fear, thinking, `Oh, God, I hope Donna doesn't mention the church and I'm terrified to think of how he will react if she mentions Christ to him.' Thank God, she didn't. We just talked about meaningless things and I sighed with relief when she left. I was so ashamed of Jacob's behavior, but it could have been worse if he had found the right opening to speak his mind. He could have been pleasant, but he wasn't and I'm not sure, but he was probably more miserable than I was. `It's probably better to live in tension than be eaten up with hatred,' I decided.

When I saw Donna at church later, she met me teary eyed and said, "Destiny, I'm so sorry, but I couldn't witness to your husband. I was so terrified when I saw that look in his eyes that I just wanted to get away as soon as I could. It was like meeting Satan face to face and only the Holy Spirit has the power to deal with Jacob. I will pray for your safety most of all and that God will touch his heart." I cried, "Thank you for trying to help me, Donna. I understand your fear since I deal with it every day."

One day shortly after that, I looked out the kitchen window and saw Ted and Pauline driving up to the house. They got out hurriedly and Pauline was trembling and crying. "What is wrong, Ted?" I asked. He replied, "Destiny, I came to you because I can depend on you to protect Pauline until I get back. If Mother calls, don't tell her Pauline is here. I have to work tonight, but I'm going to move my family to Lufkin tomorrow and I'll work there. In the meantime I need you, Destiny, because you know how mean Mother can be when she gets mad about something. She will hurt Pauline if she can get her hands on her and that's why I came to you because I can trust you to keep Mother away from her." I was completely bewildered and confused because I couldn't imagine Pauline doing anything to make Mom that mad. Mom had always bragged to me what a good girl she was and she was so quiet and never said a word out of place. "Certainly Ted, I'll watch after your wife and no harm will come to her as long as she is in my house." Ted told Pauline that she would be all right and he left after thanking me for my help. Mom called later, but she didn't mention the incident, probably because she knew that I wouldn't tell her anything anyway. Neither Ted nor Pauline ever explained what had happened and I didn't really want to know because I had so many problems of my own to deal with. When Ted picked up Pauline and the two girls, they moved to Lufkin and I didn't see them again for quite a while. I was surprised that Mom didn't tell me what happened though, because she was always spouting off about some of the kids doing something that she didn't approve of.

Our problems weren't improving and when my Aunt Mae, Granny's daughter, came for a visit and Jacob invited her to stay with us too. My uncle had died recently and she was homeless. She was very happy as she joined us in the church activities. She wasn't with us very long after she fell in love with one of the Deacons who was a widower as his wife had died recently. They were like two kids in love and they were married and she moved into his house. Up until this point, the Lord had kept a tight rein on Jacob, but that was about to change very soon.

I was having so many problems and my nerves were close to the breaking point, when one Sunday evening while the family was all gathered around the dinner table, Jacob suddenly announced to me in no uncertain terms what he had planned and what I had to do. Jacob shouted his demands, "Destiny, go to the bank tomorrow and borrow the money that I need to buy a house I'm going to have moved on our land next to us for Mother and Daddy." He added sternly as he gritted his teeth, "Destiny, get it in your head right now that I'm not asking you how you feel about it, I'm telling you to do it even if you have to put this place up for collateral." He had so much hate in his eyes and his demands cut deep in my heart like a sharp knife and my eyes filled with tears. I felt trapped with no way out and it made me miserable. Jacob got up out of his chair and suddenly he turned around with his eyes glaring at me and said, "Destiny, it's not going to do you any good to cry, my mind is made up, so you get busy and do what I told you to do."

I looked at the children and Granny who were terribly nervous and afraid and I didn't know what to say to them as Jacob stormed victoriously out of the house as we all sat stunned and unable to say anything. I knew Jacob could be cruel, but this was uncalled for. It wasn't right to involve the entire family in our problems and I was so embarrassed. "Are you going to do what Daddy told you to do, Mamma?" Isabella asked near tears. "I don't have much choice in the matter. If I don't, there's no telling what he will do," I told her, heartbroken.

The forces of Satan were drawing me into a trap and only God could find an avenue of escape for us all. This bitter battle was directed toward me and it didn't seem to bother Jacob how much it was hurting the rest of our family. Evidently, he was set out to destroy me and with his mother living right next door, that net would be reinforced even more. I shuddered in terror knowing that the greatest battle of my life was coming and somehow I had to find a way to escape. Who is the victor in such a war as this? Only God has the power to deliver His children from the clutches of Satan.

I went to the bank and borrowed the money for Jacob. My heart was breaking as I talked to the banker hoping that he would turn down the loan. I wanted to blurt out my story to my old friend as he sat there, so business like not noticing the terrible ache and fear that I was going through. When he handed me the money, there was such a feeling of impending doom and hopelessness. My last hope was gone and Jacob had won yet another battle in this war. I needed a miracle just to bring peace back to my family. It was hard enough to live under Jacob's domination, but with his mother living next door, it would be unbearable for us all. Jacob was so strange and often hard to understand. His whole attitude could change in an instant. When I gave him the money, he acted as if nothing had happened. Suddenly, all the hateful things he had said were erased from his mind completely and everything was wonderful. `How could he go through life trampling all over me without any remorse or guilt time and time again? He has won this battle,' I thought miserably, `but he hasn't won the war, which could go on throughout our lives if he keeps resisting the love of God.'

A big lump came up in my throat when I saw the house he had bought coming down the road. I just wanted to run away from all of my heartaches and problems, but Jacob was jubilant knowing he had the reins and was completely in control of the situation. Now he would have his mother as a watchdog over his family while he was away and he wouldn't need to come home very often after she moved in.

After the movers left, Jacob wanted me to go over to look at the house with him. I went with him reluctantly because the house symbolized something more than just a house to me and I hated it and the idea of it sitting on our land. I felt terrible when I walked in the door and when

Jacob walked through it; he pointed out some of the things that he wanted to do to improve it. I was heartsick that he seemed so obsessed with the house and I realized even more how hopeless our situation really was. He didn't seem concerned that Sam was going to have surgery the next day.

Sam had been ill with tonsillitis quite a lot lately and the doctor said that he needed his tonsils removed. I admitted him into the hospital the following day and when he came out of surgery he was very sick. Wayne and Cindy were looking after Isabella and Granny so I didn't have to worry about her, so I stayed with Sam day and night.

I was weary from sitting up all night with Sam. When Isabella and Cindy came the next morning, and Isabella suddenly burst into tears and she cried, "Mamma, Daddy told me that he would whip me if I told you what is taking place at home, but I have to tell you anyway. Grandma Quinn is throwing her weight around already. Daddy said that you had enough to worry about and I'd better keep my mouth shut, but Grandma stomped into the house and told us all, even Daddy, that she was going to straighten us all out. She said the first thing she was going to do was to get rid of Granny or anyone else that we had taken into our home. Granny was so afraid, and Daddy didn't stand up to Grandma. He just sat there like he2 was afraid to open his mouth. Oh, Mamma, what are we going to do?"

I was furious with Jacob for allowing his mother to march into our house and throw her weight around. I couldn't believe that he would put up with that, not even from his mother and I knew that I wasn't going to stand for it when I got home. I asked Isabella where Jacob was and she told me that he was sitting in the lobby. I told her not to worry about her Daddy whipping her, but if he did I wanted to know about it immediately. "Go and tell your Daddy to come in here right now, Isabella," I said, trembling in anger. Then she went out to find her Daddy while I seethed inside at the very idea that everything had gotten so bad as soon when I turned my back. Jacob entered the room as though nothing had happened. He thought Isabella was too afraid of him to tell me what had happened after he had threatened her. As soon as he walked in, I got straight to the point. I told him that I knew the whole story and that if he touched Isabella I would have him arrested. He tried to lie for his mother, but I knew better. I stated firmly, "Jacob, you'd better understand right now that nobody is going to take over my home, not even your mother. Nobody had better not upset Granny either. When I get back home, I'm going to take her to live with Mamma and get her out of the hell at our house." Jacob tried to calm me down, but he couldn't. When he realized that everything he said only infuriated me more, he said that he had to go load the truck.

Sam was all upset about everything going on around him, but I couldn't stop the chain of events that were getting out of hand. I was understandably mad, but I couldn't control my temper when Mom walked in the door on the pretense of visiting with Sam. She started in on me as soon as she sat down, telling me about her plans to straighten my family out. I turned on her with all the pent up fury that I'd been suppressing all those years and I shouted, "You'd better enjoy this victory that you think you have won because things are going to change as soon as I get Sam out of the hospital. I'm so sick and tired of you and Jacob dominating our lives and interfering in everything we try to do for Christ. I'm going to leave your precious son when Sam is discharged and I pray to God that I never have to see either one of you again as long as I live. You are not ruling my house or running anybody off. You can have Jacob and the house as far as I'm concerned. I just want to be free and I'm going to fight for the freedom to worship God wherever I choose." She started crying, but I knew those tears were only temporary and she wouldn't ever change and not one time did she tell me that she was sorry for the way that she had treated me. I knew she was crying because she had lost this battle and her pride was hurt.

She left the room and Sam cried, saying, "Mamma, Grandma doesn't care about me. She didn't come to see me; she just came here to jump on you. I just wish they would all stay away if they are just coming here to cause trouble. I'll never forget the way Grandma has hurt me though, but I can't believe she didn't show me any respect and treated me this way."

Dad came later, which I expected him to do. He came on the pretense of visiting Sam, but I knew that he was going to try to smooth things over for Mom and Jacob if he could, but the damage had been done. He didn't have any tangible proof that I had a boy friend somewhere to make me feel guilty for this time as he had when he used Ted while we were living at Fort Worth. I despised their tactics of deceit and I wasn't interested in anything Dad had to say. He started to cry too, when he realized his cunning efforts had failed miserably and he left the room just like Mom had when he finally came to the realization that my mind was made up and it wasn't going to be changed.

The doctor was planning to discharge Sam Wednesday, so I started making preparations to leave when I went to pick him up. Jacob would be out of town for several days on a trip, so I wanted to get away before he returned. First of all, I moved Granny to Mamma's. Then I paid all the bills which were due, because I didn't want Jacob accusing me of running off and leaving him in debt. I didn't want to leave Jacob without any transportation so I left the best car for him. I left everything except our clothes, in the hope that he would leave us alone. Everything was packed and ready to go when Isabella and I picked up Sam at the hospital. When we were all set, we drove by the church and told them our plans before we started out to Ruston, Louisiana where Joyce and Gentry lived and were expecting us to arrive around midnight Wednesday night. I made the decision to go there because I thought Jacob wouldn't bother us and think that I had run off with another man.

I kept looking out the back glass for a long time watching to see if Jacob was following us. He could very well be if Mom could have known how to contact him and tell him what was going on. As we drove further from Cleveland, I began to relax and finally feel free. Sam insisted on driving the car, even though he wasn't strong enough yet. It was as if he wanted the pleasure of steering our escape from all the tyranny and lack of freedom we had endured for so long. We hadn't known what freedom from fear actually meant until that night, just driving down the highway and singing praises to God for the escape route He had made for us. The older children had experienced some of his bitter rage, but Isabella and Sam had suffered the most since they had stood for the Lord in spite of his threats to stop us all. And even though he had been cruel so many times, they still loved him. They knew as I did that Jacob needed Christ more than anything else. I felt like a tiny bird that had finally been set free from a trap, flying free at last with its tiny wings outstretched. "Oh, my God, my Father," I cried. "No one can possibly understand how precious the gift of freedom is unless they have been under some sort of bondage, Father. Please, Jesus, don't let Satan take our freedom to worship you away. Please grant us a new way of life, I pray."

We arrived at Joyce's very early Thursday morning. Even though we were exhausted, we were too excited to sleep. We were anxious to find a place to live and a job for me. Also, Isabella and Sam had to get started in school as soon as possible. We were so excited when I found a job right away. It was as if the Lord guided every step that we took, especially when we found an apartment very near the school and everything was wonderful. Sam said, "Mamma, I'll get a part time job and work after school to help out too, so don't worry, we will make it just fine." We were so happy and excited about beginning a new life never once thinking anyone would stop us.

I thought Jacob would be glad that we had left, but he was so full of the devil and old Satan wasn't going to let us go that easily. He needed someone to dominate and control and I was naive enough to think he would simply let us go. However, I soon learned that he hates to lose any battle and he certainly doesn't know what love is, because love causes you to think of another's needs and not your own selfish desires. He had to win whatever the cost, no matter who gets hurt, and what belongs to him, no one dare touch or take away.

Only the Holy Spirit of God is able to penetrate such a stony heart of pride even though we give up and throw up our hands in defeat. That night Joyce and the kids went to buy some fried chicken so we wouldn't have to cook. I was exhausted, so I stayed at home. They weren't gone very long before I heard someone driving up and I became very frightened because I had a very strong feeling that it was Jacob. When he started knocking on the door, my heart began pounding so hard in fear that I felt certain he could hear it and I didn't know what to do. He knew that I was terrified of him, so instead of his usual forceful demanding way, he used devious and sly methods to get me to open the door. He would plead, "Destiny, please let me come in so we can talk about our problems together. I didn't come to harm you in any way. I just want us to sit down and really try to work things out at least for the kids' sake."

Whatever gave me the hope that Jacob would ever change is something that I will never understand. I knew that he would do anything to get what he wanted and he had proved to me that I was his possession and not someone that he loved. I let him because I was so afraid. All hope of our marriage had ended. I knew how cruel he could be and he would kick the door down, if necessary to get in. I was actually trapped again without any avenue of escape and I had to face my situation with courage and look to God to keep me from harm. I thought, `Lord, if I let him in and he finds out that I mean business, that I'm not going anywhere with him, maybe he will leave before the kids get back. Father, they have been through so much and I can't bear to see them hurt anymore because of me, but, oh, my God, Jacob just won't let me be free.' I didn't have any choice, I had to open the door and face this angry man that stands just on the outside, because if he has to force his way in here, he will surely kill me and probably even the kids if they happen to come in.

I opened the door and he came inside and sat down on the couch without saying anything. I started telling him how much we needed to make a fresh start. We just couldn't go on living the way we had been. He held his head down and said kind of sheepishly, "I thought we were happy," but he knew that that wasn't true and he was lying to himself if he thought we had a good marriage. "The kind of marriage we have had, Jacob, has been one with me trying to satisfy your every whim. I'm sick and tired of trying to please you and every member of your family just to keep peace. My mind is made up and I am not going to change it, so you might as well accept it and go back to where you came from. I refuse to walk back into that pit of hell that you have made for the kids and me. Now, I doubt that you wanted to hear the truth, but you knew that we wouldn't leave without a very good reason."

Jacob got to his feet and I hoped that he was going to leave. My first reaction was a sigh of relief and I thought this miserable heartache was finally over and both of us could start a new life. I was horrified, however, when I saw a shiny silver object sticking out of his back pants pocket when he stood up and I knew that it was a pistol. My tongue became paralyzed and I couldn't speak. I began crying out of fear and disappointment. It was then that I realized Jacob would never change and he wasn't going to let me go. Then I knew his intentions were to shoot me if I didn't go with him. When he walked to the door, he turned around, took the pistol out of his pocket and pointed it at me. Even though I was horrified that he threatened my life in this way, the look in his eyes terrified me even more than the gun pointing in my face. This wasn't a man standing in front of me; it was old Satan with his eyes blazing with fury and hate. His face was so distorted and it was as if old Satan himself was standing there. He was determined to make me pay for what I had done. Jacob shouted, "Destiny, you are coming with me. If you don't, I'll wait right here until the kids come in and I'll kill everyone of them and you!" I could smell liquor on his breath and knew he had been drinking to build up his confidence, but I couldn't bear the thought of the kids being hurt and I really didn't want them to see their Daddy in the state he was in. I didn't want to believe Jacob would hurt his own children, but he felt betrayed because the children had chosen to go with me, so there's no telling how far he would go. I had to stop him before the kids came home.

I jumped up quickly and said, "Don't hurt the children, Jacob. I'll go with you because I can't bear to see them hurt anymore because of me, please let us go before they come back."

Jacob wasn't a fool and he'd never been. He always used the children to get his way. Suddenly I heard a car pull up in the driveway. I was terrified. The kids were back and Jacob was standing by the door with the pistol in his hand. He had to decide quickly now what he wanted to do. Jacob glared at me and said, "Destiny, if you let on as to what is going on when the kids come in, I'll kill all of you, just like I told you, so you had better keep your mouth shut until we can leave so they won't get suspicious." Jacob stuffed the pistol into his front pocket and calmly sat down next to me on the couch. The kids came into the house babbling away and seemed to accept the idea that we had patched things up and Daddy and Mamma were back together again. Jacob said, "Isabella, I want you to promise that you will wait until you are married to have a baby." Isabella looked at me because she knew that her Daddy was acting kind of strange, but she didn't argue the point. She said, "Okay, Daddy, I won't." Jacob took out his billfold and gave Sam and Isabella fifty dollars each. I didn't understand why he did that, but he had always tried to buy their love when he did have a little money in his pocket. Evidently he was drawing their attention away from me so they wouldn't notice how troubled I was. `What kind of man had I married anyway,' I asked myself?

I sat very quiet while this was going on as I was afraid to speak because if I blurted out the fact that he had a pistol hidden in his pocket, they would have gone to pieces. I couldn't tell them that Jacob was forcing me to go with him. Since he was so drunk, I dare not say anything for fear that he might start shooting us. I tried to hide my trembling hands and stay as calm as I could and pretend that everything was all right. I just wanted to go before my children got hurt. After Jacob was convinced that he had them fooled, he said, "I think your mother and I will go somewhere to eat and just talk things out." Joyce spoke up quickly and said, "You don't have to go out to eat. I brought a bucket of fried chicken home for supper, Daddy." Jacob said, "We would like to, but Destiny and I have things to talk about alone." Then Jacob stood up and motioned to me and said, "Isabella, do you or Sam want to go with us?" Isabella replied, "No, Daddy, I want to stay here and eat fried chicken." My heart leaped in horror when Sam said, "I think I'll go with you and Mamma." He must have detected the fear in my eyes and near tears as I nodded no to him. Sam looked puzzled and he told us that he had changed his mind and that he would eat fried chicken instead. I was so afraid the kids would get suspicious that something was wrong.

I didn't look back as I joined Jacob on my way out of the house. I knew I might never see my kids again and I longed to hold them just one more time, but I knew if I did that I would break down. I stumbled blindly toward the prison that waited just outside for me, even though I'd been in one all those years and thought I had escaped. But my warden had hunted me down and he would make me suffer because I hated being shackled and bound for the crime of loving Christ and serving Him against Jacob's wishes. My fate was now in God's hands and I knew it. He had brought me through many heartaches and pain over the last twenty-five years of marriage to Jacob. I was ready to die at that moment if God saw fit to take me.

Tears of sorrow streamed down my face at the thought of leaving my children behind and wondering what would ever become of them if Jacob did take my life. Jacob turned the car toward Texas, took the pistol out of his pocket and placed it on the seat between us. As I glanced down at it, the thought ran through my mind that he probably laid it there just to tempt me. In his mind, it would give him just the excuse he needed to shoot me if I dare reach for it. He turned all his pent up fury on me then and cursed the day that he was born and the day he met me. He gritted his teeth as he shouted, "I won't let you go, Destiny, no matter how sorry you are. We've been together since we were kids and I don't know how to live any other way. You are mine and I won't give you up for any reason, so it's useless for you to even try to run away from me." "I thought you were happy, Destiny," Jacob cried. "If you weren't happy, you should have told me." I stared at Jacob knowing in my heart he was lying.

"Jacob, you've never been concerned about my happiness. The only one you ever worried about was you and what you wanted. You made all of our lives miserable because we love the Lord and serving Christ in the church is our joy and happiness. You seem to hate the Lord for some reason and you can't deny it. You must even be jealous of my love for Christ to want to possess me, but you won't ever be able to make me your humble slave because my life belongs to God. You have gone too far this time, Jacob," I cried.

Thoughts of being shot and thrown out on the roadside went through my mind. My courage lessened as I looked at Jacob, who was gritting his teeth like some wild animal. He clinched his fists and pounded them on the steering wheel, but I didn't pity him anymore. At that moment, I really wanted to die because that seemed to be the only way that I could ever escape this pit of hell Jacob had made for me. I didn't want to die at Jacob's hand though, because the kids would then have an even worse ordeal to go through. I told myself that I'd better brace up instead of giving in to my emotions just because I was so hurt.

We were crossing a high overpass on Interstate 20 at Shreveport, Louisiana when I said tearfully, "Jacob, you have destroyed any love that I've ever had for you because you have always completely dominated my life and made me afraid of you. I don't love you anymore because you trampled on the love that I did have for you for far too long." Suddenly I felt the terrible wrath of his fist on my face and my head crashed against the window, and I felt myself lose consciousness. When I came to, I looked down at the winding streets under the overpass, and my first reaction was to open the door and jump out so I could end this horrible nightmare. As I caught the door handle in my hand, I thought about Jesus and all the suffering that He had gone through. I knew if I deliberately jumped out that I would spend eternity in hell since it was wrong to take my life. `I must hold on for Isabella and Sam's sake,' I told myself. `Oh, God, how long will Jacob make me suffer? You are the only one that can stop him. Even if he doesn't kill me, I feel dead already and feel as though my whole life has been lived for a mad man. Are you allowing this to happen to punish Your child too,' I inwardly cried out to God?

Jacob seemed calmer after he hit me. I'm sure he was feeling better after he had gotten some of the rage out of his system when he hit me with his fist, but there would be questions asked when my face turned dark and bruised and I'm sure that thought occurred to him.

We drove for miles in silence until we reached Longview. Jacob turned to me and said, "We'd better stop at a telephone booth and call the kids. Remember though, when you talk to them you had better tell them you are all right, because I'll be standing next to you. I want them to think we have worked our problems out and we are going on a short vacation, which we are, Destiny."

Jacob dialed the number himself, then grabbed my arm as he spoke to Joyce, while I stood by him trembling with fear and hurt. He told Joyce that we were fine and we were going on a vacation. Joyce told Jacob that she wanted to talk to me and when he handed me the phone he held my arm tightly so I couldn't get away from him. I knew I had to be very careful of what I said and mustn't cry when I took the receiver. Joyce asked, "Mamma, are you all right?" I replied, "Yes, Honey, I'm all right. Just please see after Isabella and Sam until I get back. Jacob told me that we are going on a short vacation. I don't know where though." "Where are you now?" Joyce asked. I couldn't tell her where we were because Jacob was glaring threateningly at me, so I told her, "I'm not sure, Joyce. I'm talking to you from a telephone booth outside of a little store somewhere on the side of the highway." "Mamma, we know Daddy has kidnapped you and forced you to go with him. I saw the pistol in his pocket, Mamma. He thought he had it hidden, but when he got up to leave I saw the shiny object and knew what it was. Mamma, I went straight to the judge and filed a report on Daddy. The State Troopers are looking for him, but don't let on that I have told you about it." I knew that no one would find us now that we had crossed the State Line into Texas, but I didn't tell her how hopeless it was. I said, "Baby, I have to go now, just pray for us and take care of yourselves." Then I hung up the phone and Jacob opened the car door while I sat down feeling numb and heartsick.

Jacob was very quiet as he drove back upon the Interstate 20. He seemed pleased because he had everything in his control now. We continued going West on Interstate 20. He had always run away from his problems and this time his plan was no different. In the days ahead, Jacob was so afraid I would try to get away from him and have him arrested that he wouldn't leave my side. He even went to the bathroom with me in the motel rooms, as if I would try to escape or lock myself inside and start screaming for help. He made sure that I didn't write a note either so someone could find it after we left.

No one seemed curious enough to ask why I had dark bruises on my face when we stopped to eat and that surprised me. I also knew I was his prisoner and it was very hard to keep a straight face as I pretended to go along with him because I decided that would be the best if I wanted to get out of this alive. Jacob became paranoid and suspicious of every move I made and he was so troubled that he cried out in his sleep. He was so afraid of being caught and being locked up for kidnapping.

It seemed that the further we went away from Texas, Jacob's confidence was built up and he told me when we were crossing New Mexico, "Destiny, I'm going to take you to some of the places I've been on the truck. I want you to know what I do for a living and see what I've seen." Jacob tried to make me feel guilty for the way he had made a living, as though I had forced him to drive a truck and had to be away from home, but he had made that choice himself and he knew it. "Destiny, it's not easy to go away from home for weeks at a time and worry about what is happening at home. Truck driving is a lonely life which you don't seem to understand," he cried in self-pity. "But, Jacob, you chose to be a truck driver. You were always ready to go when problems at home got too rough for you to handle. The only time you wanted to come home was when things were going smoothly. You wanted all of the attention and you got it, but you didn't want to share your family with God. You set yourself up as the one that you wanted us to worship. You were always able to escape with the excuse that you had to make a living, but you could have chosen another way to make a living, so don't try to make me feel guilty or sorry for you after all these years." Nothing I said affected him, however, because he had closed his mind to everything I said and his ideas were all that mattered. Jacob took me up in the mountains where the Indian Tribes lived on reservations. As we drove along, he told me about some of their old traditions which they still carried on. He said the Indian women walked several feet behind their husbands to show respect. They didn't walk side by side or hold hands the way we do. When they went shopping, the woman would sit outside on the sidewalk while her husband went into the store and picked out what he wanted to buy, then after the purchase he walked out and she would go inside and carry the groceries out. Her husband walked proudly in front of her in his best clothes while his wife followed him from a distance lugging all the groceries in her arms. Jacob smiled cunningly, and I thought, `Oh, yes, you would like it just fine if I showed you that same honor and respect, but, Jacob, you haven't earned it, and you never will, because you're not my god and you never will be.'

My prison didn't have any bars that you could see, nevertheless, they were there and I knew what it was like it be a prisoner. `Lord, you know that I can't mend all the suffering and hurtful things that Jacob has caused all these years, You know that only You can change his heart. I can't undo what has been done or right any of the wrongs that he has done. I can only plead for Your love and understanding, as well as for the forgiveness of our sins and for You to heal my broken heart, but most of all, Lord, I need the freedom to worship You without fear,' I prayed inwardly.

CHAPTER 17

VISIONS OF HELL

Jacob and I knew we couldn't travel forever and eventually we would have to face our problems. They weren't going to disappear so Jacob started back toward Louisiana. We were actually gone only one week, but it seemed like an eternity.

The children had witnessed a lot of things that were almost as bad as this while they were growing up and it came as no surprise when we got back to Ruston to find that the kids were just as glad that this ordeal was over. Isabella and Sam had made new friends around that area while we were away. They were attending the same church as Joyce and they were already happy in doing the Lord's work there. This was their first time to be able to serve Christ with a free spirit and I prayed that Jacob wouldn't discourage them by his hateful attitude as he had done in the past. The roots of faith were deeply planted in the hearts of the children and they had learned the meaning of self sacrifice for Christ when we had lived at Cleveland. By enduring persecution they were even stronger for the cause of Christ and I was so proud of them.

The first thing Jacob did was apologize to Joyce and Gentry for making a fool of himself. Joyce said, "Daddy, I'll forgive you for treating me the way you did, but I don't trust you. I'm not going to cancel the warrant for your arrest either, because I know that you took Mamma by force, Daddy, and that's kidnapping. Don't try to deny it either, because I saw the pistol that you thought you had concealed. You will have to prove yourself to me before I believe you. If you try to hurt her again, I'll have you arrested. I'm still not convinced that everything is all right between you two yet." Jacob didn't tell me what Joyce said and she didn't know that I was still his prisoner with threats of harm to them even after we rented an old trailer house near Ruston and moved in right away.

Isabella and Sam started to school and I was alone when Jacob finally had to go to work because our money was running out. He got a job at a sawmill near the house so he could keep a close watch on me. He put on a good front for the kids by going to church with us and they hoped that Jacob was really trying to straighten his life out. They didn't seem to notice how terrified I still was all of the time. This threat was over me constantly, so much so that I was mentally drained and falling apart. I couldn't escape, but my love for the children kept me going day by day.

When I slept, I had a bad dream that didn't change. I would find myself cringing in a dark corner of the tiny bedroom, trying to hide and I would be crying out in fear and despair afraid that I'd be found and I would draw myself up into a crouched position and hide my head between my knees. I was afraid to come out of the dark corner knowing there wasn't any escape from the pit that held me fast and knew I could never be free. From the pit of hell I cried out to God, "Please, Father, let me die, I just can't bear anymore suffering. You know that I will never be free to work for You with shackles on my feet and my hands tied in great fear so that I can't play the piano anymore. My eyes are swollen with tears that never cease. Even when I'm in a crowd, my heart cries out with heartache. Oh, God, I pray that Your will may be done. I know Jesus suffered even more than I am doing and won the victory over hell and death so we might go free. Help me to endure whatever lies ahead, Father."

About three weeks after we moved into the rented trailer, Jacob said, "Destiny, I'm going to sell our house to my brother, Luke. I hate Cleveland anyway and always have. Luke wants to buy the house so we are going to meet him at the bank to sign the deeds over to him on Monday. You ruined all of my plans when you ran off up here, so you had better not give me any static and sign the deeds when we go to the Cleveland. If you'll behave yourself, we'll go look for a new trailer house and set it up here so Isabella and Sam won't have to move to another school."

I told Jacob that I would sign the deed if he would buy us another home, but I wanted to find one first before I'd go along with what he wanted. Jacob agreed, so we shopped around and picked out the one we wanted and the kids were really excited and I was too. They stayed with Joyce while we went to Cleveland.

Jacob was tense and nervous all the way to Cleveland and I really couldn't understand why. He kept threatening me all the way there saying, "Destiny, you'd better sign those papers. No matter what happens, you just keep your mouth shut and be quiet. You don't need to say anything even if Luke says something that you don't know about. And if Mother is there, don't pay her any attention because you know how she is, so just ignore her. I just want to get this ordeal over with and get away from there as quickly as possible."

I was puzzled by Jacob's attitude and thought, `Are you really crazy, Jacob? You must think I'm a fool and I want to live next door to your mother. Why do you think I ran away in the first place? Jacob, you don't know it I guess, but it's a relief to sell our house. You are practically giving our home away, but I don't care. I can't wait to get it over with either.'

The thought hadn't occurred to me that the reason why Jacob was so nervous had actually been the fear that I would blurt out my story when I went in to sign the papers and have Jacob arrested for keeping me his prisoner. Cleveland was my hometown and my folks lived there and all it would have taken was a sudden outburst from me and everything would have blown up in their faces. Jacob didn't have a pistol anymore and he felt insecure. The only way that he could control me now was through fear from his harsh threats and he was right as rain because none of these thoughts came into my mind until later. `What a shame,' I thought, `but the Lord must have planned my life this way and I would have to bear the cross of shame for Jesus' sake.'

Luke grinned at me as if he knew something that I didn't when we met him at the bank. Jacob was nervous and told him, "Let's hurry up and get this over with because we have a long drive back to Ruston." I was calm as I signed the deeds over to Luke and walked to the car and sat down. We didn't linger because as soon as the paper work was done, we started back to Louisiana.

On the way back to Ruston, it dawned on me that I had ruined all of Jacob's plans when I had left him. He had lost control of everything, his family and his parents too. He thought if he could get us all in one little area, he could control things better. Mom could keep us under subjection with her constant threats and when Jacob came home, she would inform him about everything and he could judge the matter. Somewhere in the back of my mind I'd known this all of the time, but I didn't want to face the fact that Jacob wanted to make our home a prison. I had spoiled his plans by running away. Even though I was his prisoner and he didn't have a guard to watch over me now, he was still having a problem trying to work and worry about me being there when he came home which kept him in a frenzy. The revelation was sickening and unbelievable. I realized that only a sick mind would even try such a thing.

Jacob's pride had been terribly bruised and he complained about how he had talked his parents into selling their place up town to move into an unfinished house and then he deserted them. He just hoped they would be satisfied with his decision to sell our house to Luke and they wouldn't feel completely deserted living in the country. Jacob felt that he had been a complete failure and blamed me for messing up his plans. Luke was happy though since he'd gotten quite a bargain by buying our house dirt cheap, but he didn't know how happy I was to see him walking into the same prison that I had just escaped from, but he would find it out in time.

"It's so sad, Father. All of this didn't have to come to pass. All that the children and I ever wanted was to love and serve You in freedom. Mom professes to be a Christian, yet she became my greatest enemy when she set out to punish me because of Ted. If the truth was known I'm sure that was the motive for both Mom's and Jacob's hatred of me. In their minds, I wasn't fit to sit on a church pew, much less teach a class and play the piano. They wanted me to grovel at their feet and hang my head in shame for loving Ted when I needed him. You lifted me up from the pit of heartache and despair and helped me rise above the heartache of those days. You set my feet upon the solid Rock and gave new purpose to my life. You gave me the strength to stand and lead my children in the right way. In spite of being hated, You gave us peace and a beautiful song of deliverance that only Your children can sing. Now, Lord, help me put the past behind me and find a church where we can worship You again, even though the war isn't over. You won this battle, Father, and I praise Your Holy Name! Glory to God, thank You for deliverance," I prayed.

When we settled into our new home, our lives got better. Jacob's wounded pride started healing and he seemed fairly content most of the time. Jacob still tried to dominate our lives and he fussed and complained when Isabella and Sam attended church services without his approval, but I was so proud of them for their dedication to the Lord. Once in a while he would let me go to church as long as he was with me. But, I couldn't feel free, because I could feel him glaring at me in disgust and the look in his eyes revealed his thoughts that this wicked woman was making a mockery of God as she played the piano and this hurt me terribly. God knew how much I longed to serve Him faithfully, and I wasn't happy attending the church that I'd visit a few times with Jacob because I didn't agree with some of the doctrines they believed. It wasn't very long after we moved into our new home that I heard a knock on the door. When I opened the door, a man stood smiling up at me. My heart leaped with joy because I knew immediately that he was a child of God because his face seemed to glow with his joy in the Lord. His voice seemed like music and gladness as he introduced himself. "My name is Bro. Shook and I'm the pastor of a Baptist Church near Ruston and I want to invite you and your family to attend church services with us." I'll never forget the joy that swept over my soul and the peace of God was wonderful and I knew the invitation to attend that church was from my Lord.

Suddenly, I felt free and happy, as if all the chains that had held me so tightly for all this time had suddenly fallen off and I wanted to shout to the whole world that God had set me free at last. I responded quickly and told him that I had two teenagers that would be coming with me Sunday morning. He was very happy when he walked to his car and I rejoiced all the rest of the week, because God had opened a special door for the kids and me to worship Him. I wasn't afraid of Jacob anymore either and my old fighting spirit had returned and not even Jacob could stop the mighty power of God on my life anymore.

When I told Jacob about my intentions, he frowned, but he met such a resistance that was too overpowering and he knew that he couldn't stop me from having my way. He knew right away force wasn't going to work this time and I would fight him all the way so he went along just to see why I was so excited. Bro. Shook was a special servant of God and he loved Jacob. Jacob resisted being loved by anyone though, especially his wife whom he would rather dominate and rule over instead of loving her the way a husband should. Jacob watched me suspiciously and made fun of me when I played the piano by saying ugly remarks which cut deep into my heart. Jacob was jealous of his family, but we ignored him when we could. I was so happy as I watched the children grow in grace and faith in God. Bro. Shook took Sam under his wing and taught him a lot about music, especially how to lead singing and Sam gave his first devotional while we attended that church.

It really seemed like our lives weren't meant to be like other folks though. For some reason we would be moved away to another area when we least expected it. I don't know if it was Divine providence or Jacob's restless behavior that never seemed to find rest and contentment anywhere we went. I learned to accept our role without complaining and placing all my faith in God to use us wherever we went. It wasn't easy to say goodbye to our friends, who thought we lived like gypsies and had no roots anywhere.

It wasn't long until Jacob quit his job again and of all the places he could have gone, he went back to Cleveland and hired on with his former employer. He told me, "I want you and the kids to get in the car this weekend and drive down Highway 190 between Livingston and Bon Wier and look for a place to park the trailer. I'll be hauling board road lumber into Louisiana and I refuse to live in Cleveland. If you can find a place around Jasper or Newton, it will be perfect and I can go by the house on my way to Louisiana and when I'm going back to load at Cleveland."

At first we were heartsick because we hated to move again and leave our friends behind, especially Joyce and Gentry. `How long will Jacob drag us from pillar to post?' I thought. We set out in search of a place to move the trailer early Saturday morning. We entered Jasper on Highway 96 and turned left on Highway 190 and started looking for a trailer park along the highway. We laughed at Isabella when we drove through the small town of Holly Springs. She shouted excitedly, "Look Mamma, it's Holy Springs. We are going in the right direction." Oh, how I prayed we were and this move would please the Lord. I prayed that God would guide us to very place He wanted us.

As we drew near Newton, I could see the sleepy little town from the small hill as we entered the city limits. It looked like a story book world with the high steeple on the courthouse rising high above the other buildings. I felt welcome as we crossed the creek at the entrance of the tiny town, which added to my romantic idea of a story book world. The stores were located in a perfect square around the court house, so closely entwined that it seemed like loving arms reaching out to say, `you are safe here, Destiny.' Then on down the highway we spotted the high school and I thought, `Father, everything is perfect, now if we can only find a trailer park.' No sooner had I thought this than there was a trailer park just after we passed the high school. `Now what could be more perfect, Lord?' I thought. We turned into the trailer park and asked for permission to park our trailer on their lot. I told them it would take a few days to get it moved and everything was working according to God's wonderful plans. There seemed to be something very special about the little town of Newton. Maybe one of the reasons is the kids and I picked it out with the guiding hand of God. We were very excited about moving now and couldn't wait to tell Jacob about it.

The church members were very sad when we told them we were moving away. The song leader cried more than the others did. "Losing a family is a great loss," John cried. I said, "John, if it's the Lord's will that we have to make this move, He will send others to fill our places," but John couldn't believe it would actually happen. The very next Sunday though, while we were preparing to move, John called and said, "I can't believe it, Destiny, God did send a family to church today just like yours. The mother plays the piano and she has a boy and a girl the same ages as Isabella and Sam. That's remarkable, I think, don't you?" We were very excited knowing God had answered our prayer. He had supplied everything we needed and confirmed His will by sending others to fill the places we had filled at the church. Now we were anxious to get moved because the Lord had something wonderful waiting for us at Newton.

Jacob left us to do the moving and he gave Sam all of the dirty work to do, he had always done that before and this time was no different. Sam was only sixteen years old and I don't know what I would have done without him. He fulfilled all the duties that his Daddy should have been responsible for. He helped the movers get everything ready to move, disconnecting the electricity and the water lines and unblocking the trailer as well. Jacob always found an excuse to be too busy some place else, but he expected his instructions to be carried out precisely. I was ashamed of Jacob for putting such great responsibility on our young son's shoulders, but Sam never complained.

God blessed our efforts and we made it safely to Newton on Saturday. While Sam and I were blocking up the trailer, a young man who lived in the trailer park walked over to see us. He introduced himself as Kim. He was Sam's age and it made me happy that Sam had already made a friend with someone in Newton. Kim told Sam about the school where he would be attending, then Kim said, "I want to invite you all to the Newton Missionary Baptist Church. I hope you can play the piano," he said smiling. "We sure need a pianist badly." Sam turned to me and smiled, God had confirmed His will again and we knew the Lord had truly sent us here.

We were all so excited and Kim couldn't wait when he found out that I actually played the piano. He said, "Come with me and I'll introduce you to our pastor." We put down our work immediately and went with him. When we met Bro. Harrell, we couldn't wait to get started in the ministry at Newton.

Bro. Harrell and his wife were wonderful Christian workers for Christ. They loved our family and Jacob couldn't resist the love and attention that the pastor and the church showered on him. The church began growing and quite a large group of young people took an interest when Sam started a youth choir and they went to various churches to sing. We were all happier than we had been for many years, even Jacob. He still didn't surrender his heart to Jesus, but he began to see the results from bringing up our children in the church could be. He was very proud of Isabella and Sam now and helped carry the group of young people to different churches to sing.

Isabella met Steve at the trailer park one day when he was visiting his cousin. His parents went to the same church that we did and Steve started going to church regularly. They fell in love and started planning their wedding after a short courtship. Isabella invited a lot of her old friends from Cleveland to her wedding, including Jacob's parents. I worried about them coming, but there wasn't any mention of the past when they came. I was happy that everything was peaceful and the bitterness of the past was behind us. I was relieved to learn that Mom and Dad had sold their house and moved back to town as well.

We all laughed at Jacob because he hated to wear a tie, but Bro. Harrell insisted that he wear one when he walked Isabella down the aisle. He wore it, but took it off just as soon as he could. He said, "Destiny, the last time I wore a tie was at our wedding and I was miserable then too. Promise me that when I die you won't let them bury me with a tie around my neck." I laughed and promised him that I wouldn't.

Sam fell in love with a girl from Bon Wier named Karen. They were married at the church three months later and they moved to Woodville. A lot happened while we lived at Newton which had to be the Divine providence of God. Four grandchildren were born in one year while we lived there and I was so busy that I didn't have time to worry about Jacob.

Our lives were changing and the adjustments were hard to make, especially when I couldn't avoid seeing the restlessness building up in Jacob. He wouldn't keep a job long and I knew that he was looking for an excuse to move again. I didn't want our lives disrupted by moving again since we finally had a nice home even though it wasn't paid for yet, but we were getting behind on the notes, so I went to work at the nursing home as a nurse's aide to help out. I should have known Jacob would find a way once he made his mind up. He quit his job and went fishing and lay around on the couch while I worked for a small salary that only fed us and paid our rent.

He made fun of me for working while he enjoyed his leisure. He burned the food and would laugh when I complained about it. He made life miserable for me and then he would laugh and say, "Why should I work? I have a wife to make a living for me." One day I came home from work and Jacob was on the couch and I lost my temper. I said firmly, "Jacob, get up, I want your undivided attention." He sat up and looked sort of sleepy and disinterested, but he woke up when I told him, "Jacob, I quit my job today. I went to work to help out, but you didn't appreciate it, so listen up, Jacob, from this day forward until I die, I refuse to work anymore for you. Now if you think I'm kidding, you are mistaken. I promise you, Jacob, if you don't get off your behind and go to work and make me a living, I'll find a man who will!" He knew I meant business so he got to his feet and stretched. Then he turned around and said grinning, "Well, I guess I'd better find a job now, but I sure have enjoyed my long vacation and hate to see it end." I felt like hitting him as hard as I could, but I just walked away in disgust. Jacob went back to work for his former employer at Cleveland and he hauled board lumber to Louisiana.

As time passed, it was as if I was just waiting for another drastic change to take place. I continued going to church, even though I went alone most of the time. One Sunday afternoon after lunch, I lay down to take a nap. I drifted off to sleep right away and began to dream.

I found myself in a terrible place and was holding my small grandson, Kevin, in my arms. I held Kevin tightly as I looked around and cried out in terrible fear, "Oh, God, I am standing in the very belly of hell! Father, how did we get here and why are we here? I know I'm Your child and You washed away my sins and saved my soul from hell, and yet, I'm here and I don't understand." Confused and bewildered by our situation, I clung desperately to my small grandson who was only a few months old in my dream. Kevin wasn't alarmed as he nestled in my arms and it amazed me that he wasn't crying in fear. As I looked down at him, I thought, `I mustn't let him see how afraid I am. I know there's a special reason for us being here and God will provide an avenue of escape for us.'

I looked down at my feet and saw that I was barefoot and so was Kevin. I was standing on a smooth gray colored stone that protruded above the ground just wide enough for my feet to stand on. Red hot lava ran all around the stone and smoke rose up as the thick liquid fire that flowed slowly and had no particular destination that I could tell. I nervously looked down and realized that I was wearing the little cotton dress that I'd purchased at a bargain store many years ago. I couldn't understand why I was wearing it now. We were very poor back then and I marveled knowing the little dress didn't even exist anymore. I looked down at it, thinking, `It looks as new as it was on the Easter Sunday that I wore it to church.' As I thought about the newness of the dress, I realized that it wasn't scorched or even warm, even though fire was all around me. The stone that I was standing on felt cool to my feet also, even though hot lava was encircling it.

Kevin nodded sleepily, as I looked at my surroundings. I was so terrified; that I was afraid to move for fear that both of us would fall in the thick hot lava that swirled around the stone threateningly. I could hear the screams of lost souls as they suffered and their agonizing cries could be heard far away in the distance. Hell seemed to go upward toward a small hill and I knew it must be even more horrible on the other side, because the screams seemed to be even worse in that direction than here where we were. Smoke rose up from the fire and brimstone as far as I could see. Old scorched tombstones protruded out of the ground here and there. There were disfigured people walking around with only stubble of what looked like had once been hair. Their faces weren't recognizable and their distorted features were twisted like melted wax. They wandered aimlessly about and they were groaning in agony. There wasn't any love or pity for another, because each one was suffering in their own misery. I was so afraid they would see us and push us off the small stone into the fire, but when they wandered close they would turn and walk away as if they were afraid to touch us.

I looked to my left and to my surprise, there was a beautiful sea. I could tell that a soft breeze was blowing out over the water, but I couldn't feel it. There was some sort of clear wall that seemed to separate the beautiful sea from hell, but I didn't know what it was. I watched the ripples on the vast blue sea which sparkled like diamonds as the light from Heaven shone on it. `Oh how miserable hell must be, to have cool water so near and yet no one in this horrible place could get one drop on their parched tongue. With the glorious light streaming down from Glory, a constant reminder is ever before them. They had refused to accept the Son of God as their Savior and Lord. Now it was too late. They must suffer terrible pain and agony forever because they had rejected Jesus Christ, the one who had made the complete sacrifice on the cross for our sins. Oh, God, You didn't prepare this horrible place for mankind. You prepared it for Satan and his angels. The devil is leading so many down the path of destruction as they seek their pleasures instead of the way of righteousness. No one need go to this horrible place if they would only repent of their sins and ask Jesus to come into their heart. Oh, Father, I can see our Savior in my heart, standing with His arms outstretched, beckoning, "Come unto me and I will give you rest."

`I don't know why I'm here today to witness these terrible things, but I am placing all of my faith and trust in You, Father, to deliver me and my grandson,' I prayed in confidence. I realized that I must act on faith as I looked down and saw another stone in front of me. I was almost paralyzed with fear, but I raised my right foot and stepped across to the next stone. As I did, I stopped and took a deep breath thanking God that we were safe, then I saw another stone appear and I followed the stony path that God had provided, crying out in joyful praise to God as we continued carefully stepping from one stone to another. "Oh, Kevin, we are going to make it safely home. I know in my heart God has provided an ark of safety just ahead where we'll be carried to the safe haven on the other side. Just one stone at a time will take us to that dock where an angel of God is waiting for us." Kevin was content to be in the arms of his grandmother as we continued slowly down the path. Suddenly, I saw a green grassy dock just ahead and a man in a ruddy brown garment was standing on the bank watching for me. The red lava ran a short distance from the bank so I had to watch my step until we reached the lush green grass. Tears of joy blinded me as we drew near the bank and the man of God called out to me, "I've come to take you safely home. Destiny." He reached out his hands to me and took Kevin in his arms, then he held my arm as he helped me get in the crude flat wooden raft that would take us over to the large wooden ark that waited just off shore. As we approached the Ark of God, I was crying praises to God, "I love You so, my Lord, thank You for delivering my grandson and I from the horror of hell. Thank you for the peace and safety that You provide for Your children," I cried. When I planted my right foot firmly upon the Ark, I woke up from my dream.

I sat up on the side of the bed and tried to understand why I had experienced such a mysterious dream. I shuddered, thinking, `Lord, I don't ever want to go to that horrible place. I can't bear the thought of any of my loved ones dying in their sins and spending an eternity in that awful place. Why did You take me there, Father? Do I need to live a more sacrificial life? Haven't I done my very best to teach the children how important it is to follow Christ? I've suffered a lot of abuse from Jacob too, Father, and he needs You before it's too late. I realize now that no matter how much I have to suffer, I must win Jacob to Christ, even with the knowledge that I might have to suffer more than I ever have before.' As I dressed for church, I committed my all to the Lord and if I had to walk through hell and suffer for this one lost soul, I knew the Ark of God would take me safely home.

Our lives began to change immediately. Jacob found the perfect excuse to leave Newton. He got into a fuss with the finance company over the trailer and he let other people take up the notes on it. He gave everything we had away, except for what we could get by on to live in an apartment. He quit driving a truck and started roughnecking and we wound up in a small apartment in Lufkin, Texas. It's strange how quickly my faith was put on trial by sending me to the town where Ted was living at the time.

CHAPTER 18

UNSETTLED TIMES

My heart ached as I packed just enough to get by in a small apartment that Jacob and I would rent when we moved to Lufkin. Any hope of having the security of a home should have been gone from my mind by this time since I knew Jacob didn't really want a home that would tie him down. I tried very hard to get as excited as he was and think of these changes as an adventure, but I couldn't hide the disappointment that I felt in my heart. I just wanted a home and settle down like normal people. I should have known after twenty-five years of moving here and there that our lives wouldn't change and it would be even worse now that the kids had married and left home. There just wasn't one thing to hold Jacob down any longer.

My heart ached as we drove away from Newton that day as I realized another chapter of our lives had come to an end. I wondered how soon I would experience that walk in hell, just like I had dreamed about. Now that the kids were gone, would Jacob try even harder to keep me from serving God? He seemed so happy and free as we drove toward Lufkin. I realized suddenly that he wasn't running from God all alone now. He was carrying me with him and there seemed to be no avenue of escape. I knew I couldn't escape my fate even if I had tried and that I had to fully trust in God with all my strength and take each day as it came if I expected to survive.

When we arrived at Lufkin, Jacob went straight to Ted's house first. Ted and his family had lived there for quite a while. I always felt uneasy when Ted was around and with Jacob moving us to the same town where he lived was more than I could understand, but who could make any sense out of anything that Jacob did. I was so stunned that I couldn't speak when Jacob asked Ted to quit his steady job and work with him roughnecking. Ted's wife frowned on the idea and she tried to convince Ted that he was making a mistake. I didn't open my mouth because it wasn't any of my business, but I had my own ideas as to why Jacob wanted Ted to go to work with him. Jacob made the proposition sound exciting as he told Ted that he would get a big bonus if he stayed with the job until it was finished.

That convinced Ted and when he told Pauline that he could find another job when this one was finished, she seemed satisfied. I'm not even sure that Ted didn't have an ulterior motive for taking the job as I suspected that Jacob did by insisting that Ted go to work with him. Since we would be living in the same town, Jacob needed Ted working with him so he would know where he was all of the time. Jacob wasn't going to take any chances in spite of Ted having a pretty wife. Jacob thought Ted would consider it a privilege to work with his brother. I knew that Ted would take chances and that he would see me one way or another. My only hope was that Ted had changed toward me. `God help me,' I cried out in the Spirit, `I'm in a situation that I didn't create.' I knew that I must be very careful around them both, because Jacob would be watching everything we did. Jacob didn't know about the new commitment that I had made to the Lord and I hoped that my suspicions were wrong, but I couldn't take the chance and be on guard constantly. I knew right away that Ted's feelings hadn't changed toward me, but I was determined to hide my true feelings from everyone, especially from Jacob who seemed to enjoy placing us both in a bad position and it upset me terribly.

I tried to be friends with Pauline, but for some reason a wall had built up between us. We should have formed a friendship easily though since we had a lot in common except for our age. We both played the piano and organ and we both liked to sew, but she didn't seem interested so I put that idea out of my mind after I began to realize the Lord may not want us to be real close friends.

Jacob and Ted went fishing sometimes when they had a day off. I thought I had been wrong when they would come in laughing about the good time they were having. I started feeling easier when Ted came to the house and brought his family with him. Then I realized that Ted sensed my fears and he wasn't letting his feelings show either. Eventually, the barrier grew weak and that pretense on both our parts didn't last long. Couldn't Ted see how afraid I was of Jacob, but he took every opportunity to be near me. I would snap at Ted over nothing and I thought my hateful attitude would discourage him, but it hadn't when we lived at Fort Worth and I couldn't see any signs that it was working this time either.

It was a relief when Jacob got mad and quit his job, even though he didn't stay there long enough to get a bonus. I didn't mind because I was the one who wanted to run away this time since I was under such pressure because of Ted. Jacob found another roughnecking job near Woodville, Texas and we moved there right away. Ted went to work on the same rig after he got his bonus for staying until the job was completed. One night I heard a car pull up in the driveway. I thought it was probably Jacob and that he had probably quit this job too. I went to the door, frustrated, thinking, `When will this merry-go-round ever end?' When I opened the door, Ted was standing there. I couldn't believe my eyes, even though I really wanted to see him in my heart. Ted said, "Destiny, can I come in?" I said, "Yes, but where is Jacob? Didn't he come along too?" Ted replied, "No, he isn't with me, he's still at the rig. I just had to see you, Destiny, and since I had tonight off I took the chance since I knew Jacob was working." "Oh, Ted, don't you realize how much danger we are in? If Jacob had any suspicion that you were coming by to see me he will follow you and could drive up at any moment and I wouldn't be able to control his violent temper."

Ted took me in his arms and tried to kiss me, but I shoved him away. I was trembling with mixed emotions, wanting Ted and at the same time remembering my promise to God. I pleaded, "Please, Ted, go home to your wife and family because it's hopeless for us. I couldn't live with myself if we did anything against the Lord tonight. I'm trying very hard to be faithful to Christ and even if I loved you, I couldn't break up your family. I couldn't bear to have a cheap love affair. Oh, Ted, I can't live like that, I would want to die." I was so upset that I wasn't sure when he left. I felt so guilty because Ted and I loved each other in such a hopeless situation.

I cried and cried after Ted drove away. I didn't know if I would ever see him again. I was sure our feelings for each other weren't going away, but when we met again, we would suffer the same hopelessness. `What will Jacob do when he comes home from work?' I thought. `He's going to see the car tracks and question me about them.' I walked the floor praying that he wouldn't harm me when I told him the truth. When Jacob got home from work, I told him that Ted had come by and he looked at me questioningly, then asked me what he wanted. I told him he needed some money to buy gas so he could make it home so I gave him a few dollars and he left. Jacob seemed satisfied with my answer and didn't mention it anymore. I calmed down then and praised the Lord that everything was peaceful once more.

It wasn't long until Jacob decided that we needed to buy a travel trailer and then we wouldn't have to rent an apartment every time we decided to pick up and move to another area. It was in the middle of winter when we bought a used travel trailer. I was so happy just to have a home of our own again. It was a stupid idea to set out on the highway in January, but Jacob said that we would travel until our money got low and then he would find a job on a rig until we decided to move on. I knew it was a crazy idea, but that's the way Jacob was. He didn't worry about our future so we drifted along with the tide. We traveled to the edge of San Antonio and the north wind almost turned us over so Jacob turned around and went to Winnie, a small town near Beaumont and parked the trailer in a trailer park. He started working on a rig, but it became a nightmare for me with Jacob working the graveyard shift and him trying to sleep in the daytime in such close quarters as the trailer. Jacob had never been hard to wake up until now and one night after trying to get him awake to go to work I cried out in frustration, "Jacob, I know you hate working in the oil field, so please go back on a truck. I can't keep living like this." He laughed and said, "Do you really mean that?" I replied, "Yes, Jacob, I know you won't be happy until you're back on the road again." He jumped to his feet, laughing happily and responded quickly before I changed my mind. He said, "Let's go to Cleveland right now and I'll see if I can get my old job back." He got his job back and we moved the trailer to Cleveland that evening.

We enjoyed our peace for only a short period of time, but our life had always been that way. Much like a roller coaster, I think. We spent short periods of peace on a high point, and then suddenly we would come crashing down, powerless to control the destiny that drove Jacob to do the things that he did. I wasn't able to attend one particular church anymore, but I hungered for the beauty of serving Christ the way I had done when the children were at home. I was more or less drifting along with the tide, not wanting to irritate Jacob and so afraid to make a commitment to any church right now. Besides, how could a church depend on a person who lived the way we did?

Our lives drifted along without anything dramatic happening for quite a while. Then one Sunday morning Mom was rushed to John Sealy Hospital at Galveston to have emergency gallbladder surgery. At the time I was sick with a terrible cold. I felt so bad, but Mom insisted that I stay with her the first night after her surgery which I did against my better judgement.

Jacob rented a room at a motel on the waterfront that was large enough for the rest of Jacob's family to sleep. After sitting up all night with Mom, Jacob took me there to get some rest so I could sit up with Mom again the following night. I was so ill that the only way I could go to sleep was to look out the big bay window and watch the waves of the Gulf slap against the shore. He didn't seem to realize how ill I was and I certainly didn't need to expose Mom or the other patients to my cold. I hadn't slept very long until Jacob woke me up saying, "You've slept long enough, Destiny. Get up and come eat with the rest of us." So I drug myself out of bed and went with Jacob to the restaurant. I ate very little and sat quietly while the rest of them laughed and cut up, as if they were on a vacation.

Jacob took me back to the hospital after eating supper and after he visited with Mom a little while, he went back to the motel. When visiting hours were over, a nurse came by and told me that I had to go. Mom started crying, but the nurse insisted so I left the room. When I got to the lobby, I called the motel and told the manager to tell Jacob what had happened. While I was waiting, a security guard walked up to me and said I had to leave the hospital right now or he would have me arrested. I was so frightened and almost in tears, because I didn't know where the motel was located and suddenly Ted and Dad appeared smiling at me. It took all of my strength to resist rushing into Ted's arms. I didn't expect him or Dad, but I was never so relieved and happy to see Ted in all my life. He told me that he volunteered to come after me and Dad came along. I wondered about that, it seemed strange that Jacob and Pauline didn't kick up a fuss. `Oh well,' I told myself, `I imagine Dad kept the peace by telling Ted that he would go with him.' Ted was always doing things like that, however, he took every opportunity he could find to be with me, but I would have been terrified to go without Dad.

When we got to the motel Ted said, "Destiny, you need rest so go on in the bathroom, Pauline is in there too." The bathroom door was open halfway and Pauline was standing in front of the sink. She just stood there not inviting me in and I felt like a fool when I walked on in. I was speechless when I saw what she was wearing and I thought, `She needs a housecoat on before she crosses the room in front of the men.' I looked around, thinking she had left it in the bedroom, but as I glanced around the room, I didn't see one anywhere. It made me nervous and uneasy and I felt sorry for her. I almost cried when she walked through the door and brazenly walked across the room in her scant black lace thing.

I slipped into my granny gown and lay down by Jacob. I knew he was awake and had seen Pauline cross the room. Tears rolled down my cheeks as I thought, `I can't believe Pauline would do such a thing because she had always presented herself as the perfect Christian and I was so disappointed that she didn't seem to be one bit ashamed of flaunting herself before all the men folks.' Jacob put his arms around me and said, "It's all right, Honey, I was shocked too, but go to sleep now and don't worry about it anymore. Ted didn't seem to mind so after deciding it must be all right, I closed my eyes and slept between coughing spells

Pauline wanted to go back to Lufkin the next day so Jacob asked Ted if he would take me home because I was sick. Ted told Jacob that he would, but we went by the hospital first before we left and Mom asked, "Destiny, will you help me out when I get out of the hospital?" "Sure I will," I replied and she seemed happy and relieved because she would need someone to help her until she got on her feet again.

I climbed into the back seat of Ted's car and it was a miserable trip and I wished that I had stayed with Jacob. Pauline wouldn't say a word to Ted or me the entire trip. I knew she was mad about something, but I felt so bad that I just sat quietly. He was trying so hard to please her and I felt sorry for him. I thought, `I'm not the only one that has problems, Ted does too and his just may be as severe as mine are with Jacob.' Finally, Ted drove up to our little trailer and I thanked them for bringing me home. `It may not look like much,' I thought, `but it sure looks good to me.'

When Mom came home from the hospital, I went to take care of her. She became concerned about the rattling sound in my chest and told me, "Destiny, you need to get to the doctor right away. I believe you have pneumonia." I followed her suggestion and went to see the doctor. He wanted to admit me in the hospital, but I didn't have any insurance, so he gave me some prescriptions to get filled and told me to stay in bed. Lord, I was so sick that I couldn't move around much and it was so frightening to feel water sloshing around in my lungs. Dad told me it would take about two months to recover from my illness. I didn't want to accept that idea, but I found out he was right. Since Jacob was away from home so much, he decided to carry me to Isabella's so she could take care of me.

I packed some things and we were just starting to Newton when we received the message that my Daddy was in the hospital at John Sealy in Galveston. I was heartsick and wanted to see him. Jacob had kept me away from my folks for so long because of his jealousy, but he didn't know that Mamma and Daddy came to see me one day while he was working. My whole life with Jacob had been so confusing and because of his bitter jealousy and hate, I lived in terror. I loved my folks and Daddy knew it, but he stayed out of our lives because he didn't want to add to my problems. I broke down when I got the news and Jacob said, "We'll go by John Sealy and see your Dad on the way to Newton." I knew only God could have touched Jacob's heart that day and I'm so grateful He did.

When we got to Daddy's room at the hospital, he was hopeful since the doctors had located his problem and they were treating him for it. He seemed to doze a lot, but between naps Daddy witnessed to Jacob. He said, "Jacob, you need to settle down and live for Christ now that you are older and all the kids are married. Why don't you get off those trucks and get a job where you can be home at night. If you don't, someday you will regret it." It seemed as though all the bitter things in the past were forgotten as we visited with Daddy. Jacob seemed to realize that Daddy loved him in spite of the way he had treated him and Mamma. I felt such peace when we left Daddy and I kissed him feeling that any hurt I'd ever caused him was forgiven. I didn't have to tell him about my heartaches. He sensed the pain that I had been going through so many years and even though he didn't want me to suffer, he knew that I was suffering for the cross of Christ Jesus to win my loved ones to Christ before it was too late. Jacob knew Daddy just wanted us to find true happiness in spite of all that had happened in our marriage.

When we arrived at Isabella's, Jacob visited for a while before he left. Isabella took me to her doctor the next day and he started me on some vitamins to help me recover from my illness. One day that week the call came that Daddy had died. I had sacrificed not being with my parents to keep peace with Jacob and it was too late now to change anything. I had sweet and precious memories of Mamma and Daddy and I was especially grateful that God had touched Jacob's heart to go an see him before he died. Daddy had been a faithful soldier for Christ Jesus for many, many years and served as a Deacon in the church. One of the main things he taught us was that it was very important to be faithful. He would tell us that whether or not we had an office to fill in the church, it didn't take much effort to go to the worship service. I know Jesus met him at the gates of heaven and said, "Welcome home, my good and faithful servant." `One day I'll see Daddy again and all the many who have gone on before him. What a glad and happy day that will be when I join them,' I thought, praising God.

CHAPTER 19

SATANIC FURY

After Daddy died, I became very restless. I wanted a home, not a tiny trailer. I started searching for a place and found a trailer house for sale near the bank of the San Jacinto River near Coldsprings, Texas. The place appealed to Jacob, because he could fish any time he wanted to, so we sold the travel trailer and made the down payment on the place. We were both so happy when we signed the contract. We shouldn't have had any problem meeting $100.00 a month. We sure couldn't find a place to rent that would be any cheaper than that. When we moved in, I felt free and happy and fixing up the house was my joy and pleasure. I was especially happy to see Jacob so content and doing things he had always wanted to do. Jacob bought a boat and took the kids fishing every weekend. Our home was a special place and all the members of our family visited often.

On the first Thanksgiving at our new house, I invited all the family for dinner. All of our children came, as well as his parents and other members of his family. We had such a wonderful time that day. After dinner, Mom played the piano and sang, "Chewing Gum" for the kids as they stood around her so amazed that Grandma Quinn could even play a piano. Later I played the piano, everyone sang the old familiar church songs and Gentry recorded all the happy activities on a tape recorder. It was the last family gathering that we would all spend together this side of heaven though.

Jacob looked for every excuse he could find not to work. He was like a child again and didn't worry about the bills. We were behind on the house payments and when I worried he would ignore my constant warning that he needed to stay with a job. The owner began complaining about the notes being behind and finally he told me that he was going to anull the contract if we didn't pay up by a certain date. Jacob still ignored it as if he wasn't concerned, thinking the payments were so low that he could catch up easily.

One morning Jacob was sitting at the table and talking about the weather which was exactly right to go fishing. He remarked lazily, "Destiny, I'm going to town and buy some fish bait, do you want me to pick up anything while I'm there?" I replied, "Well, Jacob, while you are in town, you need to buy a tent." He looked puzzled and asked, "Now why in the world would we need a tent, woman?" I snapped, "We are going to need a place to live very soon and if we have a tent we can set it up on some deserted spot along the river bank and you can fish to your heart's content." Jacob looked surprised and asked, "Why did you make a remark like that, Destiny?" I replied emphatically, "Jacob, you haven't listened when I told you how far behind we are on the house payments and the owner wants his money and I don't blame him for being upset. You are going to cause us to get kicked out. My God, Jacob, we are three notes behind, what did you expect the man to do?" I felt like hitting him with a skillet when he got up and stretched and yawned, and grinning sheepishly, then he put his favorite cap on his head and started out the front door. He turned around and said, "I'll be back as soon as I can. I guess I'd better look for a job before we lose our home." He found a job and went to work that day. Everyone always thought everything Jacob did was funny. He was quite a character, but they didn't have to live on the edge like I did from day to day.

One Saturday we went by to visit with Mom and Dad for a while and she told us they planned to be away for a couple of weeks. Shane, their grandson, lived in Mississippi and he told them he would drive to Cleveland and bring them to his house to spend some time with his family. Shane would take them to Carol's, their only daughter, later. Carol lived in New Orleans, so Mom and Dad were excited since they didn't get to see them very often. Shane planned to pick them up the coming week, Mom said. We had a nice visit that day and it felt wonderful to have our family enjoying the peace that we should have had all those years.

On Monday morning, I heard a car drive up unexpectedly. I was surprised when I walked to the door and Mom and Dad were getting out of the car and she had several items in her arms that I recognized immediately as various things that I had given her over the years. I didn't understand why she was bringing them back, but I didn't ask her why as I invited her into the house. Dad was acting strange and he lingered outside instead of joining us.

Mom was acting very strange as she placed the things she had brought on the kitchen table. "What is wrong, Mom?" I asked, bewildered. "Why did you bring all these things back that I gave to you?" I was really confused when Mom started weeping and I stood there unable to find the words that would comfort her. Then she wiped her eyes and began telling me the reason why she came on this special visit. "Destiny, the Lord impressed so on my heart to come here today and bring these things back to you. Among these items is an old pin that you gave me many years ago when you and Jacob married. The rest is mostly crocheted items that you made over the years.

I told Daddy that if I should die I want you to have my sewing machine and if he didn't bring it to you then I would come back and haunt him." "But why, Mom?" I cried. "I don't understand." She replied, "Destiny, I've been experiencing strange dreams lately and I want to go on this trip without anything left undone that I need to make right before I go. These are things I wanted to be sure that you got back since I don't trust my family to give them to you." I didn't know what to say, so I sat and listened to her without interrupting anymore.

I felt uneasy as I put the items on my bed and went back to the table. Mom had never been a friend to me all those years until lately. She had treated me like I wasn't really a part of her family and then they only tolerated me. My heart went out to her now as she tried to make things right and tried to express things I had needed to hear all those wasted years.

It was as if I could feel a giant wall crumbling away that had separated us for so many years. I felt closer to her at that moment as she tried to correct her past mistakes. She began sobbing and her lips trembled as she confessed that she had wrongfully judged me in the past. "Destiny, you have been a good daughter-in-law. You have respected my family where Ted is concerned, but I never really appreciated it. You brought up your children to know the Lord against all sorts of opposition and you were faithful to the church you loved that I resisted so strongly because we didn't agree on what they taught. I've been so wrong all of these years and I regret all the pain and heartache that I put you through. I just couldn't face the Lord with this terrible weighty burden on my heart," she cried and I put my arms around her and said, "Mom, I love you and everything is going to be all right. You just go enjoy your trip now and let's forget the past." She said, "I love you too, Destiny." We held each other crying because of all those wasted years. Old heartaches seemed to melt away and a true mother-in-law and daughter-in-law relationship began. In a moment of time, the love of Jesus washed away the harshness of the past and formed an everlasting bond between Mom and I.

As they drove away, I watched until they were out of sight and wondered if I would see her again this side of heaven. It was almost time for them to come home the day the telephone rang. I didn't recognize Carol's voice at first so I didn't understand the message she was trying to tell me. Carol said, "Destiny, mother passed away. She had a heart attack and died in the Emergency Room at the hospital." I was completely stunned, but Mom's last visit flashed through my mind. I felt frozen to the receiver and felt weak as Carol explained the circumstances surrounding her death. Carol said, "Will you tell Ted and Luke what happened and tell Jacob that I'll make the arrangements to send Mother's body back to Texas. I'll bring Daddy when I come." She seemed to be calm and I told her, "I'm so sorry, Carol. Yes, I will notify the others right away. God be with you," I cried.

Mom's death came so unexpectedly and it was a shock to everyone, especially Jacob. He took her death very hard as we all did, especially since my Daddy had been dead only a year. His death had taken its toll and torn us apart and Mom's death only added to our sorrow, but it seemed to bring Jacob and I closer together. For the first time in our marriage, Jacob reached out to me and I held him in my arms while he cried. Mom was buried at the Plum Grove cemetery next to the church in 1979.

Ted had moved his family to Fort Worth where Pauline's family lived. Mom had told me many times how afraid she was for Ted to go there. She would cry and tell me that she had experienced a horrible dream and when Ted would even mention going there for any reason, she would beg him not to go. I guess since Ted and his wife seemed to be doing quite well and Pauline was climbing the ladder of success that no one suspected the way that Ted was falling into the very grasp of Satan. Luke would brag about their good fortune and how happy Ted was since this was always what Ted wanted - to have a nice home and plenty of money to spend. They were flourishing when Dad went to visit them and he came back home telling us how wonderfully well off Ted and Pauline were, but Dad was a very sick man and had to be admitted into the hospital shortly after Ted brought him back to Cleveland.

As soon as Jacob and I learned that Dad was in the hospital, we went to see him. Dad was in such terrible pain and I was very worried as I sensed something dreadful was about to happen. I checked his pulse and it was running away with skips between beats and I told Jacob to go get a nurse or a doctor. Jacob didn't waste any time when he saw my deep concern and he ran out the door, but before a nurse could get there, Dad started projectile vomiting of blood that splashed on me and everywhere. The nurses rushed Dad to ICU and we followed them. The doctor chased Jacob out, but he told me to stay and I'll never understand that unless the Lord wanted me there. The doctor and nurses worked with Dad while I stood by his bedside and held his hand and prayed. Dad looked up at me and said, "Destiny, I know I'm dying, Honey, but remember this, I have no regrets as I leave this old world, because I've made peace with God." Tears were streaming down my face when I looked up and saw Ted walk in, so I left the room and walked alone to a deserted area to pray. The doctors operated on Dad, but he never regained consciousness and he died safely kept in the arms of our Lord in 1981. He was buried beside Mom and it just seemed as if we would never recover from his death.

Isabella brought Randall, our grandchild, for a visit shortly after Dad passed away. It was like a breath of clean morning air to hear her happy laughter and the joy she brought with her. She brought some beautiful plants from the nursery at Newton to plant in our yard. She thought of more things she wanted to do to spruce up the yard. So we went shopping and bought the things she wanted. It was so exciting just to be working in the yard while Randall, just a toddler, played in the soft dirt helping us too. I was so happy to have my daughter home and we enjoyed being together, but my happiness never lasted very long. We had just gone inside to start supper when Jacob came home from work in one of his foul moods. He sat at the table saying very little. We tried to ignore it, thinking he might eventually join in later. Isabella and I were so excited about the improvements we had made and I could see pretty blooms already on the flowers she had brought in my mind. We chattered away like old friends that hadn't seen each other for years, but Jacob just sat sullen and I didn't understand why.

Jacob had that look on his face that I had seen so many times in the past. Suddenly, without any kind of warning, he stood on his feet with a look of madness and sheer hatred as he moved quickly and determinedly to destroy his own flesh and blood just to punish me. I couldn't seem to move; I stood frozen in terror as Jacob lunged forward and grabbed a barstool and slammed it across the bar toward Isabella. Isabella screamed, unable to understand the reason why her Daddy had suddenly attacked her and barely missed the terrible blow of the barstool that he slammed on the bar with every ounce of his strength. If she had not reacted so quickly and jumped back, she would not have survived the terrible blow, I felt sure. Isabella started screaming as she cried out in terror, "What is wrong with you, Daddy?" Jacob wouldn't answer as he reached down and raised the other barstool over his head and barely missed the blow again as he brought it down with all the strength he could muster. Isabella grabbed me by the arm and drew me from the corner where I was cringing in fear and complete disbelief. Jacob was cursing us as we ran toward the front door. Isabella snatched Randall up in her arms as we ran out with Jacob hot on our heels trying to hit us with something he had in his hand and his blows seemed to come very close as we ran toward the pickup. Randall was crying so that he was trembling all over, and I was calling out to God for help and deliverance from this monster. Every second was vital to our escape from the bitter rage that Satan had placed in Jacob.

`This has to be a horrible nightmare and I'll wake up soon,' I thought, and it was as if my feet were paralyzed; yet they were moving because Isabella was pulling me along. Isabella shouted as we ran to her pickup, "Get into the pickup, Mamma, or Daddy will kill you." I could almost feel Jacob's breath on my back as I opened the pickup door and jumped into the seat. Isabella gunned the motor in a desperate attempt to get away from this furious animal who was charging fire and brimstone with his cursing tongue, shouting that his vengeance would be worse than I'd ever known before. I couldn't bear to look back as we sped away and Isabella didn't slow up until we were completely away. Randall was still terrified of his Grandpa's behavior and he sobbed as I held him tightly in my arms and kissed his little face. As we drove toward Newton, we both cried and there were so many questions in both our minds. It was unthinkable that any man would hurt his own family and much less a helpless baby. Isabella burst into tears and said, "Mamma, do you think Daddy has lost his mind?" I replied, "Baby, I don't know. I think we just encountered Satan in your Daddy. I've confronted that terrible demon in him before, but God has stood between us and struck him to his knees. This Satanic force hasn't struck out at my children until now, although he has used you children to hold me in his clutches. It may very well be some type of drug he has taken while he was out on the truck, or he may have been drinking whiskey and mixed drugs with the alcohol. I'm so ashamed, Isabella. Steve won't ever allow you to bring Randall around us after this and I don't blame him. This night isn't over yet, Honey, and I'm afraid of what Jacob will do next."

Steve was surprised when we pulled into the driveway and he asked what had happened. Isabella blurted out the whole terrible story between sobs, still shocked by this experience. Poor little Randall had fallen asleep from complete exhaustion and I put him in his warm bed. Steve had built Randall a bedroom next to the driveway adding it onto the house after he was born. Then I went into the kitchen and joined Steve and Isabella where Steve was listening to Isabella give a better account of what had happened now that we were all safe. Steve sighed in relief that we had escaped Jacob's wrath, but I just knew that he couldn't really believe how terrifying the experience had actually been. He said, "It's all over now, so don't worry about Jacob tonight. Destiny, you can sleep in Randall's room and we'll all go to bed and get some rest."

As I dressed for bed, I thought nervously, `Oh, God, I hope this terrible nightmare is over, but we both know Jacob won't give up that easily.' I went to bed, but I didn't sleep. I listened intently for any sound that might be that of a truck engine. It wasn't long before I heard the sound of a truck coming down the country road slowly and I knew it was Jacob coming after me. Isabella and Steve were still in the kitchen when I jumped out of the bed and ran into the kitchen, trembling and crying hysterically and fell into Steve's arms. I cried, "Steve, Jacob is coming, don't you realize that he won't let me go?" Steve said, "Destiny, go back to Randall's room and don't come out for any reason." I went to Randall's room sat on the side of the bed as the truck drew nearer and terror gripped my heart. "Please, God, don't let any harm come to my family because of me. They don't deserve being terrorized by a mad man like this," I prayed.

Jacob drove up into the driveway and I heard the truck door slam behind him. Steve probably thought naively that he could talk some sense into this mad man. As Jacob reached the door, he started accusing me of running around on him. As always, he accused me of cheating on him with Ted, which he used to get his way by making me feel guilty and of course he enjoyed letting everybody know just how sorry I had been years ago. He shouted, "I'll never forgive her or Ted." He spoke very loudly, because he knew that I was hidden somewhere, probably in Randall's room. Steve tried to reason with him by asking, "Jacob, how long ago did that happen?" Jacob replied loudly, "That doesn't matter." Steve said, "Jacob, you know that happened many, many years ago. Why have you waited all these years to punish everyone? You haven't been perfect yourself, Jacob. I know, because you've bragged about some of the things you've done yourself. This is just an excuse to use against Destiny."

Jacob began shouting louder, "Destiny, you had better come out from wherever you are and get in the truck because I'm not leaving here without you. I'll back that load of lumber over this whole house and I'll kill everyone that tries to stop me. I mean it, Destiny. I'll start by backing over Randall's room. I intend to have you with me and I won't take no for an answer." I could hear Isabella sobbing like a child, not believing that her Daddy would actually hurt her or her family. She just didn't want to believe it, but I knew Jacob was capable of anything and my heart broke when Isabella pleaded saying, "Oh Daddy, Randall is sleeping in his bed. Please don't hurt my baby."

Jacob was seething with fury and hate, knowing he had ruined everything. He knew he had caused wounds in his daughter's heart which might never heal or be forgiven, but Jacob trampled on the innocent when they stood in the way of what he wanted. I knew that he was getting desperate as he shouted again for me to come out. I prayed, "Lord Jesus, I don't have a choice anymore now than I did when he kidnapped me with the same threats of killing the kids if I didn't go with him. You know I can't place my children's lives in jeopardy and take the chance that he might be bluffing. Lord, give me the strength and courage to walk out of this room and if my life should be sacrificed, then God grant me the grace to bear it. Walk with me, oh, God, through this fiery hell until You see fit to end it. Please, God, help me to bear the shame that Jacob has brought upon us."

I rose to my feet as I felt my courage return and I walked into the kitchen calmly and said, "All right, Jacob, let's go." Isabella gasped in fear and Steve rose to his feet and took me by the arm and said, "Destiny, you don't have to do this." I looked up at my son-in-law and said, "Steve, take care of Isabella. I'll be all right. I couldn't live with myself if Jacob hurt any of you because of me." Then I turned and walked outside and climbed into the truck. I could hear my baby crying and saw her hanging on to Steve and my heart throbbed with pain as I sat looking straight ahead not knowing if I would ever see them again.

Jacob climbed in the driver's seat without another word. The truck rumbled back down the old dirt road while I sat numb and unfeeling. I had been through so much that I simply didn't care anymore if I lived or died. When we reached the highway, he headed toward Lufkin and we didn't speak to each other all the way. I wouldn't look at Jacob who seemed satisfied and now that he had me alone with him, he was in full control again. As always, he didn't say a word about the terrible nightmare that he had put everyone through. It was as if the whole thing had never happened at all.

Jacob parked the truck in front of a small cafe on the outskirts of Lufkin that night. He finally leaned over the steering wheel and broke down in tears. I couldn't find any words to say to him. I had loved him all these years, but I couldn't love the man he had become. Still the love of Jesus filled my heart with so much compassion that I held him in my arms until he stopped crying. I knew that I was his prisoner again and I accepted my fate that I would never be free. He didn't once say he was sorry for the way he had treated me. I suppose he expected me to accept whatever misery and shame he decided to bring on me because I was his wife and he had the right to do whatever he wanted to do. It was as if he couldn't let go of the tight rein he held or maybe he was just afraid that I would run away again, and he was willing to sacrifice anyone if he felt the least bit threatened. Jacob was a tormented man and he wanted to possess me and I was powerless to stop him.

We unloaded the following morning and started toward Cleveland. I assumed he was going by our house before he picked up another load. I could tell something was troubling him and I wondered if it was because of his terrible outburst the day before. As we drew near our turn to go home, Jacob told me that we didn't have a home anymore, that he had set it on fire before he followed me to Newton. He seemed so cold when he told me, as if that was part of my punishment and that I deserved everything I got because everything that happened was my fault.

I cried out in despair, "Oh, God, what will ever become of us?" He just sat there and stared ahead while I cried pitifully. "Please stop and let me call Wayne, Jacob," I begged. "Maybe he will be able to salvage something and we won't suffer a total loss." Jacob pulled over in front of a store that had a pay phone outside and I got out of the truck and called Wayne myself. I was horrified because of all of the horrible things that were happening. Since Wayne and his family lived right across the street from us, he would know if our home was completely destroyed. I was crying when Wayne answered the phone, but Wayne was elated when he heard my voice. He said, "Mamma, don't worry, the house didn't burn up. Cindy and I ran over to the house as soon as Daddy drove off. Daddy had set the couch on fire so Cindy and I carried it out in the yard so the house wouldn't burn down, Mamma. You can come back home if you want to now." I cried, thanking God that I still had a home to go back to, but Jacob hurt me even more by refusing to take me home.

I was totally defeated and would never recover this time, I decided. All of the guilt and shame lay heavy on my heart that was still suffering for everything that had happened at Fort Worth and I realized that I would suffer punishment for that as long as I lived. `Oh, God, I can't understand Jacob not wanting to at least go back and gather some of our things,' I cried in my heart. His mind was clearly made up to walk away again because he couldn't face the shame he had brought on his whole family. By now, my heart was so broken and I tried desperately to mend the broken pieces of our life. It was such an awful shame to waste our lives away by running from the love of God. `If only Jacob would accept Christ then our lives would have been different,' I told myself. He could find a lot of excuses for what he had done, but the truth was clear to me that he wasn't going to share his wife with anyone, especially the Lord, who continually stood between us.

Like a dying man gasping for air, I prayed that this would be the last episode of his temper, but unfortunately, our lives became even more tragic as Jacob ran from the love of God. The Lord was the only one that truly loved me and I held fast to His hand as He led me by His grace through many more troubling and unsettling times.

CHAPTER 20

THE UNSEEN HAND

I was very depressed when Jacob took me by Mark and Peggy's house to stay until we figured out what to do next. He had told the kids that if they would go to our house and clean up his mess, they could have all our things. Peggy had gathered a lot herself and brought them to her house. I could see all the things that Jacob had given away and I didn't want to live. All my hope of ever living a normal life was gone, but it didn't seem to bother Jacob at all. He seemed so happy to be in full control again. Evidently, he must have been pretty miserable being tied down with a house, even though it was near a river where he could enjoy fishing when he wanted to.

He kept working so we could eventually move, but the last thing I wanted right now was a home of our own. I just couldn't bear the thought of going through the pain of continuously being uprooted over and over again. I didn't think I could bear to face my friends or my family. Not only did Jacob force me to believe all this had happened because I'd been unfaithful loving Ted years ago, but I also had to believe that Jacob had convinced the kids that I was a terrible mother and a bad influence on the children. I was at my lowest point and believed I couldn't sink any lower than I already was. Peggy didn't give up though. She scanned the newspapers in search of a house to buy or rent. She got mad and accused me of not having any faith when I wouldn't take any interest and I didn't seem to care what happened. "Don't you understand, Peggy, I don't want another home. God only knows how many times I've had to walk away from the security of a little house just to please Jacob. Just a little apartment will do. Something that won't hurt when Jacob decides to leave again. Unless you have walked in my shoes, you can't possibly understand the terrible hopeless feelings that I have," I cried bitterly.

Peggy just frowned and I knew she just thought I was feeling sorry for myself and nothing could be as hopeless as I made it out to be. She stubbornly kept searching while her remark cut me to the quick. I had allowed Satan to win this battle by giving into despair. I wondered if I could pick myself up by the bootstraps again and begin to look to Jesus. It seemed as if I had left all my strength behind and had no will to fight back. Fear of Jacob's tantrums had kept me from the church and the beauty of God's house. I'd lost the only peace and joy of the one thing most lovely to me. It was the music in my soul that Jacob had deliberately stolen. The will to fight to fill the role that God had called me to do was in my heart. Even though I was afraid that if I had the opportunity to serve my Lord again, I knew I would have to battle Satan again, but no one wanted to face Jacob's wrath and invite me to church around Cleveland and I really couldn't blame them. It was as if I was a tiny bird caught in a vicious trap and had lost the will to fight back. Only God could release the lock in my heart which seemed so much larger than the trap where I was held prisoner while my warden pretended to be kind and understanding toward his victim. It wasn't long before Peggy found us a place that we could afford. A tiny ray of hope began growing in my heart once again. She found a small trailer house at Shepherd for sale. We paid the down payment and the owners financed the rest for us. It was a nice place even though it was small and some of the kids gave back some of our things which was a real blessing.

I found a small Baptist Church right away too, and gradually I forgave the past and found happiness again. I met new friends at Shepherd and the Lord smiled and rained down showers of blessings in every way. I played the piano at church as well and everything was peaceful for a short time.

Jacob went to work driving a truck for a well known truck line out of Houston. He drove a lease truck for an old friend he had known for many years. Jacob was very excited when he found out the company policy had changed from the way it used to be, and I could go along with him on the truck. He insisted that I go with him right away. Jacob didn't care that my health was bad and it didn't matter that I suffered while riding in the rough truck and my condition would only get worse. It was a horrible nightmare bouncing around in the off seat, but if I complained he would get very mad. I stayed at home every chance I could, but he kicked up such a fuss I didn't get to stay there much.

Jacob had convinced himself that I was happy on the truck with him, so I made up my mind to have an open mind and try to understand what his main interests were. I learned first of all that the truck was his home and the only home he had ever wanted or loved. `Lord, we are worlds apart and all our interests are as different as night and day,' I thought as I realized these worlds would never meet and both of us would find the happiness that I had longed for. I wasn't sure that I could bear to leave my world behind nor even try to make his world mine. The very thought broke my heart, but I knew in my heart that Jacob would eventually force me to live in his world no matter how much I loved my home, my church, the family gatherings and friends dropping by for visits. Jacob took such pride in the truck he drove, just as I did in our home, washing and polishing it until it shone to perfection. He would back off and look at it with pride and smile, feeling very proud to drive it down the highway. Everything inside the cab was solely his possessions and each item was carefully placed at his fingertips. If I moved anything out of place, he would throw a fit so I was in a terrible strain constantly and afraid to touch anything without his permission.

I realized very soon that I was just another fixture, sitting in the off seat to be used at his command. I tried to convince myself that he didn't realize what I was going through, even though it was obvious that he didn't care. It was as if I should consider it an honor to be a passenger in the truck that was truly his domain. Besides fear of him, only God's grace held me there as I began trying to understand the man that I had married.

Jacob told me about some of his adventures as we drove down the highway in hopes that through them he might arouse my interest in the trucking industry. Jacob had driven for this truck line in the fifties when the oil industry was booming. He told me one story that I found hard to believe, but Pat White, who had traveled the country with Jacob, verified his story. He said the dispatcher sent several trucks with oil field pipe to the Northwest Territory and he was one of the group. They had to go past Yellow Knife, which is about as far as a truck could go. They made the trip in the winter before the ice bridges began to melt. Mosquitoes hid under the ice bridges and if you got out of your truck they would swarm all over you like a thick black cloud. I suppose Jacob must have traveled everywhere across the United States and Canada, as well as Alaska and parts of Mexico. He took great pride in the adventures he had experienced, and he didn't mind telling me that his favorite dream was that I would go with him someday. He wanted me to give up everything I loved and make the truck my home. All of my suspicions were correct and he was determined that I learn to love this way of life as much as he did.

I had gone with Jacob on a trip to the east coast when the kids were young. He was hauling produce at the time. Pam kept the kids while we were away so it would give me a short vacation. There weren't very many women who were seen in a truck back then and I knew then that I didn't want any part of that kind of life. I was really frightened when Jacob took pills to keep him awake. I didn't know the danger of drugs back then, I only knew they couldn't be good for him. Sometimes he would be so high on drugs that when he stopped to fuel up the truck, he couldn't seem to find any solid ground. He would step high as if the ground was higher than it was and I watched in disgust, thinking, `Jacob, you don't have to live like this.' When we arrived at the produce market, we had to wait for our turn to get unloaded. Drunks wandered by and stared in my window and pressed their faces against the glass. I would shrink back in terror, but Jacob just laughed at me. I would lean back as far as I could to get away from them so they couldn't touch me. I kept the window rolled up and my door locked, but that made Jacob laugh even harder. He said, "They are just curious, Destiny. They have never seen a woman in a truck before." I promised myself that if I made it home that I wouldn't go with Jacob anymore.

Later that night, we watched another man staggering down the street, swinging around one street post and eyeing up the next one. While he weaved and swayed Jacob laughed and said, "He's going to miss the next post and fall down and when he does he'll have to lay there because he's so polluted that he won't be able to get back on his feet again." Sure enough, he missed the post and wallowed on the sidewalk unable to get to his feet.

It was terribly sad to see women in tattered clothing digging in the garbage for food. As I watched, I thought about the times Jacob had left on a truck, staying gone for weeks at a time and leaving us to fend for ourselves. Although we didn't starve while he was gone, the flour would get awful low in the barrel and one time we completely ran out. God had been merciful to the kids and myself and now as I witnessed women scrounging for food in this way, I prayed that we would never be that hungry. Tears streamed down my cheeks as I wondered if she was scrounging for food for her children and as I prayed I felt so helpless, hoping and praying someone would help them.

The trucking industry had changed tremendously since Jacob first started driving a truck. He took great pride in being a tough guy back then and he joined his truck driving buddies in many a brawl. Once taking a cue stick, he cleared out a bar. There was nothing Jacob liked better than a good fight and he tried to outdo all of them by holding his liquor better than the rest and still be standing up and bragging about his adventures while the rest had passed out on the floor. The older truck drivers talked about him at the terminal and on the road. If anything unusual had happened at a truck stop or at the truck terminal, you could rest assured that Jacob Quinn was in on it. He had told me about some of these experiences and I'd let it go in one ear and out the other. But while I was with him on the road, many of his stories were verified by strangers who had known such a truck driver years ago. He had frightened me half to death when we were on our way to the east coast and a man with long hair was standing on the road thumbing a ride and Jacob slowed down and I thought he was going to pick the man up. The man started cursing me when Jacob didn't stop and Jacob grabbed a hatchet out of the truck and chased the man down the Interstate. Lord, I was so afraid that I thought my heart was going to stop beating as I watched the race in my rear view mirror and all the traffic on both sides of the Interstate came to complete halt. Everyone was looking and some were out of their cars. Some were laughing at the show, but I was terrified. The only thing that I could think of was about the big load of cabbage in the trailer and the thought of what I would do if a State Trooper came along and threw the idiot in jail. The man escaped, and I'm not so sure that Jacob wasn't just scaring him as he whacked away and I'm sure the man felt the wind as it slashed very near his back. Finally Jacob turned around and came back to the truck and I lit into him with fury. "How dare you pull such a stunt, Jacob. What on earth would I do with all of these cabbages if you had been arrested?" He just laughed and drove back on the Interstate and I suppose the crowd that stopped to see the show wondered about the idiot truck driver that would do anything to get a little attention. I guess Jacob had the biggest ego of anyone I knew and was determined to be the best at everything except being a loving husband.

It didn't come as any surprise when Jacob quit his old friend, Dude, and started driving Norman's truck. Dude's little truck was smaller than Norman's, but Jacob like the challenge and working for Norman would offer him a challenge that he hadn't experienced since he was a young man. The higher pay also appealed to Jacob and besides that most of the other drivers envied anyone that drove for Norman. Jacob was very excited when he told me the news. I was happy for him, but didn't want to go with him on this truck. I'd seen some of the huge loads Norman's other drivers hauled and I was glad Jacob didn't haul such monstrosities. It may be adventurous, but I preferred the dull life of just being at home.

Jacob drove a blue KW for Norman, which he called `Old Blue.' Besides it having more power, it had a bigger sleeper too. It was bad enough just going with Jacob now and then, but I knew he wouldn't be satisfied until I went every trip. He was gradually taking me away from everything I loved, but he didn't want to push too hard just yet by forcing me to go against my will. Jacob was convinced that in time I would like the things he did. He liked the idea of me being with him every minute of the day, but I felt like a caged animal because I needed my space and my needs included the church. He really worked very hard trying to make me believe that he worshiped me and wanted me to worship him in the same way. He would tell me that he really needed me and simply didn't want us to be apart anymore. He seemed to be fine when things went to suit him. But if they didn't go according to his plans, he would start his old habit of blaming me for everything. So I had to take the brunt of all his rages and this was the way he thought he had to be in order to possess me and to hold me firmly in my prison. I'm pretty sure every woman that has been on a truck with her husbands has experienced what I'm talking about. Jacob insisted that I go with him one Friday morning in 1984. He said, "We are going to haul a tank to a steam mine at Middletown, California." When I thought about a tank, I didn't think it would be so large. It wasn't only a huge round tank; it was also very heavy. The crew worked for hours getting it loaded, and by sundown we were ready to go.

We slept at the terminal that night, because our permit wouldn't allow us to travel after sunset. Jacob told me that night that I was the second driver. I said, "Jacob, you know that I can't drive this truck and I would certainly be terrified if for some reason I had to." He replied, "Don't worry, Destiny, you won't have to drive, but don't let on when we get to the location because that was one of the requirements. Norman knows that you don't drive." "All right," I said, "But I'm not capable of taking over if the occasion should arise." Jacob laughed and told me to go to sleep and let him do the worrying.

We set out at the break of dawn and started west toward San Antonio. We got out of Houston before the Saturday traffic got bad, but we ran into heavy traffic in San Antonio. Jacob frowned when he read our permit that routed us through the main stream traffic in downtown San Antonio. "Whoever wrote this permit hasn't hauled a tall load on this route," Jacob sighed. "There is at least one low underpass on our route that we can't get through that I know of, but we'll follow the route or we'll be in bigger trouble." I didn't know anything about low underpasses or where they were located, but I knew Jacob did.

We were both tense as we continued on Interstate 10, and the Saturday traffic whizzed by us in a hurry to get somewhere. Jacob drove very slowly when the sign appeared that the underpass was just ahead which was far too low for us to get under. Jacob eased up to the underpass and stopped the truck when the high load touched the overpass, then he got out and looked up to see if there was even a possibility of easing through somehow. I was anxious and nervous as I sat glued to my seat, wondering how we could possibly get out of this situation. We were trapped with no way out unless we backed out in all this traffic. I just wanted to close my eyes, hoping the problem would disappear, I guess.

The Lord always hears the cry of His children though and He provides an outlet in His own way. This time I looked up and saw a Law Officer above the overpass. He saw our dilemma and shouted down to Jacob, "I'll be there shortly." "What a relief, Father," I cried, "You are wonderful!" The Police Officer guided the traffic so we could back up, then he escorted us around the low underpass and then waved us on our way. As we drove out of the city I thought, `How many times has God made an escape route for Jacob and he never once seemed to realize where that deliverance had truly come from?'

We arrived at El Paso around dusk on Sunday. We parked in a Rest Area near the State Line, I knew that I had to sleep before entering New Mexico on Monday. I couldn't help noticing how tense Jacob was and wondered why. He listened intently to the truckers talking on the CB radio and I had a strange feeling as chills crept up and down my spine. I'd heard from other drivers how certain truck drivers were dare devils and that they would do just about anything to please their bosses. Dumb me, I wondered as we left Houston, how would we ever reach Middletown, California by Wednesday? `Gee, it's an awfully long way to go and we are still in Texas. Oh well, Jacob knows that and promised me that he would drive legally if I'd just go with him, but then, he has lied to me before,' I thought. I stared at the logo on the hood, which read, (JUST RIDIN' AROUND.) "Oh, I wish we were headed back to Shepherd,' I was thinking as my instincts were telling me that Jacob was going to do something stupid, such as sneak around the New Mexico Scale House and it made me even more tense and afraid.

My suspicions were correct and I shut my eyes in disbelief as Jacob started moving slowly toward Anthony, New Mexico, down a highway not on our route. I held my breath and I could hear my heart pounding fiercely as he started down the main street of Anthony. I forced myself to look over to my right as I shook with terror, knowing we should be one of those trucks which were in line to be weighed at the New Mexico Scales. The place was lit up with bright lights and I was sure the officers could see our truck. Even if they couldn't see us, they could hear us without any problem. Jacob had to make things worse than they already were. Just as if he dared the officers to chase us or maybe he simply got a thrill out of scaring me half to death as he crept along, ever so slowly through town with the jake brake blaring on and off. Every tiny bump on the highway made my air seat squeak when it bounced and it was like a death sentence being passed on me. Jacob was laughing. I didn't think it was funny and shouted, "Jacob, it's bad enough that you are bootlegging this load through town, but you don't have to sound a trumpet by using the jake brake to let the whole world know we are coming through and defying the law. He just grinned, seeming to take advantage of every second so he could fully experience the thrill of terrorizing me.

`What kind of man had I married anyway? He doesn't even know the meaning of fear. He seemed to enjoy frightening people, particularly me. I can't understand why he is this way,' I thought. I sighed in relief when we left Anthony behind and got back on Interstate 10. He didn't stop again until we reached the Arizona State Line.

Things went according to plan through Arizona and then we crossed into California. We traveled over mountainous terrain most of the time and we had to climb the mountains in low gear and descend the same way. Many times we had to pull over to cool the brakes. They would get so hot from the pressure on the trailer brakes that smoke would boil up as if they were on fire.

Our route took us across the Tehachapi Pass in California. Every mile was an adventure that I didn't want any part of, but I held my breath in wonder and amazement when I viewed the beautiful country side around Bakersfield from the top of a high mountain on Tehachapi Pass. As I looked, I thought, `How great our Father is.' Golden reeds waved in the wind, shimmering like pure gold. Then a beautiful picture of perfectly sectioned off rich farmland around Bakersfield added to the loveliness that our Lord had made. I was awestruck by the view as I marveled at all of God's beauty. Jacob wanted me to see the places he had been, but what I actually found was the beauty of the One who had died for sinners like Jacob and myself.

God's creation held me spellbound and I didn't want to leave. I wanted to remain on this spot where Jesus filled my heart with such peace and tender love that I could hear Him whisper in the wind, `I love you, Destiny, and I'll never forsake you. Even though you must suffer now, it will pass and one day you'll be free.' It was wonderful standing in the presence of God as He refreshed my spirit, yet I knew we had to go on to finish our course to fulfill whatever purpose God had planned for the future. When we started north on Interstate 5 we made better time. Long before we drew near Sacramento, I could see steam rising in areas on the mountain range to our left. When I asked Jacob what it was he told me, "Destiny, everywhere you see those puffs of steam rising up there are plants built on those locations. Instead of drilling for oil, they drill for steam. And we are headed to one of those locations somewhere on top of one of those mountains near Clear Lake. I've been to Middletown before and it's a treacherous trip up that mountain with a load like the one we are hauling. I just hope `Old Blue' has enough power to get us there safely, but as soon as we get this load off, I'm going to Bakersfield and get it fixed. We'll spend the night at Clear Lake and climb the mountain in the morning because we'll need all the rest we can get." I had such an eerie feeling as I looked at the mountains. The steam mines didn't look that large from a distance, but I was frightened because I knew Jacob was worried about the truck. When we woke up the following morning, a blanket of thick fog surrounded the area where we were. I felt certain it wouldn't dissipate anytime soon, but we had to get started anyway. The fog was so thick that my eyes burned from straining to see the center stripe which divided the highway. The work traffic was behind us too, and this added to the tension that tied my stomach in knots and they passed us when they could. I clung nervously to the seat which squeaked and irritated Jacob, then he would shout, "Stop that seat from squeaking," and I wanted to cry because I couldn't quiet the noise.

Tension mounted as we crawled along very slowly in the lowest gear he could find, twisting and turning on a winding road which was barely wide enough for cars to travel on. I tried to see through the thick fog to see how far it was to the valley below, but it was impossible and we were following a blind course which put us in the hands of God. Right then, I just wanted to go home where it was safe. I cried softly, but couldn't let Jacob see my tears. I wondered, `How can he truly love me and subject me to such fear? I don't want to believe that he brought me with him just to make me suffer, but I can't stop thinking that he would do anything to get revenge.'

About the time Jacob would get the truck straight in the road, another crook was ahead that caused the load to lean and sway across the stripe in the highway. As we crept ever so slowly upward, Jacob told me a story about another trucker who had carried his load up a mountain such as this. His truck suddenly quit running, he lost the air in his brakes and then the truck started rolling backward. The only thing he knew to do was to jump out of his truck, but that was a mistake. When he jumped out, the truck ran over him and crushed him to death. I looked at Jacob frightened and asked, "Jacob, what if this truck quit running too?" Jacob replied quickly, "Destiny, whatever happens, if this truck quits running, don't jump out of it. No matter how afraid you are, ride it out. Just remember that. At least you'll have a chance if you will stay in the truck."

His story had been frightening enough, but I froze in sheer terror and was near panic when `Old Blue' did quit running. I couldn't say a word and felt numb with fear. I could hear Jacob shouting, but his shouts seemed far away. "Get out of the truck, Destiny, and find a rock to chock the wheels or we are both going to be killed!" Since he had just told me about another trucker doing that, I wasn't going to move. He could shout and scream all he wanted to, but I was glued to the seat horrified and couldn't move even if I had wanted to. "No, Jacob," I cried, "I'm not moving out of this seat. If I'm going to die, it won't be because I was stupid enough to listen to you." No matter how much he pleaded, I refused to open the door of the truck.

It was as if he regained his senses when he calmly stated, "I'll try to start the engine and see if it will run." When he did `Old Blue' made contact immediately and the engine hummed as the air built up again. Jacob took a deep breath, then said, "I don't have a choice, I have to find out what kind of truck I'm driving." He gripped the steering wheel as he released the clutch, then as the drivers dug into the pavememt; the front end lifted off the ground. I held my breath unable to understand our situation, wanting to scream; yet nothing came out. I couldn't believe that the hood of the truck was weaving and swaying above the ground as the heavy load pulled hard against the truck, but God was with us and He was the power source in `Old' Blue' that settled the front wheels on the pavement again.

We were barely moving when the front end settled down and we continued climbing upward at a snail's pace. I strained my eyes in the dense fog for some sign of a plant off to the side. Suddenly a dim light appeared, but I couldn't tell if this was the plant we were looking for, because it was so foggy that I couldn't read the sign at the entrance. We continued our climb until we reached the top of the mountain, then we turned around and started back in search of the location. The fog began clearing some when we found a place to pull off, and a man in a pickup came up behind us to lead us to the location. When Jacob stopped the truck, he told me to stay in the truck because the area was wet and slippery and he got out to take the binders off so the men could unload. I was so relieved and sighed gratefully. This trip had been mentally and physically exhausting along with all the terror we had experienced earlier. I thought about the incident as tears of relief streamed down my face, thanking God for intervening when we were so near to being killed. "Lord, I can't bear up under this life that Jacob has chosen to live," I cried. "Oh, God, why must our lives be lived from one tragic experience to another?"

I listened to the men shouting commands as the load was lifted off the trailer. Then I heard Jacob rattling the chains as he placed them on the headache rack, thinking, `We'll be leaving this terrible place very soon now, but Jacob will only find something else that is sure to be just as treacherous to haul.'

Suddenly, I saw men running toward the truck through the rear view mirror. My heart seemed to stop because I knew something terrible must have happened. I looked out the window and saw Jacob lying on the ground. "Oh God," I cried, "Is Jacob dead, Father?" I was beside myself as I fumbled for the door handle, so confused and horrified that I didn't even know what I was doing. Finally the door came open and I stepped down, almost falling. Then I staggered around the truck to the area where Jacob lay lifeless on the ground.

Something seemed to hold me back from racing to his side. I could hear my voice, but it wasn't coherent I'm sure since the men kept telling me to stay back. I could only keep repeating, "I'm his wife," as though I had to convince them that I wasn't just a woman he had picked up on the side of the road. I leaned against the truck unable to understand what was happening. My legs were trembling and I couldn't seem to stand up as I gasped in desperation and terror. Jacob had the strangest coloring and his arms lay limp on the pavement. Two men hovered over him while one rolled up a slicker and placed it under his head. The man in charge shouted, "This man isn't breathing." Then they started CPR immediately. I stood on the sideline crying helplessly and agonizingly as I prayed, "Oh, God, please don't take Jacob right now. He is still lost, Father. I can't bear to see him die and go to that awful place I dreamed about to suffer an eternity in hell."

The leader of the group looked at me and then told an elderly man to take me to the office while they tried to revive Jacob. As the man led me away I heard the man say, "This man is dead." I was numb as I stumbled and leaned on the elderly man while the words, "This man is dead," rang like an echo through my head.

Crazy thoughts went through my mind as I waited in the office, such as, `Lord, we're 2,000 miles from home and I'm afraid. What will I do? I can't drive this truck if Jacob doesn't make it. How can I tell all of the unbelievable events which have taken place today to the children and find a reasonable excuse for all that has happened? I only want to find some peace and don't have any idea how to ease their minds either.'

It seemed like hours passed before a worker came and told me that Jacob was alive. "We are carrying your husband to the hospital at Clear Lake," he said. "He is being loaded in the company ambulance right now and someone will take you to the hospital." I was so happy as we started down the mountain, knowing Jacob was alive and hoping that he would recover quickly. Another ambulance met us about halfway and Jacob was transferred from the company ambulance into one that had professionals who took over his care immediately. Finally we arrived at the hospital, but they wouldn't let me go in for a long time, so all I could do was wait in the lobby and pray.

Eventually a nurse called me to come to the treatment room. The doctor on call was puzzled and didn't understand what had actually happened. "Mrs. Quinn, I can't find anything wrong with your husband, except for a heart murmur that he said he has had since he was a boy. Will you tell me what happened at the plant, because the reports reveal that the paramedics didn't know what happened." I explained that Jacob was putting the chains back on the headache rack and he slipped on the trailer and fell into the headache rack, then he fell on the ground. When I got out of the truck, they said he wasn't breathing and they started CPR to revive him. The doctor said they hadn't told him the men at the plant had administered CPR on him. "He will be awful sore Mrs. Quinn, but I think he will be all right. If he has any problem get him to a hospital. I'm going to release him because he wants to go. A company car will be here shortly to carry you both back to the plant so you can get your truck," he said.

A worker picked us up around 3:30 that afternoon and took us back to the plant. Jacob was so embarrassed about the incident that he didn't have much to say so after picking up his paper work and I thanked them for their help, we left and started to Bakersfield to get the truck fixed.

I will never forget all the things that happened on that day. Jacob's life had been snuffed out and he didn't acknowledge that he believed any of it. My heart was so burdened with sorrow as I recalled the awful experience on our way to Bakersfield. Did my cry to God reverse His decision to take Jacob's life? Was heaven silent for a fleeting moment while the Lord made a decision which would affect our destiny? It was a crucial period in our lives as Jacob's life hung in the balance and he actually died and only God breathed new life into Jacob, granting him more time to accept Jesus as his Savior. It hurts to know that Jacob didn't believe God had by His unseen hand reached down from heaven and snatched him out of the clutches of Satan. One more time, and he didn't give God the glory for God's gift of life, neither did he thank God for the great miracle our Heavenly Father performed that day on a high mountain top 2,000 miles away from home. God heard the cry of His child and extended His merciful grace out of pity and love for my lost husband and me.

We wonder about the ways of God and it's hard to accept His will sometimes. During that time, I felt unable to go on without Jacob. In spite of our inability to communicate or agree on how to live, I loved him and couldn't bear the thought of him dying without Christ. However, God will scan the whole situation and His judgement is right and good for everyone concerned. I realize now that if Jacob had died on that mountain not only my life would have been different, but also Ted's. I didn't know Ted was going through hell himself at the very same time and needed help too, but somehow the Lord would work things out in His own time and no matter what we have to suffer, one lost soul is worth it all. We can't see into the future, only pray and place our hope and faith in God that all this suffering would one day be over.

CHAPTER 21

MYSTERIOUS BEAUTY

After getting the truck fixed at Bakersfield we drove to the truck terminal at Fontana and the dispatcher got a load to Houston. When we got to Houston I went home to get some much needed rest, but Jacob stayed with the truck at the Houston terminal. Jacob came home on Friday and told me that I could stay at home this trip. He had a load waiting for him at Tyler, Texas and its destination was Moses Lake, Washington. He told me, "Honey, pack my clothes while I take a shower. I have to hurry so I can get the load out of the plant before quitting time."

Jacob was gone on this trip about a month and I took advantage of being home and enjoyed many of the things I'd missed when I was on the road. It was wonderful attending church services again and being with my old friends. I was able to put the terrible experience at Middletown out of my mind for a while. I knew these things wouldn't last long and no matter how much I tried to convince myself that I wasn't going to let Jacob draw me back into his way of life, I knew that he would insist that I go with him. He simply wouldn't take no for an answer. I hated being away from home and going back into that living hell. If he wanted to live that way, I didn't care if he would just stop trying to force me to live in his world we could have been happy, at least I would, but he wouldn't listen.

On March 28th late in the evening, I heard the truck rumbling toward the house. `Okay,' I told myself, `I'll stand up to Jacob this time and I refuse to back down no matter how mad he gets, I will not go with him anymore.' He was always promising me if I would go with him, he wouldn't ask me to do anything. `Just be by my side and keep me company,' he'd tell me. It never worked out that way though. I had to endure his tantrums and fits of cursing when things didn't go to suit him. He would rant and shout profanities when he got off the route, shouting, "Look at the map and tell me which way to go!" Whether it was in the daytime or the middle of the night, the vibration of the truck made it difficult to read the map and it was next to impossible to see by the dim map light. I would strain my eyes trying to see the tiny numbers that refused to keep still, much less be able to pin point exactly where we happened to be at the time. I was so afraid of giving him the wrong directions and I would frantically search the map all the while trembling inside. He would get beside himself if you cried out, "Jacob, I can't see." If I could find what he needed, very often he wouldn't believe me and turn the wrong way and go for miles before he would turn around. `Oh, God, I have to escape somehow,' I pleaded, `I can't bear this way of life anymore!'

When Jacob slammed the truck door and walked slowly up the steps, I knew something was wrong and my stomach tied in knots. When he walked inside I could see he was very ill, but I didn't know what was wrong with him. He sat down at the table while I fixed his plate, but he wasn't hungry and he ate very little. I'd never seen him like this, so pale that his skin had a yellowish cast. He looked up at me like a small child with pleading eyes and said, "Honey, will you please go with me on this trip. I don't feel well at all and I really need you this time. I have been through hell on this last trip to Moses Lake and I have to pick up another load tomorrow and go back to the same location."

Everything I'd promised myself earlier flew out the window. If he had acted tough, I could have spoken my mind, but my heart melted so that I couldn't tell him no, so I told him that I would go with him. Jacob's face lit up and he smiled. He was really sick this time and he needed me, but he always had some way to make me do what he wanted me to do. No matter how I tried to change things, it was as if a higher power had full control and I couldn't escape my fate.

The next morning, I packed our things while Jacob rested, then we set out to go to Tyler. As we drove into the plant I couldn't believe what I saw, the tank we'd hauled to Middletown was like a toy in comparison to this load. Men worked feverishly getting the load ready for shipment which we had to get out of the plant by quitting time. They had actually assembled a whole section of a carbide plant and nailed plywood around it, encasing the whole structure. It seemed incredible that we would ever be able to deliver this cargo without at least losing some small part of it. The truck looked so small in front of the load and when Jacob backed the truck up to it I watched in awe and wonder. After the load got its final inspection, we started covering it with tarps and securing them down tight. When we eased out of the gate I knew we were about to experience the adventure of our life, but since Jacob had hauled a load just like this one a few weeks ago I felt better.

Both of us were tense as we wormed our way through Tyler. Once we reached the city limits I began to feel better, but Jacob never relaxed. When we got to the first truck stop on our route we shut down for the night. We got an early start the next morning and checked the load after breakfast. As soon as the sun peeked over the horizon, we started off again. It looked like a big house on the trailer with plywood covering it. Our permit took us on a northern route and we headed toward the Texas panhandle. Jacob was upset because this permit routed him a different way from the previous trip. He also had had two women escorts on the last trip across Texas, but the permit didn't require them this time.

We weaved slowly though the countryside over narrow highways, only meeting a farmer now and then, or someone travelling in a travel trailer. The route took us through parts of Texas that I'd never seen, so the trip through that area was nice and pleasant. I looked at the scenery as we drove along on a ghost-like highway that had once been heavy with traffic. I knew this was a familiar highway to Jacob, however, because he had hauled loads through here in the past. Jacob didn't talk much about this area; his mind was on the awesome responsibility of getting his cargo to its destination.

Jacob told me how important good escorts are and how the driver's life and his cargo depended so much on them to get them safely to the destination. He said his former escorts were very courageous when they encountered several difficult situations. Maggie was the experienced escort and led the way and Susan was on her first trip with no experience, so she followed behind the load. Jacob loved and admired their grit. They had to stop when a sudden flash flood crossed the highway and the water was too high to cross, but they needed to keep going if they made their destination on time. The only solution would take tremendous courage and Susan was afraid, but they trusted Jacob's experience as an older truck driver so they were willing to try anything. Jacob told them, "I'll go ahead and both of you follow as close to the trailer as you can and we'll make it across." Susan was so frightened that Maggie put Susan in front of her and Jacob drove into the high water and the girls followed. The big tires separated the water and cleared a path so that they could cross over safely. Jacob said they made it across and the girls probably wouldn't forget him after that experience. Jacob praised them continually and he wanted them to escort us on this trip. He would say over and over, "I hope Maggie and Susan will be waiting to escort us across Colorado Monday morning, but the company seldom uses the same escorts every trip." I had never seen Jacob so obsessed about escorts before.

We shut down Saturday night somewhere in West Texas. Jacob said that he and the girls had spent the night here on their trip. He told me that we should reach the Oklahoma panhandle Sunday and then we could rest until Monday morning. Everything went according to plan and we made it to the Oklahoma and Colorado State line Sunday around noon. We parked at a Truck Stop and tried to rest, but Jacob was awfully sick. I thought he had a terrible cold and he was miserable. I could hear the rattle in his chest and his face still had that yellowish cast. I was worried about him because he really needed to go to a doctor, but he would tell me, "I have to get this load off first. I just probably have emphysema like Daddy had." The old truck stop had been closed up for quite a while. We were alone and afraid because it was really a deserted area. We spent a miserable day as I tried to make Jacob comfortable and prayed for him while he slept most of the day. He was so short of breath that he really couldn't rest well though. Our escorts met us at daybreak on April 1st. They were two men instead of the women Jacob hoped for, however. When we entered Colorado we faced a fierce winter storm, which made our trip even more treacherous through the blinding snow. We crept along slowly, tense and nervous and just trying to keep the truck on the highway was nerve racking. We only traveled 66 miles that day and shut down for the night at a Truck Stop. It took three days to cross Colorado since our route took us along the high elevations, then along the Kansas border and then we turned west for a few miles. At that time, our permit sent us on a more northern route toward Wyoming. Since we didn't need escorts in Wyoming, our escorts left and we set out alone.

Thelma Quinn

We were on Interstate 25 in Wyoming when a State Trooper pulled us over to check our permits. It was so cold that Jacob and the officer sat in his car to check the papers, but it wasn't long before the officer walked up to my door. I was frightened when he told me that Jacob had passed out in the car. He said, "Your husband is a very sick man, I believe, so I'm going to follow him to the next Truck Stop just to be on the safe side." He kept his word and followed us on in to Cheyenne and we spent the night there. The next morning I noticed that the swelling in Jacob's feet hadn't gone down over night like as it usually did. In fact, the swelling was much worse. Still, Jacob refused to seek medical help. He insisted stubbornly that he would make it until we could unload at Moses Lake. I prayed every waking minute that he would get better, but I didn't know how seriously ill he really was and how easily he could stop breathing at any moment. We were completely in the hands of God.

We left the Interstate the following morning and took State Highway 20, which took us across the Bridger Teton National Forest. I'd seen herds of antelope running free in Wyoming and I envied God's creatures because they were free. I sat in wide-eyed amazement as I had never in my whole life seen so much beauty as I viewed that magnificent mountain range. It made me realize the awesome power of our God who had formed those mountains had also formed the whole world by just His Word and all he had to do was speak it into existence and it was done. Now I sat in awe and wonder and thanked Him for the opportunity to see this majestic scene while I was still alive. Jacob had said he wanted me to see all the things that he had seen, but he didn't realize that through all the marvelous wonders that I saw that it just made me draw even closer to my Lord and God.

The highway was narrow and almost deserted at this time of the year. The lodges were closed too. We would meet a car once in a while, but they had to leave the road to let us pass. Somewhere along the terrain we met a State Trooper. He stopped us to check our permit and the load. He said he was surprised to find anyone travelling on the frozen highway, especially with a load of such huge dimensions. He just shook his head and smiled, then he told us to be careful and to watch out for the icy road as we drove on toward Idaho.

As we made our way to Idaho Falls, I thought about the brave pioneers who had blazed this trail for us. I could almost see men like Lewis and Clark as they camped by the winding river with a warm fire blazing just about dusk. I could picture them in my mind, wearing ruddy clothing, sitting by the fire and looking at the parchments and maps that they had brought along. They couldn't have walked many miles over the rough terrain in a day while they charted the route so very carefully.

The rivers roared loudly as they ran by in such a hurry to get to wherever they were going. The swift water slapped the rocks in a steady beat with such power that no man could stop it had he tried. Only God could contain such power in His hands and I realized the course that God had planned for each of us was very much the same. The river twisted and swirled along its banks, through deep ravines and down mountain slopes in a mighty rush, untamed by man, very much like Jacob's life as an adventurer.

I often wondered how the wagons had made it over the mountains with women and children walking along beside them. Sheer determination must have driven them on. Were they not adventurers just like Jacob? Didn't they have the same spirit that wouldn't let them give in to sickness or cold weather just like he did? There was so much that I didn't understand about the spirit of man. Only God Himself designed these incredible people and He led them by His Hand. Along the lonely snow laden highway, a beautiful elk appeared at the edge of the woods facing our truck. He made a beautiful picture in contrast with the deep snow, and in my delight I thought, `This handsome specimen of God's creation seems to question our being in his domain anyway, especially something so monstrous that I felt sure he had probably never seen anything like it before.' Jacob was delighted too and he smiled happily, very pleased that I was excited about the wonderful things he had told me about and he was overjoyed to be able to share these experiences with me by his side. He exclaimed, "Now, Destiny, aren't you glad that you came on this trip with me?" "Yes, Jacob," I replied.

From Idaho Falls, we headed toward Salmon, Idaho on Saturday morning. Snowdrifts were so deep that the only way we could tell we were on the road was by the fences on each side. I saw a big truck coming toward us and judging by his speed I decided he was familiar with this highway and evidently had quite a bit of experience driving over ice and snow. I grew very worried as he drew near, because our load was very wide and I cringed in fear. I covered my eyes as we met the truck and Jacob just laughed as the truck whizzed by.

When we got to Salmon, Idaho we parked at a deserted spot in front of a plant. Jacob rolled the landing gears down and pulled out from beneath the load, then we went to town to eat and to find a place to rest over the weekend.

We slept in front of the plant that night and got up on Sunday morning and went to buy supplies in town. Jacob said, "Honey, let's go to the Rest Area nearby and rest there today, maybe we can have a picnic too." I said, "Jacob, that would be nice," so we went to the Rest Area instead of staying with the load. We really didn't have to worry about anyone stealing it anyway.

It was such a beautiful Lord's day. The sun was shining and even though it was cold, it was nice to be out in the fresh air. Jacob parked in a secluded spot so we could enjoy our privacy. We just sat in the truck for a while at first watching two men fishing for trout. I marveled knowing the river must be icy cold, but the men wore fishing gear that covered them from their feet to their hips. We watched as they waded the cold river where ice and snow was formed on the banks. Later, Jacob and I shared a picnic when the fishermen left. Jacob was still quite weak and ill, so he crawled up into the bunk and took a nap.

I sat looking at the river as Jacob drifted off to sleep and I compared the river to my own life. It roared like thunder as the rushing water dashed across the rocks and splashed against the banks. The water had no will of its own as it rushed onward toward its destiny and I knew that I didn't have any control over my life either and wondered if my life would always be lived in a continual turmoil just like this river. Surely these raging waters will reach its destination and probably further down stream it will flow into a beautiful calm sea.

My heart was heavy as I opened the door and started walking up the small hill where the park tables so I could be alone to pour my heart out to God without disturbing Jacob's rest. My legs felt like lead as I made my way to sit down at a table. I looked down at the scene below and started crying out to God. "It's Sunday again Father and Jacob needs me more at this time, more so because he is very ill. I pray that You will have mercy and heal him of his illness and give him another opportunity to be saved before it's too late. I love him in spite of him taking me away from the things that are most dear to me and he would rip You out of my heart if he could, Father. It's very hard drifting aimlessly along without any hope that things will ever change. Oh, how I long for You today and the peace that I experience when I'm in Your House," I cried bitterly.

Suddenly, Jesus spoke in a sweet and tender voice to my heart, "Destiny, look up, you are sitting in the cathedral that I created." I raised my head and through tear-dimmed eyes I realized this was indeed a Holy Place. A deep blue sky was like a dome overlooking the cathedral. The walls were beautifully carved out of stone in a variety of brilliant colors. Red, yellow, brown and gold and other harmonizing colors, all in beautiful contrast, something that no artist could ever capture on canvas. The cathedral was encased by the mountain, which seemed to reach up to the sky and it was as if the walls wrapped me in God's tender embrace and I knew Jesus loved me with all His heart. God spoke continually as the river roared loudly, "Listen, Destiny, see how the river of life runs freely. Don't you see, my child, oh, don't you understand, all you see with your eyes tells you that I am here with you and I'll never forsake you nor leave you alone. You have a mission for which you must suffer for My sake, but in time you'll rejoice, Destiny." "Thank You, Father," I cried, happy now and satisfied.

Jacob got out of the truck and joined me. He told me he felt some better after a nap as he sat down beside me. I said, "Jacob, it's so nice and peaceful here, I hate to leave. The Lord fills this place and I feel so near to Him. I would like to stay here forever." "It is nice, Destiny," Jacob agreed. We just sat quietly for a while, drinking in the beauty that God had provided and then I felt led to ask him some questions that had bothered me for many years. I said, "Honey, we both know you have been very sick, but I want to ask you some questions that you may not want to answer, but I need to know the answers for myself so that I can understand you better. Just be completely honest with your answers though." He looked surprised, but he told me to go ahead and ask him whatever I wanted. I said, "Honey, why have you hated God all these years and made my life so miserable when I would take the kids to church in spite of your threats? Why do you despise the church anyway, and why does the mention of the Lord's name make you cringe?"

I didn't expect Jacob to answer my questions and that he might just simply change the subject, but he didn't. I became frightened when I saw anger building up in him and I decided that I had made a terrible mistake by bringing up such a touchy subject which he wouldn't want to talk about, as if he wanted to forget something very hurtful that had happened his past. I sat quietly, watching his reaction and my heart went out to him as he bowed his head and I knew whatever had happened had been very painful. He gritted his teeth and I cringed in fear as he turned to me and said, "All right, Honey, I will tell you why I don't want any part of the church or God." Jacob clenched and unclenched his fists, as he grew more agitated and upset. You could feel his anger as he spoke, "Mother made me go to church when I was a boy. I kicked and cried when she made me wear those stupid short britches she thought looked so cute and nice. She wouldn't let me wear long pants like the other boys wore to church. She whipped me every Sunday morning screaming threats at me. Then she would drag me to her friend's car who carried us to church and would force me to sit in the back seat. I despised her friend who had three girls who sat in the back seat and stuck their noses up at me. All the way to church, Mother would yell at me and those smart aleck gals would poke fun at me. When we would get to the church, Mother would drag me inside and make me sit between her and her friend. When the preacher gave the invitation the `old Bitty' and Mother would grab me by the arms and drag me to the alter and hold me down while they poured oil all over my head. They would hold me down and pray that God would rebuke the old devil in me. They would cry and yell real loud, as if their God was hard of hearing. It was some sort of a ritual, I guess, at least they did me the same way every Sunday morning. I hated the church and their God, because it seemed that all their God wanted to do was just to punish me."

I trembled with heartache as Jacob continued and some of the things his Aunts had told me went through my mind. "Well, my resentment didn't end at the church though, because Mother didn't take me home after church. We always went to her friend's house for dinner and we didn't get to go home until the evening service was over. I had to endure those three snooty daughters of Mother's friend all afternoon, but every chance that I could find, I would sneak into their Daddy's room where he sat drinking alone. I didn't blame the man for drinking all the time. They didn't want anyone to know he was there because they were ashamed of him, but we became good friends and I enjoyed his company. When Mother would miss me, however, she would yell, `Jacob, come here, I don't want you in that room.' Mother's old hypocrite friend would agree with her, and I blamed her for the way Mother treated me, because I believe she would beat me all the time just to impress that `old Bitty.'"

Jacob was pouring his heart out and he started telling me more about his childhood. He said, "I really couldn't do anything right. If I lied, I got a whipping. If I told the truth, Mother wouldn't believe me. She'd whip me real hard and then she would start praying that God would rebuke that old devil in me. Oh well, I guess I deserved those whippings and probably deserved even more of them. Don't get me wrong, Honey, I loved Mother and she did the best that she could. Anyway, Daddy finally put a stop to Mother forcing me to wear those stupid short pants. He put his foot down and told Mother that if I couldn't dress in regular clothes he was going to keep me at home with him. He said that he wouldn't be caught out in the public with shorts on like that and she wasn't going to force me to wear that garb either. She made me go through this same ritual every Sunday until Daddy told Mother, "Kate, leave Jacob alone. I'm not going to allow you to force him to go with you anymore." I asked Jacob if their pouring the oil on his head helped him. Then he grinned and replied, "All I got was oily hair." I started laughing and so did he, and I honestly believe his confession cleared the air. Jacob didn't realize through his story that the Lord was helping me to understand how he saw the Lord. "Oh Jacob," I cried, "God loves you. He isn't a bad monster who is out to seek revenge and punish you. He wants you to love Him and let Him be your Lord and Redeemer. God is love, Honey, and Mom did a horrible thing and so did her friend. Someday, both of them will have to stand before Jesus and give an answer for the way they treated you. I hope you can forgive them both, Jacob, otherwise, these bitter feelings will only eat you up. The love of God gave you life up on that mountain at Middletown and the many other times when your life hung in the balance from the various accidents that you have experienced. You must realize that Jesus loves you in spite of the way Mom did, which was wrong, but as you said she was doing what she thought was right. Thank you for sharing these things with me, Honey. I really do love you, Jacob." Then he took my hand and we started walking back down the hill toward the truck. As we walked, I thought tearfully, `Lord Jesus, Jacob has carried scars which are so deep that not even my love is able to wash them away, but Your sweet love can.' The mission of a soul winner isn't easy and most often it takes a very long time to win them to Christ. I decided that it would take a lot of patience and understanding and the help of God to bridge the wide gap between Jacob and myself, but in time love would win over the forces of Satan.

As we walked toward the truck I looked up at the clouds racing by, and said, "Jacob, isn't that snow clouds?" "I'm afraid it is, and they are coming from the direction we have to go tomorrow, Destiny. The escorts should be coming through that pass and they will be able to tell us how bad it is when they get here," he sighed.

Around five o'clock two cars drove up and two women got out and joined us. They introduced themselves and told Jacob they would be escorting us the rest of the trip to Moses Lake. They said they had been delayed because of the snowstorm over the pass and we would have to wait until the snowplows could clear the pass before we could start out tomorrow. "We'll rent a room at the motel and meet you in the morning. Once we get clearance from the highway department, we'll start out," one of the escorts said. It was around noon on Monday before we got the clearance to start up the Lost Trails Pass. One pilot car pulled in front of us and the other one followed closely behind. As we crawled along the winding mountain pass, the road was still white in places the snowplows had left. We climbed higher and higher and the scenery was a sight to behold, and Jacob cautioned me to sit still, but I was so excited that I took pictures from the window of the truck. It was all so beautiful and absolutely breathtaking. My heart raced excitedly thinking how gloriously wonderful our Father really is. Fir trees with snow laden boughs bowed gracefully in the sunlight and when the loud jake brake roared, it seemed to wake up the whole mountain. God granted us the privilege of seeing His beautiful winter wonderland, where

His Holy Presence caused me to watch in awe and reverence and brought me that much closer to Him. As the big truck rumbled through the sleeping countryside, little flakes of snow tumbled from the snow laden boughs and silently joined the soft snow banks around the tree trunks, already being carried away with the north breeze that brushed the mountain side like tiny angel wings. White sparkling snowflakes glimmered in the sun, swirling round and round before finally resting where they fell.

Up the winding mountain highway `Old Blue' moved steadily with the big load almost touching the mountain side as the left front wheel rolled off the pavement on the driver's side, and we were crosswise most of the time. I prayed that we wouldn't meet a car or truck on the icy highway. Jacob and I were startled by the sound of cracking wood and he told the back escort to look and see if she could pinpoint the problem. She came back on the radio and told him it was a board at the top of the load that protruded out enough to give the driver warning that he was too close to the mountain. When Jacob found out the cracking wood didn't involve the load he relaxed and we continued upward which was snow laced with the ice and had formed on the highway in thick white patches. I was tense and afraid and could feel the wheels slide as they lost traction every now and then. However, Jacob kept control of his emotions, while I sat in my fear, picturing us crashing down the mountain side in spite of everything we could do to prevent it.

As we drove on through those mountains in the ice and snow, I watched Jacob driving over the treacherous roads and thought how strong he was in spite of being so sick. He never wavered, never lost control as he held `Old Blue' steadily moving on the icy road. It was as if I were seeing Jacob for the that man he truly was, just as he had been in California, his strength and courage could have only come from God. We inched our way up the steep inclines and descended every downward turn in the same low gear. The front escort drove ahead, sometimes out of sight to warn the traffic that was on the road that a wide load was just ahead. Thank God, there weren't many cars or big trucks on the highway, because at times the truck and load would lean with the slant of the highway. It took nerves of steel to drive a truck with such a monstrous load like this and I shuddered, but I was glad that it wasn't me sitting behind the steering wheel. Jacob had taken on an awesome responsibility, but I couldn't imagine anyone wanting to live like this.

As Jacob communicated back and forth with the escorts I sat as still and as quiet as I could. I was proud of Jacob since I knew he was one of those strong men who had a lot of true grit which very few men possessed, but the Lord had given him all these traits which I couldn't seem to understand. Although I admired his strength under these circumstances, the thought of living this way day after day was a terrifying thought. My continual prayer was that God would take care of us and help us to get safely home again. `Once this trip is over though, Father, Jacob would just get excited with the challenge of another one. How long suffering will Your love be and will You continue to extend it to us as we go on living so dangerously? I can't bear much more Father,' I cried so many times, `but one day would pass and another sunrise would peek over the mountain and I will have to trust in Your mercy again.' We reached the summit on April 9th and then we reached Montana. We shut down for the night near Missoula and took off again as soon as it was light. We crossed Lolo Pass that day and through a small part of Oregon and I praised the Lord for every mile as we drew nearer our destination.

As we drew near Moses Lake we ran into a construction area and were held up for quite a while. We were all concerned about the delay, because it was Friday and we didn't have time to spare if we were going to get unloaded before the plant shut down for the weekend.

We sighed in relief when we pulled the load into the carbide plant. We had been two weeks getting this load to its destination. Even though I was extremely tired, Jacob was in a much worse condition. He was having so much trouble breathing that I told him to stay in the truck and I would drag the tarps off and get it ready for the men to unload. He said, "Honey, the workers can't help you, because they aren't allowed to, so just take your time and maybe I'll be able to help you when I get my strength back." Finally we got the load off, and the men watched me just like Jacob had said and they didn't offer to lend a hand.

After they took the load off, we went to the nearest Truck Stop and called the dispatcher in Houston. Then we went to the restaurant to eat supper. As we sat in the booth, I heard a commotion behind me and turned around to see what was going on. A man sat against the wall at a table and it looked like he had a baby bear in his hand. Everyone in the restaurant turned their attention on the man as he made the little bear talk and placed his little paws over his eyes as if he was shy. The man was such an expert at this that I actually thought the baby bear was alive. Evidently I wasn't the only one who believed it because a waitress went to his table and said, "Mister, animals aren't allowed in this restaurant." Jacob started laughing because he knew the little bear wasn't real. And I was afraid when the man became very indignant and got up from the table and stated very firmly to the waitress, "Well, if my bear ain't welcome here, then I ain't either," and he stomped out of the restaurant. The waitress' face turned red with embarrassment when one of the men told her that the little bear was just a puppet.

When Jacob called the dispatcher later he told him to go to the terminal at Tacoma and they would try to get a load going back to Houston Monday morning. We didn't start toward Tacoma until Saturday evening though. Jacob felt so bad that he just lay around in hopes that some of the swelling would go down and he would start breathing better.

It was around 135 miles or so from Moses Lake to Tacoma, Washington. We should have been able to drive that distance in only a few hours, but since Jacob was so sick, it took a lot longer because he had to stop and rest at intervals all the way. We arrived at Tacoma before daylight on Sunday morning and Jacob told me to get some rest. He couldn't lay down anymore, so he had to sit up to sleep. I went to sleep from complete exhaustion, because I always stayed up when Jacob did.

The sharp sound of chains rattling woke me up with a start and I jumped up. I panicked when I realized that Jacob wasn't in the truck and looked quickly at the rear view mirror to see if I could see him. I was relieved when I saw him raising the landing gears on the trailer so he could pull away from the trailer. I was so worried as I watched him struggling to breathe and it took so much effort for him to climb back up into the truck. When he sat down, he leaned his head back breathlessly and said, "Now, I can search for the hospital and get help." There's no doubt that God had His merciful hands on us as we went directly in the area where the hospital was located. He drove the truck straight up to the Emergency Entrance. When we walked in, the medical staff took charge immediately and led him to a examination room.

I waited in the lobby until someone came up to me and told me that Jacob was in congestive heart failure. They rushed him straight to the Cardiac Unit and started treatment on him and because he was so sick, they allowed me to stay with him. Jacob and I were so naive then about so many things. Jacob had been very near death all this time and we hadn't realized how seriously ill he was. "Oh God," I cried out in prayer, "Thank You for bringing us so far. It was only through Your loving tender mercy that we have survived. Now once again I come to Your throne of mercy as I bring Jacob before You again, just as I did at Middletown. Oh, my Father, why can't Jacob see that time seems to be running out for him to be saved? Please God, save him before it's too late and grant me the strength to stand by him until the end. If it be Your Divine will let him get well again and we can go back home together."

The Cardiac Unit was formed in a circle and the nurses' station was located in the center. Jacob's room was fairly large and the nurses brought me a cot to sleep on. The entire medical staff was very nice and went out of their way to make us both comfortable. The hospital furnished my meals and also pajamas for me to sleep in and it pleased Jacob that I didn't have to leave the room for any reason. We weren't there very long until a lady chaplain came to visit. She seemed puzzled and asked, "Mrs. Quinn, aren't you afraid to be so far away from your children with your husband in his condition?" I replied quickly, not even considering the thought that Jacob might die here, "No, I'm not afraid, but then I'm never afraid when I'm with Jacob away from home. We just came through a dangerous experience, so being here in the hospital is a haven of hope and refuge for us both actually. He is getting the best possible care now and I don't worry and the thought hasn't entered my mind that he won't recover. The Lord provided this help for us and He has everything in control. It doesn't really matter where we are as long as we are together." She seemed so amazed at our positive attitude and tears filled her eyes as she looked at Jacob smiling with joy and pride because of the things I told her. "I've never witnessed such devotion in a married couple before. You have a marvelous testimony of faith so few couples have these days." Then she left the room with a smile on her face which glowed with joy.

I called the children about Jacob's condition as soon as I could and gave them the telephone number to Jacob's room. I was so stunned that I couldn't be positive just who I was talking to on the phone, but I think it was Luke, Jacob's younger brother on the other end of the line. He got straight to the point immediately as he exclaimed, "Destiny, Ted shot Pauline! She's dead! Oh, Destiny, I know it's a shock, because we all thought everything was great for them, but they weren't. Pauline wasn't what everybody thought she was and Ted went nuts when she left him! It's a long story and I can't tell you about it all on the telephone, but Jacob needs to know his brother is in a lot of trouble. Right now he is in the county jail." I felt faint, but I hung on and tried to get a grip on my emotions so Jacob wouldn't be upset and hear our conversation. I said, "Jacob is very ill and can't help anyone. I have my hands full with him so I can't help Ted." He replied, "I'll stay with Ted as long as I can, but I can't stay very long." His words seemed to echo through my mind and my heart felt as though it was crumbling in total hopeless despair. I looked down at Jacob as he slept peacefully and I knew that I had to pull myself together, because this news could undo all the good that the doctors had done.

As I fought back tears, I told Luke, "I can't believe what has happened. The last time I saw Ted, he seemed to be on top of the world and so did Pauline. I can't tell Jacob about this until he gets better, but I'll pray for Ted." Tears stung my eyes as I hung up the phone and went to the bathroom and poured my heart out to God. "I don't understand what has happened to Ted, Father, but You know all about it. I know that I will have to tell Jacob before he hears about it from a someone else, but I need to wait until he is stronger. I'm just glad that Mom and Dad died before this horrible thing happened because they would be as completely devastated as I am. Please, Father, have mercy on our family and help us through I pray." Jacob didn't get suspicious when he saw I'd been crying since he knew that I had been praying for him throughout his illness. He was a handful though when he started getting better and I forced myself to put Ted out of my mind.

Jacob was ready to leave the hospital as soon as possible and when Norman called to see how he was, Jacob told him to find him a load going back to Houston. Norman said, "Let me talk to Destiny," and he asked me if Jacob was well enough to leave the hospital. I said, "Jacob insists that he is, Norman, but he is still in ICU with IV's going as well as being on oxygen. He's lying in bed making everyone miserable and insisting on going on the truck when he's not really able yet." Jacob took the receiver out of my hand and said, "Norman, I'm getting out of here tomorrow, so find a load for me." I could hear Norman laughing, because he knew Jacob had made up his mind and he would do it too.

Jacob told me to start packing because we would leave tomorrow, so I obeyed, even though I didn't agree with his decision. No one could change his mind, not even the doctor. "All right Jacob, I can't get you to change your mind so I'll give you some prescriptions to get filled before you leave the hospital. "I'll say one thing though, Jacob Quinn, you are one tough Texan and that's probably why you have lived this long," the doctor remarked and just shook his head as he walked down the hall. `These Texans can be so stubborn,' I thought in disgust.

When we left the hospital we went to the Tacoma Terminal, but we didn't get a load out until the next day. Jacob was still so pale and the medicine wasn't helping and it seemed to only make his condition worse. When the dispatcher found Jacob a load he came up to my window and said, "Destiny, aren't you afraid to leave here with Jacob? You both could get killed or kill somebody else. He is very sick, but he is determined to go and I can't talk him out of it." "It will be all right. We'll just have to stop along the way and let Jacob rest, but we'll make it home," I reassured him. Norman had told Jacob before we left to go by Odessa on our way home and pick up the new Peterbilt that he had bought for him. Before we got to Odessa I told Jacob about Ted. I was afraid that he would get very upset, but he took it better than I thought he would. He said, "Don't cry, Honey, I'm sure Ted had a good reason for what he did, anyway, there's nothing we can do about it."

By the time we reached Odessa Jacob had thrown most of his medicine away because the medicine was making him worse than his condition and he had improved a lot when we drove in the Peterbilt place. Jacob was upset because Norman had traded `Old Blue' in though. The new truck was very nice, but it just wasn't the truck that `Old Blue' was and he complained all the way to Houston about it. Oh, how right he was because we soon found out when we hauled a huge load to San Francisco. Later, we hauled a load back to the steam mine at Middletown and the truck creaked and whined and there were times when I thought it would break in two and we'd plunge down the mountain side to our death.

Finally, an opening came up for an LTL driver at the Tulsa, Oklahoma terminal and Jacob took it. We moved in the company house and he worked around the terminal as well as hauling LTL. We hadn't been living there very long before the company sold that terminal and Jacob quit his job and we moved back to Shepherd. I never gave up hope that Jacob would settle down to an ordinary job and we could live a normal life. There were times I thought my dream just might be coming true, but my dream wasn't meant to be, I guess.

CHAPTER 22

THE TURNING POINT

Jacob and I moved back to Shepherd just before Thanksgiving in 1984. We weren't even unpacked before I received a message that Mamma was very ill. We went to see her right away and I was so glad that I went to see my Mamma then, because she passed away on Thanksgiving day. It was the saddest Thanksgiving I have ever lived through. Mamma was the last of Jacob's and my parents still alive and when Mamma died, we were both devastated. Jacob and I hadn't communicated very well in the past and now we drifted even further apart and we dealt with our grief separately, instead of leaning on each other.

Through the testimony of one of my nieces I found peace. She said, "I went to visit Grandma and told her I would come and take her to Mamma's for Thanksgiving dinner. Grandma looked happier than she had been for years. She was all dressed up as if she were going somewhere. I asked if she had some place special in mind to go and she answered, `Yes, I'm going to see Johnny and we are going to spend Thanksgiving together this year, so tell the family that I won't be with them for Thanksgiving dinner this year.' Mamma smiled, but I thought Grandma didn't know what she was saying." Mamma did spend Thanksgiving with Daddy that year and not only that year, but she would be with him throughout eternity.

Shortly after Mamma died, I became very ill and eventually the doctor had to perform surgery. I had lost a lot of blood and even after blood transfusions I was still very weak and run down for a long time. Jacob had gone back to work for the Houston truck line and he was gone quite a bit during my recovery. `Don't get too content to be at home,' I told myself. `Things can change in an instant and you know it. Jacob is probably just biding his time until you get on your feet and you may not be healed completely before you could very well find yourself sitting back up there in the off seat of that old eighteen wheeler again.' I lived in dread every day not wanting to leave home anymore, knowing it was just a matter of time before I would have to go back to my prison again and sensing that my reprieve was almost over.

I believe that Jacob had made up his mind that he would remove any hindrance that stood in his way this time. I was even more convinced of it when he quit bringing any money home anymore and his excuse was that the loads didn't pay enough or that they had shorted him on his paycheck. The payments on the house got behind first of all and there was very little food in the house anymore. Last of all, the power company turned the electricity off and all I could feel was the shame and disgrace of it all.

"Oh, God, I haven't asked for much in my life. Just a small place to call home, whether we rented or bought a house," I cried, knowing that very soon I would have to give up all my hopes and dreams of living a quiet life at home and worshipping the Lord in the little church nearby. As I recovered from my illness, it was as though God was preparing me for some mission for Jesus' sake and the surgery had only been a small part of that preparation. I didn't know how long I could hold on until Jacob would suddenly pounce on me like a cat on a mouse, but in my heart I knew it wouldn't be long. I prayed that God would intervene day and night and stop this madness until I began to realize that I had to put my priorities in order and go on from there.

In my search for the answer, I turned to God's word, and the Holy Spirit helped me understand that Jesus wanted my full surrender to follow Him and that I must be willing to sacrifice the things of this world if there was a need. I knew in my heart that Jesus was letting me know that in a very short time I would have to sacrifice everything and enter some sort of mission which brought me no hope for anything that this world had to offer, stripped of a place to come home to, or the joy of worshipping God on Sunday mornings.

When I went to my pastor to explain all the things the Lord had revealed to me, he became quite upset and told me that my place was in the church and not running all over the country in a truck. I told him the Lord had shown me that the Lord's House was to worship Him, but the ministry of winning lost souls to Christ lay outside that Sanctuary where the lost souls were crying out for someone to show them the way to salvation. "My greatest joy is sitting on a pew every Sunday morning and listening to the word of God, but Jesus has an appointed mission for me and I'm trying very hard to prepare my heart to pursue it in peace," I told my pastor.

When Jacob came home, I told him that I was willing to give up everything and make the truck my home if that was he wanted, but he rejected my offer and it was so believable that I didn't know what to believe. `What did he want,' I thought? Of course I should have known the reason. He didn't want me to go unless he had forced me. He just had to let me know who was the boss. When he rejected my idea, I tried to accept it, but he caught me off guard when he came home from the next trip and stood in front of me and yelled at me. "If you don't give up everything and live with me on the truck, I'll find somebody who will!" The look in his eyes was frightening as he glared down at me in hate. Oh, how I wanted to tell him to go find somebody else because I wanted to be free and he was actually so dangerous and threatening, but it was his hateful words which stunned and hurt me so much that I just wanted to cry. Why did he always have to intimidate me when it wasn't necessary just to get his way? I had told him on his last trip that I would give up everything and live with him on the truck, but it had to be his idea and not mine I suppose. He just kept standing there glaring at me as he waited for my reply and the only thing I felt safe to say was, "Okay, Jacob, I'll go with you if that's what you really want." Jacob had won again, just as surely as he had at Newton when he threatened harm to our children. He didn't have to tell me that he was going to hurt me this time, I saw it in his eyes. However, Jacob didn't know the Lord had already prepared me for leaving everything behind and making the truck my home. Jacob had placed me in a position where there was little else that I could do. He'd been very cunning and used all kinds of devious methods to force me into this situation, especially not bringing any money home lately to pay the bills or provide any food for us.

I was nervous and uneasy as I hurriedly packed what I thought we could get by with. I just wanted to leave as soon as possible and get this ordeal over with. He wasn't driving a big truck now so there wasn't a lot of room to store our things, but he was so happy and excited as he stuffed our belongings into the small compartments in the truck. I wasn't happy though, because the inevitable had happened and my heart ached and I tried hard not to cry as we drove away from our home not knowing if we would ever see it again.

Only God knew how much heartache this mission would involve. Only God could help me endure what I considered to be a walk through the fiery furnace of hell and there was no hope of escaping whatever lay ahead. I already knew what a life of trucking was all about and dreaded the suffering that I knew lay ahead. "Let's stop somewhere and call Mark and tell him what we've done," I suggested. Jacob pulled into the nearest truck stop so we could call him. My heart ached in shame, as Jacob didn't seem to mind asking the kids to clean up the mess that we always left behind. Jacob never felt the shame that I was feeling as he spoke the same words that I'd heard so many times before and sounded to me like a broken record, "Mark, you kids can take anything that is left. We just took what we could carry in the truck to get by on." Mark replied, "Okay, Daddy, we'll do it right away." `When will our children get tired of running behind us and picking up after us?' I thought. `Don't they feel any shame at all for their Daddy?'

As far as I could see or even think of, there was no avenue of escape and the truck would become my home or it would be my prison. Too many times I'd tried to escape, but to no avail and finally I accepted the awesome promise that was made to my Lord and Savior that I would do my very best to glorify His Holy Name through my life. The truck had been my home for two long years without any hope of looking forward to any of my dreams. They had been trying years, and the marvelous grace of God was all I had to see me through. The Holy Spirit was my Comforter when I cried in heartache and despair, desperately missing my family and I would dream about our little kitchen which had been left behind. Jesus shared my sorrow during all those times of despair and hopelessness, but I couldn't share my true feelings with Jacob since he was convinced in his own mind that I was happy just being with him.

During our many years of trucking, we traveled day and night. We hauled permit loads much like those we had hauled on Norman's truck. One of the most interesting was one we hauled was to St. John's, Newfoundland. We loaded at Bryan, Texas along with six other trucks and we all were going to the dock at St. John's. Jacob had been to Newfoundland before, so he knew we had to cross over from Sidney, Nova Scotia to Newfoundland on a huge ferryboat. Most of the drivers were excited about the trip since they had never been there, they were looking forward to the adventure.

We arrived at Sidney on Thursday morning. After getting all the paper work in order, we had to wait for the ferry to come into port. While we waited, the drivers cut up on the CB radio. Finally, the ferry docked and began taking on passengers. I was surprised because I expected the ferry to be like the ones I'd ridden at Galveston, but this giant could hold at least seventy-five loaded trucks, besides hundreds of cars. Besides all of this, but there were many passengers on foot. All the vehicles were chained securely in the lower part of the ship.

We rented bunks to sleep on during the crossing which took seven hours. My bunk creaked, whined and shook and I clung to the side afraid I would tumble out of it and fall on the floor. I was very sick even after taking pills for sea sickness. Jacob laughed when I tried to keep my balance the next morning, but I didn't feel well at all.

Once we reached Newfoundland and got off the ferry, we still had 566 miles to go before we reached St. John's. They say Newfoundland is a rock and all of its many lakes and rivers were as blue as the sky. I saw a huge moose in a creek bed on the way to St. John's. Since I had never seen one before, it was exciting as well as travelling in a strange country so far from our own.

We arrived at St. John's on Sunday and while we ate dinner I heard some of the patrons talking about how a herd of moose had ventured into town and had to be driven out by helicopters. Evidently that happened quite frequently from the way they talked. Later Sunday evening, we set out in search of the place we were supposed to unload the following morning.

The address was the Port of St. John's. Our cargo had to be transported from our truck to a ship anchored at the dock. Seven trucks lined up to get their load off the following morning, but things didn't go according to plans as it often happens in the trucking industry. This ship was a special one with four countries involved and neither they nor the trucking firm we worked for were concerned about how long we had to wait to get our trucks unloaded. The special ship was an exploration ship and they wouldn't set our cargo on the ground. They would remove part of its cargo off the ship and then replace the shipment with the supplies which we brought from Bryan.

Disgruntled drivers complained and I couldn't blame them. It was terribly trying to all of us because we were stuck on the dock until we could all get unloaded. Jacob and I was the last to get our load off and by then it was Thursday.

A truck driver's life is nerve racking and filled with suspense. You find yourself near tears in a situation like the one we were in. Every morning when you wake up you hope this will be the day when your load will come off and you can be on your way. Everyone gets tense and nervous waiting for someone to call your name, waiting and hoping they want you to take the binders of your load so that you can get ready for them to take the load off. Bored and unhappy, you try to pass the time by talking to other drivers, but mostly they just complained and threatened to quit just as soon as you could get back to the truck terminal.

There weren't any motel rooms on the dock either. We slept and ate in the truck, which Jacob would have done anyway. There weren't any bathroom facilities around either and we had to manage without those small conveniences.

We carried a small pan in the truck and washed as best as I could, but life was hard and we roughed it.

Jacob didn't seem to mind as long as I was with him, but if I complained He would be furious with me, so I tried not to let on and tried to be cheerful in spite of our circumstances.

A friendly policeman visited with me quite a bit. He told me some of the history about Newfoundland. One day he pointed out the Cabot Tower, which looked small from where we were, and then told me that the first radio signals went out from that tower in World War II. Newfoundland was a neutral country during the war, so ships from other countries entered their port. Every day while we were there, he stopped by to talk with me and helped me endure the endless days while we hoped that the next truck to be unloaded would be ours.

On October 31, 1985, I watched large groups of people from every nation in the world board this magnificent ship and took a few pictures of the event from the window of the truck. The truck drivers were invited to join the large crowd to see the inside of the ship. I didn't go because my clothes weren't presentable, but some of the drivers did and they said it was quite an experience. Even though those days were trying, I'll never forget the things I saw and learned or the kindness of that policeman. He gave us a nice pin from the police department to remember him by, as well as some of the history of Port of St. John's.

On Thursday morning, we finally got unloaded and loaded some oil drums on the trailer which had been stored at the dock which were to carried back to Houston. Winter had set in so the drums were covered with ice, but we managed to get them loaded and tied them down. They were slippery with oil and we were finally on our way to Houston and had made our way to Memphis, Tennessee, we started over the big bridge there when one of the drums worked loose, tumbled off the trailer and rolled into the heavy traffic. We couldn't stop on the bridge to recover the drum and when I saw it tumble off to the side of the highway out of the line of traffic, I breathed a sigh of relief.

There are a lot of women who enjoy this type of adventure and they enjoy the thrill even while it is tying your stomach in knots of fear. I never did learn to like it or appreciate the challenge that a truck driver encounters constantly. Jacob may force me to live this way, but he couldn't make me conform to this way of life. There were a few quiet times though when we waited outside of a plant over the weekend to get unloaded on Monday. During those times, we rested and watched television. Sometimes I cut Jacob's hair while he sat on a small folding chair which we kept stored in the truck. Jacob liked the way I styled his hair and he often made the remark, "Honey, I don't know how you do it with those large sewing scissors."

Sometimes we stopped by a store and bought some meat to barbecue when we had to wait over the weekend to get the load off. We would go to an isolated area and Jacob would take out the little barbecue pit and the two small folding chairs we had stored in the truck and we would have a cookout. We would catch up on our rest over the weekend and many times I would sit for hours just looking out the window with Jacob sleeping in the bunk. By the time Monday morning came around, we were rested and anxious to get our load off so we could go back on the road again and the endless cycle seemed to never end.

If we parked in a Rest Area, we couldn't rest for someone knocking on the door and waking us up. Brazen women didn't mind asking a driver if they could give him a good time for a price. It was vexing to me to be subjected to so much sin continually. It wasn't only at the Rest Areas that we were tormented, but the Truck Stops were just as bad. I despised hearing the CB radio day and night which Jacob wouldn't turn off even when we were parked at a Truck Stop. What pleasure he received from someone wanting some dope or had some for sale or sell a girl's services for a driver's pleasure, I will never know. Trucks were parked side by side with no privacy at all, so I made curtains to put around the windshield and windows. Even though Jacob had drug me to the pits of hell and stripped me of my dignity didn't mean that I had to enjoy it. I could hear my Daddy's voice in my mind saying, "Destiny, no man loves his wife that will take her into a hell hole. He has no respect for her or himself." `Daddy, I know of a certainty that Jacob has never loved me,' I would cry in my agony.

I never got used to waking up and climbing into my seat pulling back the curtain to find eyes staring at me. Diesel smoke filled the air from the trucks that ran day and night. The smoke would sift inside the truck and settle on our clothes and our hair. This way of life was trying and vexing to the soul of a child of God. There were very few drivers who respected a woman in a truck. It was a common thing to glance out of the window and see a driver using the bathroom and I'm sure they only thought if you put yourself in a man's place, then what do you expect? Many times I couldn't hold back the tears as I was continually exposed to degrading things and I despised Jacob for placing me in these situations. It had to be my walk through hell that I had dreamed about. Here I was, a mother and a grandmother, brought to the lowest point in her life. It wasn't just that alone that drug me down and broke my heart, but I saw many young runaways all along the highways and around the Truck Stops. Each one was looking for a handout or a ride to another town and these kids needed Jesus to get them going in the right direction. I cried knowing that it was only by God's grace that my own children weren't like these lost children who were destitute and in need.

During all our travels, I saw many children who were cold and dirty lying on the side of the road and it was heartbreaking to see the terrible misery of so many who were lost and undone without God or a place to lay their heads.

Once we were crossing a mountainous area out West, when a truck in front of us pulled off to the side of the highway and the driver made a young woman get out, then he drove away and left her on the side of the Interstate. I heard the driver bragging about what he had done on the CB and I cried, "Oh, Jacob, that woman can't walk to the next town, it's at least fifty miles away." I didn't like the look that came over his face before he spoke. I realized then that that woman could easily be me if I gave Jacob any trouble. `Truly God, I am his prisoner and live under a constant threat,' I thought. Then he grinned and said, "Don't worry, another driver will come along and pick her up." I felt sorry for the woman and sighed in relief when I saw another truck stop and she climbed into his truck through the rear view mirror. She was just trash to Jacob and the truck driver, but, Lord, she has a soul and You love her and want her to be Your child too. Right then all I just wanted to do was to go home and then I would remember that this truck was the only home we had.

One time when we were up in the northern states somewhere on a Sunday evening and couldn't get unloaded until morning. We were also very tired and hungry. Some of the other drivers, who were waiting along with us had brought their wives with them too, suggested that we get out of our trucks and find a place to eat. The only place that we could find open was a bar, but it also had a restaurant. The bar was separate from a huge dance floor and we sat at a large table in the dance hall. The large room was empty except for our group and one of the women said, "It's awful dull and quiet in this place. I wish someone would play that old piano standing over there against the wall on the dance floor." As if Jacob could read my thoughts he remarked sharply, "Don't you do it, Destiny."

Lord, how I ached to touch that old piano and Jacob glared at me as I got up and went over to the piano and sat on the bench. It was glorious to feel the keys beneath my fingers, and I felt so close to Jesus as I began playing some of the old church songs from memory. I rejoiced in Christ as a small group formed around me at first and others came out of the bar and joined us too. Some staggered in, but I kept playing and we sung `Amazing Grace' and `Rock of Ages' together. They were the old songs that lifted my heart and I led from memory songs such as `The Old Rugged Cross,' `What a Friend We have In Jesus' and many others. Some wept openly and testified how their mothers had carried them to church many years ago when they were young. It had brought back many memories of the past for them and myself. I pray that through that small demonstration of faith at least one turned back to the Lord. God gave me a sweet blessing that night which I will always recall with joy. It wasn't a tabernacle, but Jesus was there and He would live in my heart no matter how far Jacob took me over this land and even across the sea. He couldn't destroy the sweet presence of the Holy Spirit that dwelt in my heart comforting me through the hardest trials during my life.

The beautiful peaceful times were so few, but there were times when God touched my heart and I would love Jacob in spite of everything he put me through. Sometimes on Sunday mornings we would be driving across open country and just before sunrise on the desert, I would wake up and sit on the side of the bunk.

Everything would be peaceful and quiet, except for the sound of the truck. Jacob would be sitting beneath the steering wheel, looking straight ahead. I felt as if he might be thinking, `I hope Destiny wakes up soon and takes her seat beside me.' I would sit for a moment and drink in the peaceful feeling that I seldom enjoyed anymore, and as the sun peeked over the mountain I'd wrap my arms around Jacob and say, "I love you with all my heart, Honey." He would kiss me shyly and say, "Come sit with me." Then I'd climb into my seat beside him and for a time we'd share love and peace. Oh God, if only our days together were all so lovely as this, then I'd have been happy just to be his constant companion. I still cry when I remember many other times when Jacob would make me afraid through his cursing when things didn't go just to suit him. I would break down and cry when he was harsh and our life was a living hell instead of what it should have been. I was so afraid to speak or move in my seat most of the time because the least thing could send him into a rage. I guess I just wasn't tough enough to deal this sort of life and I couldn't make my heart turn to stone and ignore my hurt.

He let me know that I owed him because he had brought me along and that I should feel lucky because he had since I didn't have any other place to go. I was trapped because there really was no avenue of escape; I learned my lesson only too well. My life with him was like a roller coaster. There were times of peace which could change instantly to fear and deep sorrow. The Lord helped me take the pitfalls as well as the happy times when I could see my Lord, my Creator of all things lovely. I could feel His great power in the things that He made, in the hot deserts and in the mountain ranges. I could feel His tender love caressing my heart when I could see the antelope running free on the slopes of Montana, and the beautiful elk inquisitively watching us from the edge of the woods standing in deep white fluffy snow. When we drove through the redwood forest on our way to Eureka, California, the scene was so breathtaking that I marveled in the twilight at noon. The huge trees were like huge umbrellas and they blotted out the sun, but the sunlight would peek through the boughs and mysterious shadows sprawled across the road in front of us. The Lord let me see fields of wheat, which so breathtaking as the golden grain yielded to the wind and made it look like a golden sea. He took me over every major highway in the United States and parts of Canada. Still after all I had seen, there's just no place on earth more precious to my heart as the little country church where I grew up and found Jesus who saved my soul and rides every mile that I do across this vast country.

My greatest joy came after being up north for a long time, especially near springtime and to cross the Texas State line was like entering heaven to me. In comparison to the northern states where winter held on with brown grass and cold chilly mornings, Texas was like a paradise. I just couldn't get over what a difference Texas was from the rest. The beautiful green grass was like a thick carpet and the colorful wild flowers were breathtaking. "Oh, Beautiful Texas," I hummed happily, "God blessed you with such wonder and majesty. Blue bonnets in full bloom, resembling a deep blue sea. Oh Father, it's so good to be home again and in spite of my prison I feel free."

As we would draw near Cleveland, I would start hoping that Jacob would go by some of the kids to see them, especially around the holidays, but he would drive on through as if they didn't exist. One particular Saturday we had been away for such a long time and knowing Sunday was Easter I hoped that Jacob would go by some of the kids to spend the weekend with them. I would have loved to attend church services with them and see the little kids in their new Easter clothes. I would have loved to see the little ones hunt Easter eggs and listen to them play and watch them run in the warm Texas sunshine. "Oh Jacob, can we go by Mark's on the way to Houston," I pleaded. "No," he replied, "we'll stay at the Truck Stop at New Caney, so we can get an early start Monday morning before the traffic gets bad." "But, Jacob, it's not out of the way to go by Mark's house," I cried. He drove on past the exit to our son's house and I cried in heartache. "Why, oh God, why does Jacob want to lay around an old dirty Truck Stop?" I couldn't understand him at all. We had to stay at the Truck Stop and I fought back the tears all that weekend. If by chance Jacob went by the kid's house, he wanted us to sleep in the truck instead of in the house.

"Father, I hate to acknowledge the honest truth even to myself, but I must confess I can only see Jacob as a selfish self-centered man. He not only cheated me out of a little joy; he also cheated our children too. One day Jacob will cry because he threw away the precious opportunities that he could have enjoyed and chose a stupid hunk of tin and rubber instead of his children," I cried out to God.

In April of 1986, Jacob and I made a trip to Charleston, South Carolina. We were at the terminal when Jacob started complaining about being short of breath. The dispatcher got us a load going toward Houston, because Jacob was in congestive heart failure again. I prayed that we would make it back to Texas before I had to put him in the hospital, but this time his condition worsened in a hurry and we only made it to a Truck Stop near Tallahassee, Florida. I had to call an ambulance to pick him up and carry him to the hospital. It was a more trying experience and nothing like his recovery at Tacoma, Washington. Jacob was in the Cardiac Unit and I could only see him for only a few minutes at a time. I slept on the floor along with some others who were sitting up with their folks. Everything went wrong that could, I guess. No one would cash a check so I was broke and hungry while I stayed at the hospital. Finally a kind lady who was sitting up with her Dad trusted me and brought me some cash in exchange for my check.

It was strange that two years ago at about the same time Jacob had heart failure and had gone to the hospital in the same condition. When the doctor released him in a few days we took our time going to Houston since Norman had sent another driver to pick up Jacob's load at the Truck Stop. As we crossed the Texas State line, Jacob said, "Destiny, let's go by Steve and Isabella's house before we go on to Houston." I was so excited, because we hadn't seen them for quite a while.

When we got there, we found out they had sold their home and were living with Granny Smith while Steve built their new home located right behind Steve's grandmother's. Jacob and I walked across the yard to look at their new home. It was so nice and spacious and almost finished and it wouldn't be long before they could move in. I was admiring the good strong lumber where Steve had nailed large beams. `The house is huge,' I thought, `Isabella will have a nice home when Steve gets it finished.'

As I watched Steve, a lump came up in my throat and tears came into my eyes. I prayed in my heart, `Father, thank you for this beautiful dream home for our daughter. I pray that someday I can have a small home too.' Suddenly a sweet soft voice spoke tenderly saying, "Destiny, you will live here someday." I couldn't believe what I'd heard and the thought of me living in this beautiful house was unbelievable. I was stunned because I knew the gentle voice I heard was the voice of Jesus and His promise reassured me that one day my dreams would become a reality.

I wanted to tell Jacob and Steve what Jesus said, but they would only accuse me of imagining things and Steve would have been real upset. He wasn't building this house and working so hard for me to live in it someday. This house was his and I couldn't see him ever leaving it for any reason. I told myself, `Destiny, you are losing your mind. You've been too many miles and your imagination is working overtime.' I would put it out of my mind, but the day finally came when I would remember the promise that Jesus had made to me that day and I'd praise Him for keeping His promise.

Shortly after that Sam left a message with the dispatcher to call him because he had something important to tell us. We called Sam immediately and he asked Jacob if we were interested in buying their house at Goodrich. He had bought another place so he put this house up for sale. Jacob told Sam he wasn't interested, but when Jacob told me about Sam's proposal, I pleaded with him to buy it. "All right," he said, "but we don't need it. I don't know why you want a house because we'll never live in it."

I was so happy at the though of having a home, a place to dream about going home to when we went to the Houston terminal. It was located just a little way off of State Highway 59. "Oh, Jacob, we can go by there and spend the night now and we won't have to sleep in the truck all the time," I exclaimed. Jacob went along with what I wanted, but he didn't like the idea. He became moody a lot after that and I believe he knew the Lord was turning things around in my favor now. I rejoiced when Sam agreed to let us pay notes on the house, so I was careful to put back enough money to meet them on time. I praised the Lord for this avenue of hope and through that hope, life on the road became much easier for me to bear.

Things weren't working out the way Jacob had planned. He had the notion that if he should die that I would drive a truck for a living. He just couldn't get it through his head that I hated the way we lived, but he insisted that I learn everything about the trucking industry, from how to load a trailer to the way the paper work had to be done.

Most folks think when they see a truck on the highway that the driver has an easy way to make a living, besides having the opportunity to see so many different places, and that their life must be filled with all kinds of adventures. Some would think that this is the life when they drive into a Truck Stop and see rows and rows of trucks parked on the parking lot, but most of these drivers are just tired. They have a deadline to meet and every load was due yesterday. His rest is only catnaps now and then and he drinks black coffee as you wipe the sleep out of your eyes and run as hard as you can to make your delivery on time. The paper work has to be in order, not only for the company he works for, but it has to meet the specifications of the Department of Transportation. They can and will pull him over at any time and check your load as well as your paper work.

When he travels from one state to another, the driver has to go through the Port of Entry. His load is weighed and has to be evenly distributed to meet their requirements. Besides making him redistribute his load if it isn't right, nine times out of ten he gets an overload ticket as well, and his boss doesn't like that. Jacob hated getting his logbooks up to date. And he growled and complained if I couldn't tell him immediately how many miles we had traveled or how far it was from one point to the other right away, and I especially hated to see him start working on them after dark because it was so hard to see by the dim light in the truck. He tried to make me do them for him, but I absolutely refused. I did all of the other paper work and that was enough.

One day I noticed his sloppy handwriting on the log sheets and I asked him why he didn't write neater. He muttered resentfully, "Destiny, I write that way so they can't read it. They are just lie books anyway." I laughed at him because he didn't seem to mind lying about everything else.

The little house we had bought from Sam needed a lot of work on it to make it livable. When Michael, our oldest grandson, wanted to make a trip with Jacob I was elated. It gave me the opportunity to work on our house. We had a friend who lived at Shepherd who was a retired carpenter. He would come and help me work on the house and gradually our little house turned into a nice little home. I stayed home every chance I could in order to fix up the house and get my bearings after being jarred to pieces in the truck for weeks. Eventually we were able to buy a used car.

The Lord was blessing us both, even though Jacob didn't think of it that way. At least, I didn't feel like a prisoner anymore, now that I could be at home for short periods of time.

Michael would tell me excitedly about his adventures when he and Jacob came home from their trips. He said they hauled a permit load which routed them through mountainous areas in Colorado that terrified him. He exclaimed excitedly, "Grandma, we were going over this high mountain and the highway was so narrow that the truck and load stayed crosswise most of the time. Grandma, I would look out of my window and the wheels of the truck would be right on the edge of the embankment and the trailer scraped the side of the mountain. I was so frightened I could hardly catch my breath and I just knew that any moment we'd go careening down the side of the mountain. You know, Grandma, I thought truck driving would be the perfect way to make a living. I thought I'd just quit school and start driving a truck since it doesn't take much education to be a truck driver. Now I think I'll go back to school and get a good education, because truck driving is just too dangerous and they couldn't pay me enough money to take the chances that Grandpa does." Jacob laughed, then he said, "Son, this is what you have to do if you don't go to school."

It is a hard way to make a living and I knew it all too well, but Jacob never knew that his wife would lie awake at night and pray for his safe return. Many nights I'd lie awake and listen intently for the soft rumbling sound of the truck driving home before he forced me to go on the truck with him. Every time he made it home again, I would breathe a sigh of relief, thanking God that he was safe at least for a little while. He was usually so tired that he didn't pay me any attention. He just wanted to rest on the couch while the grandchildren or I would powder and rub his swollen feet. We have laughed many times when the small kids would put so much talcum powder on Jacob that he looked like Casper the friendly ghost. Jacob just slept through it all, even though they crawled all over him. They worked very hard to please Grandpa, chattering about things that Grandpa never heard. They knew that they would get a reward for their labor of love and they also knew that Grandpa kept a large amount of change in one of those purple Crown Royal cloth bags that he carried in his truck. Those days are far gone now, and those little ones are grown and some, like Michael, made a trip or two with their Grandpa and found out why he was always so tired when he came home.

Jacob and I made it home to our house at Goodrich for Christmas in 1986. We were usually on the road at Christmas time so some of the drivers could go home to be with their families. This was a special Christmas, one that I will always cherish. We didn't have much food in the house when we drove in that morning so we ate Spam and scrambled eggs for Christmas dinner. There wasn't any deadline to meet or a load to worry about. Not even the kids knew that we were home, so we just relaxed and played around like a couple of kids again, without a care in the world.

`Father, the sad thing is that every day could have been like that Christmas we shared that year and then I wouldn't have so many bitter memories of all those wasted years. Please, Father, help me deal with the broken pieces of our yesterdays and find beauty in the good times as well as the bad. I'm certain Jacob loved me in his way, and I loved him more than my own life, yet we were worlds apart,' I prayed.

CHAPTER 23

HEALING WINGS OF BEAUTY

In 1987, the truck line Jacob had worked for so many years sold out to another truck line. He stayed on the job until Skip, a truck driver and friend, approached Jacob with an offer which sounded exciting. Skip owned a big KW, which he had driven himself until he bought a big black Peterbilt and he wanted Jacob to drive his KW. Skip and his fiancée, Bonnie, were originally from Virginia and Skip owned a home near Norfolk. Jacob and Skip went to work for a truck line in Pennsylvania for a while. It worked out for a while, but eventually the job turned sour and they went searching for employment at other truck lines. We all wound up back in the Houston area and Skip and Bonnie stayed at our home a lot as they tried to find a decent job. It was a trying year as Jacob and Skip moved from job to job, but finally they found a pretty good job and Skip and Bonnie rented a place to live near Dayton and moved out.

Kevin, our grandson, came to live with us in the spring of that year too. Kevin went to Isabella and Steve's for the summer and worked at a nursery near Bon Wier. While he lived there, he went to church with them and was saved and baptized at the Bon Wier Baptist Church. Then he came back to live with us in the fall. Kevin was seventeen, but he was quite different from most boys his age and Jacob didn't know how to deal with a boy that age who acted like he was ten or twelve years old instead. He had been through a lot when Wayne and Cindy were divorced and he had a lot of problems just adjusting to the situation. He wanted to drive a truck like Grandpa, so Jacob took him along on some of the trips.

I didn't go on these trips anymore since Kevin had come to live with us and if Jacob didn't take Kevin he had to go by himself. When Jacob would come home, the strain showed on his face. It broke his heart, because he wasn't able to understand why Kevin acted just like a child. Knowing Jacob, I'm sure he would get frustrated when Kevin couldn't learn everything he was expected to do over night and I imagine Jacob treated him just like he had me. Jacob would be near tears because he wanted him to be a man. Jacob didn't seem understand how hard Kevin was trying to please his Grandpa either. I hoped that by going on the truck Kevin would learn to be a responsible young man and I counted on Jacob to help him since Kevin thought the sun came up every morning just for Grandpa.

It was the latter part of January 1988, when Jacob took Kevin along with him to Fargo, North Dakota. I was very worried about them traveling so far north this time of the year. Besides the severe cold weather, they had icy roads to travel most of the way. I was especially concerned when I saw the weather reports on television and I prayed for them as I sat by the warm fire and trembled in fear. I didn't sleep much as I lay in bed and listened for the sound of the truck driving up.

On January 29, 1988, around one o'clock in the morning I woke up with a start. I jumped out of bed excitedly because I knew Jacob and Kevin were coming home. "Thank You, Father, You have brought my loved ones home safe again," I cried happily. I ran to the door so I could see them coming down the street. The headlights beamed as they slowly rumbled toward our house. I watched as Jacob parked beside the road and I waited anxiously for them to come in. I stirred up the coals in the fireplace and laid more wood to the fire so that the house would be warm and cozy when they came inside.

I couldn't imagine what was taking so long for them to come inside. `Lord, I hope they are all right,' I thought in concern. Eventually I heard their footsteps on the porch and I threw the door open to greet them. I had an awful feeling that something was dreadfully wrong when they came inside because Jacob's face was wet with tears as I hugged him tightly. "I'm so glad you are home Jacob and I've missed you both so much," I exclaimed joyfully. I'll never forget the look on Jacob's face and the tears that he cried that night. Jacob wept bitterly as he said, "Destiny, you may not want me anymore after I tell you my story, Honey. I won't blame you if you don't and I won't try to keep you bound to me if you tell me that you can't forgive me for the horrible thing I've done."

I thought as I waited silently to hear the whole story, `Lord, what on earth could he have done that would cause him to be so overcome with regret and sorrow?' I couldn't react one way or another as his words cut deep into my heart and soul. I could hear his confession, but it was as if I were experiencing a terrible dream. Tears were streaming down his face and any wall that had ever been between us crumbled as he said, "Honey, I almost killed Kevin at a Truck Stop at Fargo, North Dakota. I was so angry with him because he lied to me when I asked him if he had been slipping out of the truck when I was asleep and playing video games in the Truck Stop. He would say, `no, Grandpa,' but I caught up with him though. When I woke up and he wasn't in the truck, I walked over to the Truck Stop and saw him playing the video games through the window. When I knew for sure that he had lied to me I was beside myself with anger, not only because he had lied to me, but also because he had been stealing the change we'd been saving in the Crown Royal bags to play those games with. I was seething in anger as I devised a devious plan to catch

Kevin stealing instead of confronting him like a man should have done."

"I'm so ashamed," Jacob cried, as he continued the story. "I went to the truck and put more change in the bag and pretended to be asleep when Kevin came back to the truck so he didn't think twice when he reached into the bag to take more money out. `Kevin, you've been lying to me,' I shouted in a terrible rage. I grabbed Kevin by his ears fully intending to kill him. I lost all control of right and wrong as old Satan led me on in such rage and anger. Nothing else mattered except my revenge for the wrong that our own grandson had done to me. Suddenly, Destiny, a sharp commanding voice shouted to me, "Jacob, if you hurt my child, I'll take your life this instant!" Oh, Destiny, I knew that sharp commanding voice was the voice of God. I knew immediately that if I hurt Kevin my soul would be doomed forever to an eternity in the pits of hell without any hope of redemption. His voice stopped me cold and I fell backward on the bunk and my heart must have stopped. When I regained consciousness, Kevin was standing over me crying, `Grandpa, oh, Grandpa, are you all right?' I gave my heart to Jesus, Honey, and from that moment on I've lived for the Lord. I pray you will forgive me, but even if you can't find forgiveness in your heart for me, I will live for Christ anyway. I parked the truck for the last time and Skip can come and get it. From this moment, I'll never drive a truck again. That's why it took so long coming in the house, because we were taking everything out of the truck that belonged to us."

We were all crying as I praised the Lord for intervening just in time to keep Jacob from doing such a horrible thing that would have devastated all of us. My heart ached as I pictured those terrible things in my mind because I knew how cruel Jacob could be from experience. Tears streamed down my face as I tried to wipe those pictures from my mind knowing the terror Kevin had suffered, yet God had delivered Kevin and struck his Grandpa down. I remembered the complete trust and innocence of Kevin during my dream when we walked in hell. That same trust in his Grandpa was as great as it had been in me. Kevin had done a terrible thing by stealing and lying, but he didn't deserve to die for the terrible crime he had done. I turned to Kevin and asked him how he felt about the situation, because my decision on whether or not I could find it in my heart to forgive Jacob really depended on how he felt. Kevin replied, "Grandma, I forgave Grandpa in North Dakota when he first begged for my forgiveness. I love my Grandpa, and I always will." Jacob cried, "Destiny, will you forgive me too?" "Yes, I will, because I have prayed for your salvation for so many years. It just breaks my heart that it had to take a terrible tragedy to wake you up." Tears streamed down my face as I thought about all the years that I had prayed for the day when Jacob would be saved. `Oh surely, Father, the walk in hell is over now and Kevin was that chosen vessel that You used to crumble that hard stony heart of Jacob and now we are all together, gloriously kept inside the Ark of Safety,' I thought.

We stood clinging to one another while tears of joy fell freely and the heavy burdens we had carried for so long were lifted and it was so refreshing.

God's power to save is an awesome thing to experience. No matter how tough you think you are, the Holy Spirit is greater. And the convicting power of His voice alone is able to crumble the hardest heart and make you see yourself as you really are in the eyes of the Almighty God and no mere human is able to defy Him.

Jacob surrendered his life to Christ and like so many that had run so hard from the love and tender mercy of the Lord, repented of his sins, his only regret was that he had rejected Jesus for so many years. He hadn't known how wonderful it would be to be able to feel `the peace that passeth all understanding' which he was experiencing now and I rejoiced in his salvation because the heavy burden that I had carried for so long had been lifted.

The following Sunday, we all went to church. When Jacob walked up the aisle sobbing his heart out as he took our pastor's hand and told him that he had been saved and wanted to be baptized, a revival in the church broke out. Sam was leading the music and he fell on his knees crying and thanking God. Our pastor beckoned to me to leave the piano and come stand with Jacob. I was glad since I couldn't see the music anyway. Sam surrendered to the ministry when Jacob made his profession of faith and it was so wonderful that he did. It was especially wonderful because Jacob and I had attended Mark's ordination into the ministry just a few weeks earlier.

Oh, how wonderfully God was blessing my family and I rejoiced in the Lord. It was all like a beautiful dream, but praise God it's not a dream, it's all so very real and gloriously wonderful. Sam joined us and the three of us clung to each other praising the Lord because of the miracle of grace that He had performed with such great magnitude, even more than I thought would ever be possible.

Brother Nelson, our pastor, had known Jacob and I for many years and knew some of the hardships and struggles we had suffered. As my pastor off and on through the years, he had seen me cry in heartbreak from living with a lost husband. Many times he told me to remain faithful to Jesus Christ and someday I would win him to the Lord. When the service ended and we started to leave, my pastor took my hand and said, "Destiny, your faith did pay off in the end. I know it's been a long time, but you have persevered." I was so happy that the war between Jacob and I was over that I said, "We won at last," but someone standing by took offense to what I said and spoke up quickly and said, "God has won the victory and only Him." I wanted to cry and I wanted her to understand why I had said what I had. But I decided she had probably made up her mind that I was seeking glory for myself, so I walked on because I knew that I didn't have to defend myself to my Father, who knew my heart. `Yes, God had won the victory over Satan today and so have we,' I thought as I remembered the awful suffering I had gone through in my prison. I'd learned that soul winning isn't easy, but one soul won to Christ is worth whatever pain you had to endure, especially if it's your husband and the father of your children.

Jacob's baptism was scheduled for February 7th, so all the children came home to witness this great event. Our little house seemed to be bursting at the seams lately with all the family gathering home. That day was such a special day, however, because Daddy had been saved and was about to be baptized. Our little house was filled with peace for the first time and I was ecstatically happy as our family gathered around the table. As Jacob stared out the window and watched the falling snow, he said, "Honey, the snow isn't going to keep me from being baptized today. Nothing is going to stop me from serving the Lord anymore." It was hard not to cry from joy because I'd longed to hear Jacob say these words. The Lord had already begun to heal the broken pieces of my heart and each day brought renewed hope that through Christ, Jacob and I would find the happiness we had searched for.

When we entered the church and found a seat, we all laughed because our family almost filled the pews on one side of the church. The baptismal service was beautiful and tears of joy filled our eyes as we watched Jacob being baptized. `Everything will be different now,' I told myself. I expected our life together to be perfect now that we could finally be as one in the Lord.

Jacob sent the children home early because of the weather. He was especially concerned about Gentry and Joyce since they lived in the northern part of Louisiana, and ice would start forming on the bridges and overpasses toward evening. After the children left, we sat by the warm fire holding hands, reviewing the happy events of the day, and since they had called church off because of the weather, we went to bed early.

It seemed to take more rest for Jacob lately, but I rationalized that it was because he hadn't recovered from the stress of driving so many miles on the truck. I couldn't fool myself any longer though, because Jacob was getting weaker by the day and I had to admit him to the hospital the following Sunday with congestive heart failure again. Jacob had slowly gone down hill since he fell at Middletown, California. No matter what the doctor told me then, I knew in my heart that Jacob had died and that God had given him his life at that time. In the back of my mind, the Lord was telling me that He had extended his life to give him one more opportunity to accept Christ, as well as my plea for his life that day.

Jacob's doctor was completely honest with us both after he studied the results of Jacob's tests. He said, "I'll set up an appointment for you at John Sealy at Galveston because I can't help you, but they have specialist there who might be able to help you. Your heart has deteriorated so badly that there isn't much hope of a complete recovery. You won't be able to work again so I'll help you get your disability Social Security started if you want me to." He bent down and drew a picture on the sheet of Jacob's bed of his heart and how it looked. Jacob was calm, but I started to cry, then he turned to me and said, "Mrs. Quinn, you have a long hard road of heartache and despair ahead of you yet, so you must brace yourself for that." Then he left the room with his head down.

I didn't know where to go to get help, but I knew that I needed to while Jacob was in the hospital. The kids had been helping us all this time, but they had their own families to take care of. Sam advised me to make an appointment with Peggy Wooten and since she was related to my daughter-in-law I felt more comfortable about telling her our situation. I had been very nervous and edgy lately and especially after the doctor made it clear that Jacob wasn't going to get well, I almost fell apart.

I felt as if the whole world was crashing in on me as I walked to the courthouse where Peggy Wooten's office was. I didn't have any idea of how or where to start getting the paperwork started, but Peggy was like an old friend as she patiently listened while I cried in fear and she took charge of everything. She sent for Jacob's medical records at Tacoma and Tallahassee, as well as the other needed documents we needed to send to the Social Security Office.

Jacob resented my being gone so much from his bedside, but I stayed with it anyway and did everything she told me to do in spite of his childish behavior. I realized that he wouldn't even try to get help because he had always the idea that if you just ignore the situation long enough that your problems would disappear. He would have been satisfied to take handouts from the kids instead of trying to manage for ourselves. Peggy helped us get Indigent Care and I applied for food stamps too. Jacob thought I was doing a terrible thing and it hurt his pride terribly, but I had to forget my pride and do all that I could to get help for us. Once the papers were processed and his first check came in, Jacob was glad that I'd gone against his wishes and he beamed with joy as he sat at the table and proudly figured out how to make the money stretch to meet all our needs. When Jacob's appointment at John Sealy drew near, I went by the hospital at Livingston and gathered the medical reports to carry with us. Along with those, I had to take some important documents of our own to give to the Administrative Department at John Sealy. The documents included his birth certificate, our land deeds, and a copy of our marriage license, as well as the few food stamps we had left over in case they asked about them. Peggy had instructed me to carry every valuable document that I could think of so if the caseworker asked for them I would have the documents available.

Joyce and Isabella came home so they could go with us to Galveston. I was so nervous, because all of the responsibility of carrying those large manila envelopes fell on me. There were five of them to keep up with and no one offered to help, but I was relieved of all of them except for one when we got to the doctor's office. After the social worker looked them over and took copies of what she needed, I sat down in the waiting room and placed the envelope by my chair. After Jacob saw the doctor, we left. Lord, I didn't realize the envelope with all the important papers was missing until we were halfway home. I thought it was with the other envelopes the receptionist gave to me, but I didn't realize until Jacob told me to get the food stamps out of the envelope that someone had stolen our documents. Jacob was so upset with me when I couldn't find the envelope. All he seemed to care about was the small amount of food stamps that were in the package. I searched the car and couldn't find the envelope anywhere. I started crying when Jacob began ranting and raving like a mad man. I was heartsick because I had lost our valuable documents and praised the Lord that our deeds had been recorded at the courthouse. The other documents could be replaced and I was relieved about that. I had made a terrible mistake by laying the envelope down by my chair, but Jacob didn't need to get hysterical over a few food stamps. After being so careful not to make a mistake, I made a horrible mistake anyway. I knew that eventually I would do something that would set him off, but Jacob didn't seem to realize how much pressure I had been under lately, but all he could think about was that $40.00 worth of food stamps. When we got home I called the doctor's office at Galveston immediately and they said the envelope wasn't there, and evidently someone had stolen it.

I was so ashamed of what I'd done that I couldn't stop crying and was hurt and disappointed in Jacob. I certainly wouldn't have treated him that way and it hurt to hear him say hateful things to me in front of Isabella and Joyce, who didn't say anything while Jacob accused me of everything he could think of. He didn't let up when we went to bed that night either. It didn't seem to bother him that I was so miserable that I couldn't stop crying. $40.00 worth of food stamps wasn't worth the hell he was putting me through, but I had done wrong so I didn't try to defend myself. He started in again the next morning and suddenly Isabella exploded. She turned on Jacob and gave him a tongue lashing about his own imperfections and he shut up when he realized the girls were sick and tired of him lambasting their mother. Jacob had said some hurtful things to me during that episode and he hadn't acted like a Christian or that he had ever known the Lord. I was so afraid he was going back to his old ways as he seemed to be headed in that direction. At least after Isabella jumped on him he didn't mention it anymore. I really think that he thought the girls were impressed by his abuse of me.

Everyone catered to his every whim because they knew he wouldn't be with us very long. He did suffer a lot, but he didn't complain about his pain until it became severe and especially when he had a headache.

He knew I loved him because I would sit at the end of the couch so he could put his feet in my lap and then I would rub them gently for hours while he dozed on and off. I knew his time was running out because he grew weaker every day and my heart would ache as I watched him sleeping peacefully and I would think, `Oh, God, how can I face life without him? He has been such a dominating force in my life and has made all the decisions. Since he has controlled my every move for years and even the little things, such as when I could go to bed, cook or wash dishes. You would think that after thirty-nine years of living this way that I should be able to accept the way he is, and sometimes I doubt I'll even know what to do after he's gone.'

On our next appointment at John Sealy we were told that Jacob's condition was far too bad for them to be able to help him. His heart muscle was enlarged and soft, like jelly, and they couldn't repair it so it wouldn't do any good to replace the damaged valves. Jacob just wouldn't accept the thought that he was going to die and he was still determined to be that tough Texan until he died. He insisted on driving the car everywhere we went and I never thought anything about it, or the danger of him suddenly dying while we were going down the highway.

Jacob had always depended on me throughout our marriage to be at his beck and call. Now he was worse than ever, but I think he was afraid that he would die alone. He was a lot like a toddler who does fine as long as he can see his mother, but the instant she gets out of sight the child starts crying. As he'd done on the truck, he told me when to go to bed or wash the dishes. I had been his constant companion for so long that I felt like an animal in a cage sometimes. Sometimes he would sit on the porch and call me to join him. We'd sit and watch the birds play in the yard and talk about our days of trucking. Sometimes I wanted to do other things and would get irritated because he constantly demanded my attention. Then I'd remind myself that the day would come when I would be able to do other things because right now I needed to devote all of my time making Jacob happy and he was happiest when I was with him and was more content.

One day Jacob suggested that we visit Oscar and Faye, our friends who lived at Shepherd. When we got there Faye was crying and Jacob asked her what was wrong. She replied, "Oscar is driving me crazy. He forgets everything that I tell him. He rambles around the house at night and once he wandered away from home and a friend happened to see him and brought him home. I'm so exhausted that I just can't go on like this. My heart condition is getting worse because I can't get any rest because I have to watch him constantly." Jacob said, "Faye, gather some things together and we will take you and Oscar home with us so we can help you with him." Faye agreed to go and that night it was a nightmare because no one got any rest since Oscar wouldn't go to sleep.

The next morning Jacob asked Faye if she had considered placing Oscar in a nursing home. "They have a nice new one at Livingston and Destiny can go with you to try to get Oscar a room there." Jacob took care of Oscar while Faye and I went to the nursing home and Faye made the arrangements to admit Oscar so he could get professional help. After she got Oscar settled in the nursing home, Faye sold her house at Shepherd and bought a travel trailer and parked it in our yard.

I guess Jacob thought every woman was like me, but he found out quickly that Faye wasn't. Jacob would get real upset if Faye didn't visit Oscar every day. He decided he had made a mistake in helping Faye put Oscar in the nursing home, but I knew it was because he couldn't dominate Faye the way he had me. He would grumble to me about her and especially when Faye wouldn't go to church, but he wouldn't tell her anything and she thought he was the most wonderful man on earth. He was jealous of her children and tried to keep her from visiting with them, but Faye just ignored him and did what she wanted. "She has to be the most hard headed woman that I have ever met and she just thinks about herself," Jacob would grumble. I would laugh and think to myself, `that's just the type of woman he needs. I'll bet it would have been a different story if Jacob had married someone like Faye.'

We had a large crowd at our house on Thanksgiving that year. Besides our children, Karen's Mom and Dad came too and it was nice because they hadn't visited us on a special occasion like this before. Faye joined us as well, so our little house was full of people. We had a good time, especially me.

It was around February 15, 1989 that Isabella called all the kids and told them, "let's all go home this weekend. I have a feeling that Daddy isn't going to be with us very much longer." They all came home except for Randall, who couldn't make it for some reason.

It was a joyful occasion, but Jacob wasn't well at all. He was retaining too much fluid again and things didn't look promising. Isabella and Joyce took lots of pictures, but Jacob felt so bad that he didn't smile or cut up with the little kids when they climbed up on his lap. I felt like this would probably be our last reunion together as I fought back tears all that day. When they all went home Jacob was completely exhausted, so we went to bed early as we so often had done those days.

Jacob had complained of being so terribly cold lately that he would snuggle up close to me for warmth and would hold me so tightly that I couldn't rest. There were times that he would giggle and laugh when he dug his toenails into my legs, which hurt terribly. Once I complained to Sam about it and he said, "Mamma, Daddy is doing that so you will remember him." I retorted, "As if I could forget."

On Sunday morning, February 19th, Jacob and I called Isabella to wish her a happy birthday. Then Faye came over and we all went to church together. Jacob was very happy, but he told me that he wasn't feeling well. After church we went home, had lunch and he was watching television when he drifted off to sleep.

I went to Faye's for a while and told her, "Faye, Jacob isn't going to live much longer. I just feel it in my heart so strongly that I can't throw off this terrible weight that makes me want to cry constantly." Faye said, "Oh, Destiny, you must be mistaken. Jacob may live a long time, so you shouldn't worry." We visited a little while longer, but I had to get back before Jacob woke up and found me gone. Before I left, I asked her if she wanted to go to church tonight, but she told me that she thought she would just stay home. I went back to the house and found Jacob still napping. He woke up around five o'clock and sat up. He said he didn't feel like going to church and I didn't think it would upset him if I went to church alone, so I said, "Honey, since Faye has decided not to go to church tonight, do you mind if I go to the church that wasn't very far from the house? Faye said that she would watch after you while I'm gone and I would love to go if it's okay with you." I realized that I had made a terrible mistake in thinking that Jacob would agree to let me go to church without him when I saw that same demon spirit in his eyes that I hadn't seen in such a long time. I began to tremble uncontrollably from head to foot when I saw that monster that was filled with such hate and fury take control of Jacob again. It was unbelievable and I couldn't understand how a man who had been saved could still have that demon living in him, but the look on Jacob's face made me realize how wrong I had been. I was so afraid for my life that I expected him to jump up any moment and kill me. I tried to avoid his eyes which were glaring so hard at me that I felt trapped like a fly in a spider web.

Somehow I got to my feet and stumbled blindly into the bedroom. I didn't know what to do as I sat on the side of the bed trembling with the greatest fear that I had ever experienced. My terror gave way to agonizing cries to God, barely whispering my tormented thoughts, afraid that Jacob would hear my cries and rush into the room with more fury than I'd ever known. I began to cry out to God for mercy and understanding, because I realized that Jacob was a very sick man. His illness in his body was bad, but his being demon possessed was even more horrible and frightening and I knew that only God could rebuke that devil which controlled Jacob. "A terrible battle is raging in our home, Father, and it's between good and evil. I thought that war was over, Jesus, when he accepted You as his Savior. Now, I'm so frightened that I don't know what to think or how to handle this situation. I have to decide quickly whether to put my gown on or defy Jacob and get dressed for church. Oh, God, I just can't live in this terror any longer. I'm so exhausted from fighting the battle to worship You, oh, my Lord. When will this heartbreaking war end, my God, that has gone on for so many years? Please, God, bring it to an end quickly and deliver us both from the bonds of Satan. I'm so weary and my heart has been broken so many times that I don't want to live. Please, Father, just take me out of this torment and hell," I cried out helplessly.

I had never experienced more fear in my life and knew old Satan was just on the other side of that door. I was trembling so hard while all these thoughts kept rushing madly through my head so I nervously put my gown on instead of a dress. An experience like this will let you know how great the power of God's grace really is and only complete faith in God gave me the courage and strength just to walk from my bed to the door. I stared down at the doorknob before I took hold of it, knowing that only a door stood between Jacob and myself. Once I turned this knob, the door will open back and I would see what lay beyond that door. The thought raced through my mind that I should have crawled out the bedroom window and ran for my life instead of confronting that demon again. I knew that whatever was there that I had to face it and couldn't run away. At that moment, I placed all my faith and trust in God because I knew He had delivered me from the clutches of Satan many times before. As I turned the knob, a great calmness came over me so that I entered the room with confidence now because the great power of the Holy Spirit had taken full control of this situation. As I walked calmly into the living room where Jacob was, he looked up at me. The sweetest smile came across his face and in his beautiful blue eyes, there was a gentle and trusting look in place of that old demon. I trembled in wonder and amazement as I sat down and wondered, `Does Jacob even realize what just happened?' I was afraid to ask him anything, but somehow I was certain that God had delivered Jacob from the demon that night which had possessed him all those years. I fought back the tears, thinking how very close to death I'd been. Relieved now, all I could do was to praise God in my heart, as I felt the sweet peace of Jesus warming my heart. `Father,

I'm trying very hard to serve You at the bedside of Your newborn child,' I thought. `Someday I'll be free to attend church because You know my greatest joy on earth is in the Chapel of my Lord,' I prayed. If Jacob felt he had won a victory, he didn't let on. I believed then and now that Christ had cast Satan out of Jacob at the very moment that I prayed for deliverance in my bedroom.

The following day, February 20th, Jacob had an appointment to have some type of breathing tests at John Sealy and then he would see his regular doctor. Jacob was so happy when the doctors found an inhaler that really helped him to breathe better. He was on top of the world when we went into his regular doctor's office. Jacob became somewhat upset when a different doctor examined him and he ran an EKG on him as soon as we got there. Jacob said, "Where is my doctor? I'll bet you are one of those doctors who are still in training. The doctor called for Dr. Morman, who had been treating Jacob since he had been going to John Sealy, and when he came in Dr. Morman told Jacob that he had been under this doctor's supervision for four years. Jacob seemed to accept that pretty well and we all sat down together as the older doctor gave us the verdict that we didn't want to hear.

He said, "Jacob, the EKG reveals that your heart condition has worsened and that you can't live much longer. If there is anything you want to do before you die you need to do it right now. Actually, Jacob, you have far outlived your time. Very few people in your condition live this long. Didn't you say that your doctor told you years ago that you wouldn't live to be twenty-five years old. Man, here you are fifty-seven years old now and you have beat the odds. God has been so good to you and I believe your wife must have been too. If you will tell me the name of any kind of medication that has helped you feel better in the past, I will write out a prescription for it. There isn't any more that we can do for you and I'm very sorry, but I have to prepare you by speaking honestly."

Jacob didn't blink when they gave us the bad news, but I just wanted to cry because it was like a sentence being handed down even though we were innocent of any crime. Jacob said, "I don't know the names of the medicines that have helped me, but my wife can tell you." Even though I was nervous and upset, I knew there had been some medications he had taken in the past that had helped him breathe better, so I named them and the doctor wrote the prescriptions. We all seemed to know this would be the last time we would see each other at John Sealy Hospital. When we left the doctor's office, we stopped by the pharmacy to pick up the medicine before we started home.

As we drove away from Galveston, Jacob was in high spirits. He told me, "Destiny, those doctors don't know everything. I feel too good to die anytime soon since the doctor gave me the new inhaler. Besides that, God can heal me and give me a new heart, Honey. You know, Honey, the Bible teaches us that when we are saved Jesus gives us a new heart. Don't you believe that too?" "Yes, I do, Honey," I told him, but I couldn't tell him the Bible was referring to the spiritual birth and Jacob had received a new heart that no doctor or anyone could ever destroy. I knew that miracles were happening every day and I prayed that if it was God's will that He would heal Jacob, but my heart felt so heavy because I knew the doctors had done everything humanly possible so Jacob was completely in the mercy of God. He was so happy that I thought to myself, `Father, dare I hope because in You all things are possible?'

It was late when we got home and Faye ran to meet us as soon as we pulled into the driveway. She knew immediately the doctors had helped Jacob because he wasn't short of breath when he got out of the car. He told Faye about the new inhaler as we walked toward the porch. Faye said, "Jacob, I've never seen you this happy since I've known you. It's possible that you will get well now that you can breathe better."

It was like the good old days when the kids were small as we watched them play ball. There was a lot of happiness flowing through the house now, especially around the dining table where most everyone gathered. Sometimes we would study the Bible after Jacob was saved and he was like a little child discovering so many wonderful things in God's Word. He had entered a whole new world that he had never known before and he cried a lot because he had wasted so many precious years on a truck. He understood why I wanted to go home and worship the Lord in peace and contentment. He had been searching for that happiness too which had been available all that time, but he hadn't recognized home and family as a gift from God until he wasn't able to run any further. For as many hours as God would grant us, we shared them together with rejoicing.

Tuesday and Wednesday were spent the same way with joy and in the hope that everything would be all right. Jacob, Faye and I went to church Wednesday night not knowing the church service had been called off. We had a wonderful time just talking as we waited outside the church and when we realized no one was going to show up, Jacob said, "That's all right. We'll be the first ones here Sunday morning."

When we woke up on Thursday morning, a brisk northern had blown in. It was a beautiful day though with the bright sunlight streaming in the kitchen window where Jacob sat. Faye came over to drink coffee with us and we made small talk as we sat around the table. Our lives seemed to be as perfect as it could been and even more so when Karen and Aaron, our small grandson, came in. Jacob beamed with joy as Aaron climbed up into a chair beside him and his Grandpa helped him eat with a fork just like the grownups. He thought he was big when he mimicked everything Jacob did and I smiled thinking, `How beautiful to see Jacob enjoying so many of the pleasures that he had been missing all those years.' "God, help him to enjoy all the little things that he can until You see fit to call him away,' I prayed silently.

After breakfast, Jacob said, "Karen, can Aaron go with me to the Post Office and to Sears. Faye has a package she wants me to pick up for her so we won't be gone long." "Yes, of course he can," Karen replied smiling. We stood on the porch and watched the two of them climbing happily into the old Pontiac. Aaron was trying to tell his Grandpa something important I guess as he babbled away. Jacob was telling him something too as he helped Aaron get settled on the big armrest next to his Grandpa. They waved as they drove away just as if they would be gone for quite a while. We laughed as we went back in the house and sat at the table and visited while we waited for them to come back. Jacob and Aaron weren't gone long and they came in still as happy and bubbly as when they left. Faye went back to her trailer so that she could watch the soap operas on television and Karen told us that she needed to go home too and they left also.

Jacob sat down at the table and I asked him if he was hungry. He said that he was still full from the big breakfast he had eaten earlier and he smiled cheerfully. "Oh, Honey, I can't get over how wonderful I've been feeling these last few days," Jacob stated with his face all aglow. I smiled up at him and said, "Honey, it's so wonderful to see you so happy and enjoying our life together." Jacob got up and came around behind me and wrapped his strong arms around me and pressing his cheek to mine, he said, "Destiny, you have been a good wife all these years and I love you so very much." A big lump came up in my throat as I choked back the tears. My heart was breaking as I looked up into his sweet face and said, "I love you too, Jacob."

He was so content and happy and even then I knew that this happy time could never last. I really couldn't understand why my heart ached so terribly when I should have been dancing around with joy because my loved one was finally happy.

Jacob looked out the window then he turned to and said, "Sugar, it's going to be colder this evening, so let's go outside and cut some of the blocks of wood that Sam brought for firewood. I'll cut it up and you can place it on the porch." It was around noon and a perfect time while the warm sun was shining, so I got up and put my coat and gloves on and said, "Honey, that sounds like a good idea. While you cut the wood, I'll carry it and stack it on the front porch." I followed Jacob to the back yard where the wood was, but there seemed to be an overwhelming sense of doom which weighed me down as that it was agonizing for me to carry on as if everything was all right.

Jacob didn't sense my heartache which cried out in silence, unable to fathom the terrible tragedy which I felt was about to happen. Jacob was so happy though that I felt guilty and ashamed for allowing my imagination to get me down like this. Every time he spoke, it felt like a dull knife piercing my soul and I fought back the tears as I carried an armload of wood to the front porch. As I walked back up the small hill to where Jacob was, I thought, `I think I'll put the rest of the wood on the back porch so I won't have to walk so far.'

When I got back to the area where Jacob was, the pain was so tremendous that I avoided his eyes. I didn't want him to see my tears, because he would ask me why I was crying and I couldn't explain why they were there myself. Through tear-dimmed eyes, I saw Jacob leaning against the axe handle. He laughed happily saying, "Honey, I feel so wonderful. You know it's been so many years since I've felt so strong, just like I did when I was a young man. Say, Honey, why don't you put the rest of the wood on the back porch so you won't have to walk so far," Jacob exclaimed. Tears were blinding me as I fumbled with each piece of wood and placed it in my arms as I answered him without looking up. "Okay, Honey," I told him as my voice cracked and I trembled in sorrow. Somehow I knew this would be the last time I would see Jacob standing straight and tall with a smile like the sunshine and his eyes as blue as the winter sky.

I raised up with my load of wood in my arms and stumbled blindly to the little back porch he had built where I laid the wood on the porch and wiped my tear filled eyes on my jacket sleeve. `Oh, God, why am I crying?' I sobbed softly. `Jacob is so vibrant and happy and I want to be happy for him too.' I turned around and started back to Jacob when I noticed the door was unlatched on the little storehouse. I stopped and closed the door and listened for the sound of Jacob cutting the wood. But there was complete silence as I started around the corner of the little storehouse with my head down and looking at the ground, so heavily burdened that I stooped as though I was totally defeated. As I drew nearer, I raised my head and gasped in horror as I saw Jacob down on his knees with his head bowed as if he were praying. I knew instantly my Jacob was dead when I placed my hand on his warm shoulder. I held his sweet face in my hands, which was lifeless and disfigured now. I heard myself screaming as loud as I could, but no one responded, not even Faye who was shut up in her trailer. My throat felt like fire, but I kept screaming for help and praying. "Oh, God, help us. Make somebody hear me!" The only thing that I could think of right then was, `Jacob, I'll never leave you nor forsake you, not even in death.'

I realized that I had to leave Jacob and get help, so I ran to Faye's trailer and banged on her door. It seemed like an eternity passed before she opened the door. When she did, I shouted, "Faye, run to the house and call the ambulance. I think Jacob is dead." Faye went to pieces, but she went to call and I went back to Jacob. Finally, I saw two of my neighbors walking toward us with a quilt in their arms. They spread the quilt out on the ground and laid Jacob on it. The paramedics arrived then and they tried to revive him. After a short time one of them told me. "We'll carry him to the hospital and you can follow us in your car." I ran into the house and started gathering Jacob's medicines to carry with me because that would be the first thing that the doctor would ask for. Faye went along and I tried to comfort her with the story about Jacob dying on the mountain at Middletown, California. I wouldn't give up hope yet and I stayed fairly calm until I reached the Emergency Room where the doctor told me that they hadn't been able to revive Jacob. Jacob died at 1:41 P.M. on February 23, 1989.

I walked around in a daze, unable to comprehend Jacob's death. Everything was like a dream and I only functioned by the grace of God, feeling lost without him, yet knowing that I must go on as I tried to pull myself together.

When the boys came, I told them that they would have to make the arrangements for Jacob's funeral. Jacob wanted to be buried at the Ford Chapel Cemetery in Newton so the kids got together and had Jacob's body carried to the Smith Funeral Home in Newton. Everything was going smoothly enough, but I couldn't get control of my emotions. I stayed at Goodrich the first night and went to the kitchen and started cooking supper like I had done when Jacob was alive. Sam and Karen stayed with me and it was terrible trying to sleep because I couldn't stop crying. I kept seeing Jacob kneeling before God. His head was bowed as if in prayer, and I couldn't get the picture out of my mind knowing he had never been an humble man. He had always been that tough Texan until death came. As far as I known, he had never bowed to any man or woman in all of his life, yet in death he had bowed humbly before his God. Tears streamed down my face as I lay in our bed, feeling so alone without Jacob lying next to me and crying out to God to help me. "How can I face tomorrow, Father? Jacob has always made every decision and I feel so lonely and afraid. Right now I feel like a small child that has been separated from its' mother. Help me have the will to go on without him and begin a new life, even though I don't even know how to begin. Right now the broken pieces of my life lie in shambles and only You can mend my broken heart. Only You, my Father, have that power and only Your marvelous grace can heal my children's hearts as well as mine." God's grace did give me the strength to face another day, but it was so strange not seeing Jacob at the steering wheel as Sam drove our old Pontiac toward Newton that next morning. Isabella and Steve invited us all to their home and the various churches around Newton and Bon Wier brought food for our family and guests. Jacob's funeral was delayed until Sunday, because Michael, our oldest grandson had to come from the Marine Base in California. He didn't arrive until Saturday night and he came straight to the funeral home.

The children and I gathered around Jacob's coffin and he looked at perfect peace. He appeared to be sleeping in pain no more, no deadline to meet, no mountain to climb and no more icy highways to travel on. He could explore the heavenly heights now and I knew that even though he had entered the haven of rest he was probably searching the heavens for adventure. I smiled as I thought of the man that had forced me to go with him against my will. It was all right, now that he had found the Lord and my race has been run for Christ Jesus' sake. Jacob's race had only begun when God called him away, but we had had a few days of perfect peace and I'll always be eternally grateful for that.

As he had requested, there was no tie around his neck and he appeared to be ready to go on another trip, with his khaki pants on and his best western shirt with his hands on the wide western belt that he always wore. `Where are you going this time, Jacob? I can't go along with you now, but I'm sure you will do fine and you can tell me all about your many adventures someday,' I thought. I could feel his presence as we stood silently and I'm sure he smiled with pride upon his family. `Sweet, gentle Holy Spirit of God, carry my loved one to the homeland, far from sin and disappointment. I have loved him, Jesus, but I know You loved him more. Now I place him in Your hands as I did all those years when he left on all his many trips,' I prayed in my heart.

We notified everyone that we could think of except for Ted. Joyce wanted to contact him right away, but I avoided that idea because he was in prison and I didn't have any idea at all about how to contact him. I didn't want to think about Ted, even though a still small voice kept telling me that Ted needed me. "When I go home, I'll find him, Mamma, and I'll tell him about Daddy. God has placed him on my heart and I won't rest until I find him," Joyce said firmly.

I grieved at Jacob's funeral because I didn't see any of his old truck driving buddies and I was bitter because he had given his life to the trucking industry. Then Pat White and

Bonnie walked up to me and I was so glad to see them. I thought, `Father, this is strange. Pat was his first truck driving friend and Bonnie was the last. For all the many others in between that are missing today, I don't mind now that they are here.' It broke my heart that Jacob's sister nor his brother, Carol or Luke, had come to Jacob's funeral, but I knew in my heart that Ted would have been with me if he hadn't been in prison.

It was sad to think how our family had drifted apart, but our children and many of my folks came to stand by me, even though Jacob had treated them so badly that I hadn't seen them in years. It was wonderful to know that we were all at peace again.

After the graveside service most of my friends went their separate ways, but the rest met at Steve and Isabella's house. Later in the day, the boys took the kids outside to play ball. Some gathered around the piano while I played and we sang praises to God.

The Lord blessed me in so many ways immediately after Jacob's death as I began to experience the freedom to worship God and His Holy Presence brought a wonderful peace that I had never known until now. All my family stayed that night as well some of my sisters. Everything seemed so strange to me because the tension was gone and I felt so free. That night we sat around the table and talked about the future which troubled me because I didn't know how I would manage until I could find work. Isabella said, "Mamma, we will be moving to Jasper in July, so Steve and I have been wondering if you would come here to live. This would be your home when we move away and in the meantime you can move in with us so we can help you get on your feet. I know right now that you have a lot on your mind, but I can't bear the thought of you living by yourself at Goodrich. You will be comfortable here and everyone around here will see after your needs." It was like a dream as I heard my daughter speaking and it seemed so unreal that the Lord was fulfilling His promise that I would live here someday. It was like a new awakening from the moment Jacob died, as if the Lord had taken me by the hand and I didn't have anything to worry about. God would be my husband and Father from now on and gently guide me instead of dominating my life like Jacob had done all these years. I felt so loved with God's hand on my life as I lay down to sleep that night. I thought about the new beginning God had already set in motion and I looked down at Faye who lay sleeping on a pallet by my bed.

`What will happen to Faye if I accept Steve and Isabella's offer,' I thought? `If it's Your will that I live here, Father, You must make a way for her also. There are so many things to consider and decide, sweet Jesus, so please guide my every decision and let us all find peaceful solutions according to Your will.' I drifted off to sleep, but I awoke with a start suddenly and thought someone was bending over me because I could feel the warmth of someone's breath against my face. Suddenly I felt threatened and afraid, thinking, `Jacob's spirit is in the room and he has come back to take control of my life again.' I was smothering as I sat up in bed fighting for breath. Then sitting on the side of my bed, I thought, `Lord, there is an evil spirit in this room I'm sure, and I refuse to just sit here and not fight against this evil spirit that is threatening my new found freedom in Christ.' I remembered Jacob telling me several times that when he died he wanted me to die too. `Had he come for me?' I thought.

I got up and went to the living room trembling in fear as I opened the Bible in search of the peace old Satan was trying to steal. `I can't bear to be a prisoner again, not by a spirit or anyone. I don't want to die when I've just begun to truly live,' I cried out in the spirit. Overcome with sorrow, I fell to my knees beside my chair. I prayed in a whisper, not wanting to disturb my sleeping family, and my heart ached as I poured my heart out to God. "Father," I cried bitterly, "I don't want to be controlled by an evil spirit. I have given Jacob my best years, even when my heart was torn between my love for him and for You. He made me his prisoner even though there weren't any bars and he forced me to live a lifestyle that truly vexed my soul. All of his life he had searched for that rainbow just beyond the horizon, not knowing that You were that beautiful rainbow that he was in search of. Please, Father, set me free that I might serve You in peace without ever being afraid anymore. It will take time for the scars in my heart to heal, but I know that beneath Your Healing Wings of Beauty this heartache will pass quickly. Jacob is now free to explore the wonders of Your Beauty throughout the whole universe. So please, Father, make his journey pleasant and fill his heart with all the joy and peace that he missed all his life. Father, I wouldn't call him back to this old world of pain and sorrow even if I could."

I sat thinking for a long time before I lay down again. A sweet lovely peace filled my inner being just like the flutter of a dove's wings and I thanked God for Jesus who had given His all on the cross of Calvary for sinners like Jacob and myself so that we might live through Him. My joy was filled to overflowing and mere words could not express the way that I felt.

The Lord blessed my new life in countless ways. He brought me to Newton and helped me sell the little house at Goodrich. He gave me a desire to prove to myself that I could rise above the heartaches of the past.

With Isabella and Steve's help, I started a small fried pie business that God blessed so much that a distributor called from Houston and wanted us to build a pie factory. The house boomed with activity day and night as I fought to prove to myself that I could do anything as long as God by my side.

Little fried pies were everywhere and there wasn't any place to sit, and one day Daniel said, "Grandma, enough is enough. When I have to sit on the floor to eat supper, it's too much." One day Steve came home from work and the pies were all around. He clinched his fist and raised his hands toward heaven shouting, "Oh, God, every day when I come home from work I pray these little pies would be all gone, but every day there are more and more. Oh, God our lives have changed, all because of a little fried pie!" We didn't build a pie factory and I'm very glad. God had taught me through that experience that I could succeed with His hand in mine. The Lord placed a smile on my face as I explored my new found freedom and Isabella and Steve stood by me. Many times I cried out in my sleep and they would comfort me. I would work far into the night while they cried, "Mamma, please get some rest."

Many times I would see a big truck go by and praise God that I wouldn't ever have to climb up into one again. It took a very long time before my fears disappeared when I went to church and when I would start toward the car that my old fear would return. Then with the realization that I needn't fear anymore, I would breathe deeply and praise the Lord that I was free at last. Deep scars remained, but the Lord watched carefully over me like a mother does her child when he takes his first steps. My steps were wobbly and uncertain at first, but God taught me how to walk alone with His hand in mine. I had nothing to fear from any man anymore and I would be able to walk with Christ Jesus, a free woman at last!

CONCLUSION

Over three years ago Christ appeared to me in a vision and showed me the broken pieces of my life which He had anointed by the Holy Spirit. Even though I cried out with agonizing tears, "Lord, why must I suffer still? The past is behind me now. Please, just let me forget the heartaches of the past and live again in peace. Jacob is in a far better place and I know he has found a place of rest and You know I can't undo any of the terrible wrongs from our past. It has been very hard to write about the abuse and I know I often lashed out at him while writing the account of our life together. Over and over again You brought this writing back to me, and I would cry with bitter tears that I couldn't do it again because I couldn't bear the pain. There has been no victory and I can find no glory for myself. Oh, my God, the work is finally completed now and You have been glorified."

Many people will accuse me of writing these things about Jacob because he is dead and can't defend himself. I have that problem too and can't really understand why the Lord would lay this burden on me. The Holy Spirit does everything in God's own time, however. While these questions plagued my mind, the Lord sent me to Mark's house after my visit with Ted one Saturday. I thought I was being sent to comfort my son, instead I learned that the Lord had sent me to comfort my grandson, Michael, who had adored Jacob and had hated me for saying those things about his Grandpa. I am certain the account of our visit must be included in my conclusion and the reader will be as satisfied as I was that Jacob was giving his final approval for this truth to be written.

It was late in the evening when I arrived at Mark's house. Michael was there and later everyone had gone to bed except for Michael and myself. All the other children had agreed that I must answer the call of God to write this book no matter how serious its contents were, but Michael hadn't understood the heavy burden that I had carried in my heart. Michael started crying when I told him about Christ appearing to me in a vision. "Michael, several years ago I received this call from God. Whether the voice was the Holy Spirit or the Lord himself, I don't know. I just know His voice was one of authority and I couldn't disregard His command as He told me on three separate occasions that night, "GET UP, GET BUSY," and each time I was startled and afraid. I knew then that the Lord wanted me to write, but I put it out of my mind. Ted had felt the urgency of the message that I had received from the Lord as well, but I told him that my life story was already recorded in heaven." I continued trying to make Michael realize that I took no pleasure in the work God had burdened me to do, but that I must do His will even though our story will bring pain and heartache to my family. Michael sobbed, "Please, Grandma, don't write the things Grandpa did years ago. I want to remember him the way I knew him." My heart ached as I said, "Son, Grandpa did love all of his grandchildren and his children too. He played ball with you and took you fishing, but Grandpa had another side that you didn't know existed. These things must be written so that anyone who reads our story might see themselves and turn to Christ before it's too late. Whether we've been good or bad throughout our life, how we lived always follows us and even after we are dead, our spirit remains in those we love. Grandpa was saved one year before he died and God forgave him all of his sins and God washed Grandpa as white as snow. I know it's hard to understand that God would call me to write those terrible things about the past and also knowing that he was forgiven for all those things. Evidently Grandpa agrees with Christ on this point and through his mistakes someone will turn their life around. I only know that I must follow Jesus, Son."

Michael sobbed in heartache and despair so that I cried out to God, "Father, please take this burden from my heart and release me from Your call, I just can't bear to see my children in so much distress. Please release me from the agony that I'm suffering too." Suddenly, Michael stopped crying and he held his hands over his eyes as if he were shielding them from a bright light. I was so stunned by his sudden behavior and I knew immediately that the Lord had taken charge of this situation. I was breathless as I watched Michael who was so excited. He exclaimed with joy, "Oh, Grandma, Grandpa is here! Grandpa is in you, Grandma, and I see him very clearly! There are bright lights flashing all around you, Grandma! Oh, Grandma, I understand now, you must write the book! I have the sweetest peace in my heart now that I hadn't had since Grandpa died and I had hated you for saying bad things about what Grandpa had done, but I love you, Grandma, with all my heart. Please go ahead and write the book with my blessing and Grandpa's too!"

Tears of joy streamed down my face because I knew God had confirmed His will in me. My grandson and I sat together rejoicing and a closer bond of love was formed between us by the Holy Spirit. Later that night I couldn't sleep because I was still on the mountain top filled with joy because of what the Lord had done that I tiptoed into Michael's room where he lay sleepless too, and I asked him to repeat the glorious event he witnessed. He repeated the things he saw once more and we held each other tightly for a while. "Good night, Michael, I love you so very much," I told him as I stood in the doorway on my way back to my room. He smiled up at me and said tenderly, "I love you too, Grandma." This glorious revelation had finally set me free so that I could complete this mission that God had called me to do back in 1991.

I couldn't wait to share the marvelous miracle which God had done with Ted on our visit the following week. We rejoiced in the Lord together as we had so many times on our beautiful visits. "Darling, God has blessed us so very much," Ted exclaimed while he held me in his arms before we had to part again. I waved goodbye to him as he walked toward the Unit and shouted, "I love you, and I'll see you again next week!" He blew a kiss and shouted back, "I love you too!"

As I drove toward Newton, I hummed a happy tune. When I started across the bridge at Dam B a beautiful giant rainbow appeared in front of me. It covered the entire area in a beautiful arch which displayed such brilliant colors of blue, green, red and gold and I knew that I would be passing under it very soon. Chills of joy covered me from head to foot as the Holy Spirit touched my heart and I began praying and praising God. "Father, use my life according to Your will. Wherever You send me, Lord, I am willing to go. Whether it's to serve You where I am right now or some far and strange place like when You sent me to Ted. Your glorious grace has been more than sufficient just as You promised and Your covenant with me has been wonderfully kept. As long as I live, I will look for Your rainbow, which shall be forever the symbol of Your promise just as You said, "My grace is sufficient to supply your every need. Thank You, Jesus!" I shouted as I drove beneath the rainbow of the Lord on toward my destiny.

ABOUT THE AUTHOR

Thelma Quinn is a native of, Cleveland Texas, and now lives a simple life in the small east Texas town of Newton. She is the mother of five children and is the pianist for the Missionary Baptist Church where she is a member.

Thelma continues to be a witness and testimony for all the things God has done in her life.

She prays that in some way, this book will be a blessing, and will show you that with God you can overcome any adversity.

ABOUT THE ARTIST

Christy McSwiggan studied art in the University of Georgia school system and has been tutored by such renowned artists as Bobby Pennebaker and Marlin Adams. She currently lives in Griffin Georgia.

Christy's specialty is in oils, which she uses to create breathtaking landscapes and portraits. Only recently has she turned her talents toward illustrating books.

To Contact Christy

CALL

(770) 233-0009

If you have been blessed by this book and would like to order additional copies of:

BROKEN PIECES OF BEAUTY

By

Thelma Quinn

Call

(409) 397-4400

or

VISION PUBLISHING GROUP
(770) 467-0039